INTRODUCTION TO SOLAR ENERGY

DR SURESH KUMAR RUDRAHITHLU

Copyright © Dr Suresh Kumar Rudrahithlu
All Rights Reserved.

This book has been published with all efforts taken to make the material error-free after the consent of the author. However, the author and the publisher do not assume and hereby disclaim any liability to any party for any loss, damage, or disruption caused by errors or omissions, whether such errors or omissions result from negligence, accident, or any other cause.

While every effort has been made to avoid any mistake or omission, this publication is being sold on the condition and understanding that neither the author nor the publishers or printers would be liable in any manner to any person by reason of any mistake or omission in this publication or for any action taken or omitted to be taken or advice rendered or accepted on the basis of this work. For any defect in printing or binding the publishers will be liable only to replace the defective copy by another copy of this work then available.

This book is dedicated to: My beloved Parents Late R.S.Yadapadithaya Shishila & Late.Premalatha

Contents

1. What Is Solar Energy?   1
2. Advantages & Disadvantages Of Solar Panels   118

CHAPTER ONE

What is Solar Energy?

Why Are Solar Panels So Popular?

Over the past 20 years solar panels have become extremely popular with homeowners, business and the agricultural industry.

There are many different reasons why people are interested in solar but we have narrowed them down to **3 main reasons.**

Money:

Firstly, the most common reason why solar is popular is because of money.

Solar panels can provide homeowners with a massive saving toward their energy bill (if not completely reduce it altogether).

When people catch wind of their neighbors slashing their energy bill in half, they simply want a piece of the pie. By having a reduced energy bill it means that you will free up your cash flow each month to spend on stuff that you like or your family.

The finance side of solar is the main reason why it has become so popular in today's age.

Environment:

The second most popular reason is because of the environment.

Solar panels are being installed to help take a stance against climate change. People are willing to invest their money into something that will not pollute the planet we live on. Installing solar panels will help by generating clean energy that can also be sold.

This is much better than burning fossil fuels and oils which has a negative effect on the planet. We are realising the sustainability of solar panels which is making them more popular.

Government Incentives :

Thirdly, solar panels are getting a name for themselves through government incentives.

It is pretty hard to resist when the government is offering to buy back any excess solar energy you produce...

Plus lets not forget the massive reduction in the upfront cost, an interest free loan to help reduce the cost even more and then a STC certificate that can be sold for money!

Even with commercial solar for businesses there are rebates and grants being offered as incentives to help with the move to solar.

We Need a PV System to Generate Solar Energy : Solar energy has been around for quite some time. In fact, now is the best time to get it if you want to cut your electric bill and do your share to protect the environment. For that to happen, you will need to buy a PV system. This is designed to reduce or eliminate the amount of electricity you purchase from the utility especially when there could be a price increase in the next few months. The best part about the PV system is that it generates clean electricity which is clean, reliable and renewable since it does not emit any harmful gases into the atmosphere. The PV system must be placed in an area that is free from any obstruction otherwise, it will not be able to capture the sun's rays. A lot of experts say that the south facing roof is best while the east and west is sufficient. If the roof is not available, it can be mounted on the ground. You should know that PV systems come in various sizes so you should get the one that matches our electrical needs. If you consume about 6,500 kilowatts a year, then a PV system within the 3 to 4 kilowatt range is right for your home. You can measure this by reviewing your past electric bills and making some projections Naturally, the size of the PV system will determine the amount of space needed. If you do not use that much electricity, 50 square feet may be sufficient. However, a larger system may require a little over 600 square feet. Just remember that a kilowatt of electricity requires an area of 100 square feet. Solar energy is converted with the help of an inverter since this is what changes direct current to alternating current. You will also need batteries so excess energy may be stored so you can still use solar energy during the evening or during a power outage. The size of the PV system is also in direct proportion with the cost. Most cost from $1 to $1.5 per watt and when you include installation, the bill may reach be from $1,500 to $2,500. The cost of the PV system should not discourage you from investing in solar energy. People who use it are able to get tax rebates and it will also increase the value of your home. With that, the only thing to do now is to call a reputable solar energy provider. One other thing you should know about the PV system is that this should also be connected to your grid. For this to work, you have to enter into an interconnection agreement with your utility. This agreement will address the issue with regards to the terms and conditions under which your system is tied up with them. This also includes what is known as net metering which allows you to bank any surplus electricity that your system generates on the electric grid in the same manner that you will be charged accordingly should you consume more electricity than what you have banked. You need a PV system to generate solar energy. You just need to know what size of a system you require so this can be installed by your solar provider.

An Overview on the Interesting Facts about Solar Energy:

There are lots of interesting facts about solar energy. Educating yourself about this will prove to be beneficial in the long run. You can share the information to your loved ones. You can teach them of ways on how they can help to conserve the energy. You can also do your share to help this method to advance if you are a genius in the field. But if you are an ordinary citizen who only wants to enjoy, then feast on. But remember that you also have responsibilities to the environment that you must accomplish in order to do your part in the whole scheme of things. The Facts that Matter

1. Solar radiation makes it possible for the energy coming from the sun to be used as power source and energy that can in turn be used for many purposes. The technology on this aspect is characterized in two ways. They can either be passive or active. This will depend on the methods that are used to get, convert and allocate sunlight. What are active solar techniques? These utilize pumps, photovoltaic panels and fans to renovate sunlight into useful resources. These aim to increase the energy supply that is why these can also be referred as supply side technologies. The passive solar techniques, on the other hand, use only selected resources with constructive thermal properties, utilize the kind of spaces that can circulate air naturally and apply the position of buildings and structures towards the sun. These will lessen the need for other sources and can also be referred as the demand side technology.

2. Solar energy has influenced many factors that surround people. This can be referred in planning and designing buildings. This process can be rooted back at the early days of the architectural history. The Greeks and the Chinese first used such factor in building and constructing their architectural pieces and on their planning methods.

3. Solar energy is also being utilized by the agricultural sector because they rely heavily on its benefits in order to gain more harvest. They developed ways in order to plant the kind of crops that will grow according to the amount of sun that they will be getting for the season. This can also be used to dry the crops, pump water, brooding of chicks and to dry animal manures that can later be used as fertilizers.

4. On seasons like the Little Ice Age, fruit walls were used by French and Chinese farmers to be able to collect and store solar energy to help them keep the plants warm and to speedy up the process of ripening of fruits. These walls serve as the thermal masses. The fruit walls that were first developed were perpendicular to the ground and faced the south direction. Over time, innovations were done and slopping walls were used to gain more advantage from the sun. 5. To convert the solar light into heat, people have developed green houses. These enable the production and cultivation of specialty crops all year round. Such innovation made it possible for crops to be produced in untimely seasons and in places where you think that those plants won't grow. And these are only some of the interesting facts about solar energy. These give you a good peek at how wonderful nature is and how people have developed ways to use it to advance in many aspects of their lives.

5. To convert the solar light into heat, people have developed green houses. These enable the production and cultivation of specialty crops all year round. Such innovation made it possible for crops to be produced in untimely

seasons and in places where you think that those plants won't grow. And these are only some of the interesting facts about solar energy. These give you a good peek at how wonderful nature is and how people have developed ways to use it to advance in many aspects of their lives.

Analysing the benefits of solar energy:

We all know that using solar energy is a good thing to do. We have heard, and there are quite a number of them, all about the benefits of solar energy and we can't agree why we can't turn this alternative form of energy source to a primary one. But despite the advantages, solar power has yet to fully make it in the mainstream. Let's go back and discuss a couple of the advantages of solar energy and see why keep going back to fossil fuels for energy resource. In the long run, solar power saves money. Initial costs of installation and operations may be more expensive that other energy forms but after settling the expenses, you have an energy resource that is free. Nobody charges for using sunlight, right? The return of investment can also be shorter depending on how much energy you use. You won't spend too much on maintenance either plus those photovoltaic cells can last for 15 to 20 years. There are no mechanical or moving parts to oil and maintain nor are there parts that need to be replaced yearly. Of course solar power is environmental friendly. First its renewable not like fossil fuels which according to studies will be gone in four to five decades. The process of converting energy to usable electricity does not involve the release of toxic chemicals which can harm the environment. Carbon dioxide, nitrogen oxide, sulphur dioxide, lead, and mercury emissions will be a memory of the past when everyone goes solar. Relying on the sun for power also helps reduce global warming. Aside from the toxic wastes and pollutants, using solar power will limit other aspects of the energy industry like hazards of working with and transporting oil or natural gas. Also, other health risks are present in the use of other fuels like kerosene and candles which are still popular in third world countries. With solar energy, these risks will be minimized if not totally eliminated. The use of solar panels is also good for remote areas where providing basic electricity services is troublesome if not totally impossible at all. Solar energy can be transported to far flung villages and once installed they can be left alone for years with little or without maintenance. Communities in Asian countries have successfully installed solar panels in their community and have been enjoying the benefits of clean and reliable power for years.

For a poor country, producing electricity through solar energy can mean independence from oil producing countries which controls the supply and prices of oil. With such independence, new policies on energy can be created which will maximize the benefit for its citizens. Countries will also not be wary on natural disasters which hampers delivery of oil. With this new found independence, countries can invest its national budget on other programs aside from purchasing oil from foreign sources. There are several disadvantages of using solar power and one of which is the costs. But thinking about it in the long run, you'll see that the benefits of solar energy outweigh the disadvantages. Plus, with the current development in the field of science and technology, solar power is becoming more and more convenient and it would not be surprising to find solar energy as a primary source of power in the next few years

Arguments against solar energy:

We all know that solar energy is a good renewable energy resource and that we should start to utilize it more especially when the Earth's fossil fuel reserves are slowly dwindling and will run out in 30 to 50 years. We better look at the various alternative energies and begin a fast tracking of development to hasten our independence on non-renewable fossil fuels. And solar energy is as good as any other alternative energy resource out there. However, several arguments against solar energy have been raised through the years. But probably the most convincing argument is the high costs of solar energy utilization. The problem with solar energy is that you can only harness it during the daytime. And even when the sun is up, the sunlight will be interrupted by occasional cloud covers, rains, fog, and even smog. So in order to harness the sun's energy we need equipment that can get as much solar power as possible at a given time and we need some way of storing that energy so we can use them without any interruptions. We do have the technology to harness the sun's energy, convert it into usable electricity, and store them for future use. And that technology itself is the primary reason why solar power has not caught on even today.

The process of making solar panels as well as the technology for storing that harnessed power remains to be quite expensive. The good thing about this fact today is that due to the recent increase in the costs of fuel and gas, solar power is no longer a far fetched alternative. The gap between the costs has gone down considerably and hopefully in the near future, the costs of solar energy production will be quite competitive. Furthermore, the costs of photovoltaic cells are indeed quite expensive that contemporary oil and gas equipment. But one of the flaws of the argument of costs is that people tend to limit their perspective of solar energy as to only referring to photovoltaic cells. There are other means of harnessing solar energy and not all of them are as expensive as PV cell manufacturing. One way of getting the sun's energy and converting it into usable electricity is the concept of solar thermal plants. In solar thermal technology, various solar collectors are utilized to generate heat which can be applied from the simplest heating and ventilation of houses to the production of massive amounts of electricity.

The use of mirrors or lenses to reflect sunlight to towers equipped with liquids that heat up and produce steam. The steam then turns turbines which in turn generates the electricity needed. The process adds another step compared to photovoltaics which converts solar energy directly into electricity. Nevertheless, solar thermal systems of power production is cheaper that the production of PV cells. For a larger consumer market, it seems that solar thermal energy is the way to go. Regardless, the point here really is to emphasize that solar energy has more to offer. The cost of production is a valid argument against solar energy but still there are ways around it. Costs can be minimized by using other techniques of harnessing solar energy or future developments in the field of science and technology will produce products that are more cost efficient that what are available today.

Countries on the helm of solar energy technology:

The US is not a leading user of solar energy for a very obvious reason: they can still afford to buy fossil fuels from the international market. In other countries the oil prices are ten times higher in the US and sometimes going for the alternative is a lot better in the long run. Today, more and more countries are looking at solar energy as a primary source of power. There are several countries which can be considered as at the helm of solar energy technology.The number one use of solar energy is Germany. It captures almost 50% of the world market of photovoltaic cells. Nowhere else in the world can you find the most number of households with solar panels installed on their roof tops. Germany has this Renewable Energies Laws (EEG) which passed in 2000. The law certainly helped Germans feel the need to go renewable.

According to statistics, Germans invested nearly US$5 billion in solar photovoltaic systems and have contributed considerable in the growth of the solar energy market. Although most of the things that we see are solar panels, it doesn't mean that Germany's solar industry is not limited to the production of photovoltaic cells for electricity. Other notable usage in Germany includes solar panels for home water heating system. Some news indicate that the German solar hot water market earns U.S.$1.5 billion per year. The "solar park" in Arnstein, Bavaria, Germany is one of the biggest photovoltaic plants in the world. It became operational in 2006 and with more than 1,400 PV solar panels, it can produce 12 megawatts of energy.The next biggest country in terms of usage of solar energy is Spain. The solar energy usage in the country, more specifically the photovoltaic cells usage, has a world market share of 27%. Spain has no sign of slowing down its aggressive and pro-active approach in solar energy. Solar fields are being constructed one of the latest ones is the 60 MW solar field in Olmedilla de Alarcón, near Cuenca. There are other big solar plants in Spain and these include the solar park 12 miles outside of Salamanca, Salamanca, Spain which have 70,000 PV panels divided into three 36-hectare arrays. The arrays produce an output is 13.8 megawatts and has been powering roughly 5,000 homes since it opened in 2007. And the rest of the world follow Germany and Spain. Japan and the US still have a market share in the photovoltaic world market. The two countries both have an 8% market share, a far cry from Germany and Spain. Nevertheless, it is quite important that countries continue to improve their status in the world solar market. Other notable country that uses solar power includes Algeria, Australia, Italy, and Portugal. Aside from the rich European countries, people in Israel. and India are realizing the importance of having alternative sources of energy. These are the countries on the helm of solar energy technology. But, other countries are slowly catching up. The government of Israel, for example, required all residential buildings to install solar water heating systems in the early 90s. Today, business establishments like hotels and office buildings are trying to use solar power as an alternative from using fossil fuels whose prices continue to soar in the world market. India is facing a similar energy crisis and they are also looking at solar energy to get them through it.

Facts about Solar Energy, Some Things to Ponder and why?:

What are the facts about solar energy that we know? It is given that this comes from the sun. This was developed by people in order to take advantage and benefit from everything that the sun can provide. You can also easily guess the goals of these people why they opt to develop such technology. For one, they want to make lives easier to live. Second, they want to find other resources that people can use in their everyday lives. Maybe they also want to profit from the experience because if this will all be successful, people, businesses and industries will gain a lot from what is being developed. During the first years of its introduction, people deem that this technological advancement can only be used by wealthy people. It used to cater mostly for the can afford types of individuals. What if it can heat pool and can run spas? .But the evolution of the solar energy is just starting.

Nowadays, the benefits can be felt even by ordinary citizens. Researchers keep thinking of ways to arrive at this state. And this is proving to be good for everybody's sake. The scientists developed solar panels that can power up homes. They made this available not only for the rich and famous, but they sold the idea to governments. The latter used the innovation to bring electricity to people in their countries who still haven't experienced to live in the comfort of having this kind of power source. As a result, many people experience how it is like to have lights. They have also resorted to businesses that can be aided by such technology. The maintenance is still on-going while the technology is still being pursued. But the fact remains that this has been made available even for the ordinary Person.
2. Aside from electricity, solar energy can be used to heat water and cook food. Life is really becoming easier as people find ways to achieve such state. While the developments are still under way, people are finding ways to make such resource available for everybody.

Different organizations and government agencies help in making this product affordable for everyone no matter what your status in life is. As time passes by, people will be able to develop more and more gadgets and tools to make lives easier. There will come a time when almost everybody can benefit from this. The first notion that the solar energy is only for the wealthy will cease to be remembered. The responsibility now lies on to people's hands to take care of nature. They must give back to nature for everything that they have also gotten in the process. Technological advancements can be better achieved if people will consider how these can affect the natural habitat in general. It is okay to get what people want and what people need. But this must always be done with precaution and by thinking of the effects that these will have on everything. It is fun to learn some facts about solar energy every once in a while. These will excite you about the process. But more so, these must open your eyes to the whole scheme of nature and how important it is to take care of our surroundings to be able to benefit more in the long run.

How to Conserve Solar Energy through Your Little Ways:

As an ordinary person who lives according to what the day brings, have you ever thought about how to conserve solar energy? Do you even care? You may think you are an ordinary worker, or a simple wife or mother. Should you even care about such things? The answer is yes.You must bear in mind that you are part of a whole spectrum of nature.Whatever you do will affect all the things around you. Everything must be conserved, including solar energy. Here are some suggestions to throw in your little efforts to achieve this goal.

1. Plant trees. Nature works wonders. Every element around us affects everything else. By planting trees, you will be able to maximize the energy coming from the sun. This will be directed to help the plants grow and produce harvests. With healthy plants and trees rooted to the soil, the soil will be firm. This will be able to hold its structure even in times of natural disasters.

2. Limit your use of the energy coming from the sun. With today's innovations, there are lots of things that are being developed to use solar energy as a power source. The source may be free. But to be able to turn it to such power source, there are things that are utilized for this reason. If you will abuse the use of such technology, the crash of the materials used to put this up will be fast. This will take a toll on you especially if you rely a lot on this advancement.

3. Teach kids about the importance of solar energy. You can gain knowledge through research and through your everyday interaction with other people about this thing called the solar energy. You must tell your kids about its importance, they must be educated about it at an early age. They are the future of the nation. What you teach them now will be instilled to them until they grow old. At such a young age, they must know about how they can contribute to conserve energy.

4. Take good care of nature. This is the most important thing that you can do to help advance such cause. The sun can cause damage to people and nature if people won't do the necessary steps to care for nature in the first place. There are lots of things that you get from the environment. It wouldn't hurt to look back every now and then and see what you can do to give back to what it has already given to you. The idea here is that everything in this life must be conserved. You cannot abuse the power that you possess to gain so much without even thinking how your actions affect the world around you. It is all right to go with the flow of the continuing advancement of the technology. Look at the options available to you nowadays with regards to solar energy. This can be used to power homes and vehicles. This can give light, heat water and cook your food. This can give you satellite television and phones for supreme entertainment and communications enjoyment. This can give you luxuries like spas and warm water at pools. You must learn everything on how to conserve solar energy so that you can do your part in making sure that such resource will be available as long as you live.

How Does Solar Energy Work:

Ever wondered how solar energy is converted into electricity? Well, this will give you an idea how it works. First, solar panels are installed over a flat surface like the roof of your home. Once activated, it absorbs the sun's rays since the panels are made of semi-conducting materials such as silicon. Electrons are then knocked off loose from their atoms so it can produce electricity. This process by which light is converted into electricity is better known as the photovoltaic effect. From there, you now have direct current electricity and when this enters an inverter, it is converted into 220 volt AC which is the electricity needed to power the home. Of course this is connected to the utility panel in the house so the lights and the appliances will work when these are switched on. If you are not using that much electricity from the solar energy generated, it is stored in a battery so will be able to supply the house with power during a power outage or at night. Should the battery be full, the excess electricity is then exported to the utility grid if your system happens to be connected to it. When your solar energy runs out, utility supplied electricity kicks in.

If you are not using that much electricity from the solar energy generated, it is stored in a battery so will be able to supply the house with power during a power outage or at night. Should the battery be full, the excess electricity is then exported to the utility grid if your system happens to be connected to it.When your solar energy runs out, utility supplied electricity kicks in. The flow of electricity of solar energy is measured using a utility meter which spins backward and forward. It will go backward when you are producing more energy than you need and forward when you need additional power from the utility company. These two are only offset when you pay for the additional energy from the utility company. Any surplus is sold back to what is known as net metering

A smaller version of this is used to power a water heater inside the home. Using the same principles, homeowners get to convert sunlight into heat to get warm water. As you can see, transforming sunlight into solar energy is very easy. But why do countries like Germany and Japan use it more often than the US? The answer is because it is much cheaper for them to use this form of alternative energy compared to oil. Also, although the US initiated this during the 1973 oil crisis, it is not as popular as it was back then because the government neither increased the budget in research for alternative forms of energy nor gave incentives so people will be encourage into doing that again.

Most state regulations also prohibit individuals from installing their own devices even if this is used to give you warm water. Chances are, you won't even find anyone to do it so you will probably have to do it yourself. Just remember that if there is a problem with the plumbing, your insurance will not cover it. Should the state allow you to install such a system, you will not be entitled to the rebate. Using solar cells is just one way to make the most out of solar energy. Your other option is passive solar energy which helps avoid heat loss so those inside will not feel too cold or too hot throughout the day. This is used by a lot of homeowners living in the southwest since they do not need that much insulation compared to homeowners who live in other parts of the US.

Net Metering and Solar Energy:

You can't help but get into net metering when you decide to invest in solar energy because you sometimes consume more or less than what you actually generate. When you consume less energy, your electric meter spins backward, if you use more then it goes forward. Net metering is simply a special metering and billing agreement between you and the electric service provider. You are eligible for this if you reside in a residential area and generate some form of energy using solar, wind energy or a combination of both. It also has to be located on your premises and connected to the grid. For this to work, you need to have a meter capable of moving in both directions. Most meters these days can do that but if your provider wants to use two meters, they will have to pay for it.

However, if you enter into a time of use billing agreement, you will have to be one to buy the unit. The net metering agreement works by letting you use the electricity you generate first before you use what you normally get from your electric service provider. Your meter should show the net which is measured as the difference between the electricity you purchased and what you actually purchased. The benefit of the net metering system is that it allows you to store electricity when you are not there and then use it the moment you get home. Since there is a law that expands net metering, you can take advantage of it by generating electricity during peak hours and then using it during off peak periods. Another benefit is the fact that you only pay the net electricity that you use. If you consume below the baseline, you pay less and more if you go over it. If what you use offsets what you normally get from a provider, then you will most likely pay a lower rate. Since you entered into an agreement with your provider, you will still be billed monthly.

This will state the amount of power you generated and the amount you actually consumed. On the anniversary of your agreement, you will be billed for the previous 12 months but you can also request for this on a monthly basis. Keep in mind that you will not be paid for the excess generation of electricity in a given year although some do. If you want to use solar energy, you have to contact your electric service provider and ask if they offer net metering. When the papers are drawn up, remember that they cannot require you to pay for any meters beyond the bi-directional meter. They cannot conduct any tests or impose any requirements if it meets existing national standards for grid-interconnected systems. Lastly, you don't have to buy additional insurance or buy power from any of their affiliates.

Net metering is a policy and also an incentive when you decide to use solar energy. This is because you reduce the number of kilowatts used by your electric service provider which in turn decreases the emissions of carbon dioxide into the air.

Solar energy in households:

The sun is a great source of energy. It would be great to use solar energy in your homes especially nowadays when the prices of oil and gas continue to increase. Because of the high fuel and gas prices, more and more people are experimenting on the use of solar energy in their households in their attempts to minimize the costs of basic utilities. The sun's energy can be harnessed in different ways depending on how you would utilize the end product. There are so called solar collectors which are placed on the roof tops or used in buildings. The main purpose of these solar collectors is to provide heating and even ventilation for the houses and buildings.

These collectors harness the sun's energy by magnifying the sunlight several times and transferring that heat to air or water. That heated air or water is stored and will provide the building or home heating and hot water whenever needed. The only problem here is that not all places have equal amounts of sunlight.As you go farther from the equator, the strength of the sun is reduced. But still, this is a much better solution than relying on electric grids which do not reach remote areas. It is just a mater of storing the heat generated from the solar collector properly. For example, some buildings in Sweden utilized an underground storage facility where solar energy is stored resulting to savings from heating the building and their water. In areas where gas and fuel are out of reach of the pockets of poor communities, residents have to rely on solar cooking for their meals. They use this bowl shaped discs equipped with mirrors or reflectors which directs all the sunlight on the middle where a pot is placed.

The same technology is being used in India, Sri Lanka, and Nepal. This serves are a good alternative from conventional fuels like coal, firewood, and gas. They can use these solar stoves during a sunny day and use traditional fuels when the weather is not that good. This reliance by communities on solar cooking should encourage more studies on how to make photovoltaic cells cheaper for an ordinary household. At this time, the use of solar cells is not economically friendly for a single household. However, the approach here is to install a series of solar panels which would be shared by the whole community. This could be a good idea depending on your usage, but for basic lighting purposes these could work in small poor communities. In some areas, community cooperatives have found ways to bring electricity to households out of reach of power grids.

In the Philippines for example, a local cooperative provided households loans to enable them to install a basic solar power module which can produce enough electricity for three light bulbs. This ay be laughable in our standards but to these people who have been living all their lives with the flickering light of the candles, three electric light bulbs make a great deal of a difference.

The story is the same in other countries. In Israel, the high costs of photovoltaic cells have clamped down the growth of solar energy in the country. It if fortunate, therefore, that the Israeli government is now providing incentives for households that would use solar energy. However, according to industry analysts, the costs of solar cells production will go down as the demand increase.

Also, most are hopeful that recent discoveries and advancement in technologies will find a way to bring down costs of using solar energy. Ordinary households using solar energy is an ideal scenario that we should all strive to achieve.

Solar energy simplified:

The sun shines, we collect the sunlight, we convert the sunlight into usable forms, and we enjoy the benefits. You can't get any simpler than that. But okay, I know you need more explanations. You've been looking all over the web for information and you need, no you deserve, more than just a single sentence. The following would be my attempt in simplifying the concept of solar energy and I just hope you get something out of it. The sun produces huge amounts of energy. But what the earth gets is a pretty small share of that energy. However, even if we get only a miniscule amount, the energy we receive from the sun is more than enough for our needs. Believe it or not, a day's worth of sunlight when harnessed properly can power a big country like the US for more than a year.

So if that's how much energy we can get from the sun, why do we rely too much on fossil fuels which will disappear in 40 to 50 years time? The main problem is that the sun shines all throughout the world. That energy is so spread out that harnessing it is really a challenge. But still, there are other factors at work here, political, economical, and even cultural in nature which contributes to the slow progress of solar technologies. But that will need a whole chapter, nay, a whole book to discuss so let's leave that alone for a moment. There are various ways how we harness sunlight and the specific way may depend on how we plan to use that energy. But we can divide the usage into two general concepts, converting solar power into heat and the other one is converting it into electricity.

Using solar power to heat homes is a pretty good example of the first category. There are two ways that can be used, the first one relies on the positioning of the house's windows and the second one involves the use of some mechanical devices to distribute the heat throughout the house. Solar water heaters are also now available. What you do is provide a solar collector where the heat from the sun is trapped and collected. That heat is then transferred to the after that goes out of your faucets and showers. Converting solar power into electricity, however, needs a little bit more explanation. There are basically two ways we can get electricity out of solar power. The first one involves the use of photovoltaic cells and the second one is using various solar thermal systems. Photovoltaic cells are more commonly known as solar cells. These cells are made from silicon wafers and phosphorous.

When sunlight strikes the surface of the silicon wafers, free electrons are produced. The electrons are then harnessed via attaching a wire to the cells. As the electrons leave the cells and pass through the wire, an electronic current is produced. One major flaw of the photovoltaic cells is that they can be quite expensive plus they only convert a small amount of sunlight. Hopefully these cells can be cheaper, more efficient and more suitable to the needs of consumers in the future.

The great thing about solar energy is that it does not produce any kinds of pollution unlike fossil fuels which spit out substantive amounts of pollutants in the air and even in the water. Plus the sun is pretty much in good health aid it is still very far from dying. We can utilize more than enough energy from the sun that will last us for a lifetime.

Solar Energy, How Does It Benefit the Agricultural Sector:

What is solar energy? To put it simply, this is the energy coming from the sun. The heat and light that the sun provides are essential to life. Can you even imagine life without the sun? It will not be normal and there are lots of things and experiences that people can no longer indulge into if ever that will be the case. Everybody relies on the sun for its benefits. Did you know that the earth gets 1740 watts of insolation or the incoming radiation from the sun? This happens at the upper part of the atmosphere. Almost 30% gets reflected back to the space. The rest of the percentage is being absorbed by the clouds, land masses and oceans.

The Agricultural Sector :

If you can think of one industry that won't survive without the energy coming from the sun, what will be the first thing on your mind? There may be many sectors that must rely on the sun's benefits. But the agricultural and horticulture industry will not thrive without it. They have no other options. If the sun will be gone, these sectors will die. The sun is need by the agricultural and horticulture departments to be able to grow their produce. The latter is needed by people as well as animals. These sectors' productivity will depend on the amount of energy that they are getting from the sun. It must be balanced in all ways. It can never too little. And it must also not be so much. If it is too little, the plans may not be able to grow accordingly. The farmers won't achieve the required harvests in order to feed the population. And if it is too much, this will damage the crops. This will also cause bad effects on people's health. But if the latter is the case, people can think of ways in order to achieve the needed produce by manually trying to reduce the amount of heat that can be directed on the plants. But if the situation becomes unbearable, it might lead to drought and deaths. Farmers must know when the sun will be up, when sunny days will be long and factors like that so that they can settle for what kinds of plants they must plant to survive the kind of weather condition.

Here are only some of the things that they resort to in order to optimize the full benefits of the energy coming from the sun.

- Timed planting cycles
- Timed planting cycles
- Tailored row orientation
- Mixing different varieties of crops to improve the yields

Do you ever wonder what farmers did in times like the Little Ice Age? It is said that English and French farmers resorted to fruit walls. These fruit walls help in maximizing the collection of the energy from the sun. These serve as the thermal masses. These walls help in keeping the plants warm to speed up the process of growing and ripening of produce.

The sun's energy is also being utilized in these sectors in vital activities such as drying the crops, pumping of water, drying animals' manure, brooding of chicks and a lot more. It is hard to imagine the agriculture and horticulture sectors to survive without the solar energy. If there are anybody who knows the importance of the sun, these people are the first in line.

Solar Energy is the Future:

We consume fossil fuels at a greater rate than we have ever had over the past 50 years. That demand is fueled by the increase of cars on the street,the number of planes that take to the air and the number of homes that need electricity. Sadly, we will have depleted these resources by the end of this century which is why we have to come up with other ways to get power and solar energy may be the future. Solar energy is simply extracting the sun's energy for power. Just to tell you how powerful the sun is, it can burn scrub lands and give you sunburn if you are out in the sun without any protection. In fact, the Greeks and the Chinese used this to set fire until the 1880's by Charles Fritts made the first solar cell.

Instead of using a heater to warm up the home, sunlight can be used to control the temperature. You will just need large windows and shades to control the amount of sunlight that will go inside and keep the heat absorbed during the day to remain at night. Solar energy can also provide warm water as it warms up cold water that passes down through the closed flat panels called collectors. But solar energy does not only give warmth to the home.

It can also be used to help power it which reduces our dependence on non-renewable resources like oil or coal. This occurs when solar cells are installed on the roof so it will be able to capture as much solar rays as possible and then converts this into electricity. You will need 10 or 12 to capture at least a kilowatt of power and more if you are powering more than just your home. The only limitation which challenges the use of solar energy is that it can only generate power during the day. The answer to this is to put an auxiliary system in place that will store the energy and kick when the sun is not available. This comes in the form of batteries which will provide power in the evening or a brownout. Advances in technology have taken solar energy to the next level.

NASA uses it to power satellites in orbit, solar panels installed onboard aircraft allow it to fly across oceans while cars can travel speeds up to 40 miles per hour. It is used to power a lighthouse so seafarers will be able to find their way at sea while aircraft can land in an airport in the middle of the frozen desert. Solar energy is safe for the environment since it does not emit any harmful gases or chemicals into the air. It is a renewable resource that has not yet been fully tapped by a lot of countries which makes it very viable for the future.

But is it the only answer to reduce our dependence on oil? No because solar energy is just one of the options. We can also harness the power of the wind, the wave in the oceans, geothermal heat, hydroelectricity and a lot more instead of relying on coal or even nuclear energy that may harm the environment. It is something we have to push for the next generation.

Technologies for harnessing solar energy:

Harnessing the sun's energy efficiently is not an easy feat. The sunlight is so widespread that finding the most effective way of capturing it requires advanced knowledge and technology. There are several technologies for utilizing solar energy and all are unique and are dedicated for specific applications. First up are the photovoltaic cells or commonly known as solar cells. These are probably the best known way of harnessing the energy's sun. Whenever one talk about solar power, the first things that come to mind include having panels and panels of photovoltaic cells or PV. These cells contain semi-conductors, commonly are made from silicon, which absorbs the light from the sun. When sunlight hit the surface of the silicon, new free electrons are created. As the electrons are channeled out of the silicon, electric current is created. The second solar power technology is the concentrating solar power systems. This one involves using mirrors to reflect sunlight to one area. Some systems incorporate high tech devices to track the movement of the sun and adjust the mirrors to maximize the amount of sunlight the system receives. The sunlight reflected from the mirrors is used to heat or power a conventional power plant. Other systems channel the light from the mirrors to an area filled with photovoltaic cells. There are several kinds of concentrated solar power systems, the most popular ones are the solar trough, parabolic dish and solar power tower. The solar trough uses large, U-shaped (parabolic) reflectors to point the sunlight to a tower at the center of the mirrors. At the center tower, hot oil is heated by the sun's energy and help boil water to create steam which is then used to power convention plants. The power tower system uses the same concept as solar troughs.

Mirrors are used to reflect sunlight to a center tower where a liquid is heated and utilized for the creation of steam which will power a power. The parabolic dish system uses mirrored dishes to focus and concentrate sunlight onto a receiver. The size of the dish varies but it is commonly 10 times bigger than an ordinary cable satellite dish. Another solar power technology used today is the solar water heating systems. This is a simple one. The process involves collecting the energy directly from the sun to heat water or liquids which in turn heats up the water.

This is more common in households are ideal for family use. In order to capture the sunlight, solar panels have to be installed in your home or in the place where you will be needing hot water like a swimming pool area. You will need a big space for this but in the long run, you will be able to save lots of money from your electric bill. For commercial establishments, an ideal solar power technology is the transpired solar collector or otherwise known as the solar wall. It involves using perforated solar collectors where outside air passes before it enters the building.

These are but a few of the technologies around which can be used for utilizing the power of the sun. The technologies for harnessing solar energy continue to evolve as new technologies and discoveries are being accomplished. Everything might change in a few years time. Plus, the whole solar power technologies will become more price competitive which will benefit the general consumers.

The downsides of solar energy:

Not that I'm against using solar energy or anything but there are some downsides of using solar energy. My intention is to illustrate these disadvantages so that people can realize the other side of the coin to prepare them and not so much as to dissuade them from using solar energy. I am for everything that can save the planet. View this explanation as an introduction where we can still improve the current technologies involving solar energy. One of the first and major drawbacks of using solar power is the costs. The expense is considerably higher than the conventional electric installation. From the purchase to the initial installations of the solar panel unit, the cost is a significant factor to consider.

The high costs of solar power panels lie on the expensive semi-conductor materials that convert sunlight into electricity. However, as technology progresses and as the need slowly increases, the costs of solar panels are expected to go down, something on the level of being competitive with other energy resources. Another to consider is space. We're talking about installing a solar panel which is not small. It requires a significant amount of space which also helps maximize the amount of sunlight it can collect and convert into electricity. Some households will have the panels installed on their roof others will designate a place for it on the year or on top of a pole. The same space problems will need to be readdressed once you decide to add panels when your current setup is no longer enough for your family's needs. Positioning is also vital.

The solar panels will need to be facing a direction where it will receive the most amount of sunlight in a day. However, there is always a solution. If space does not permit such installations, there are some add-ons that can help maximize sun exposure. Positioning is also vital.

The solar panels will need to be facing a direction where it will receive the most amount of sunlight in a day. However, there is always a solution. If space does not permit such installations, there are some add-ons that can help maximize sun exposure. At night, you might encounter a problem with relying solely on solar power. Although the solution here is to purchase batteries which you can charge during the day and use at night. You will need a couple of batteries though to be able to sustain your electricity needs through cloudy, stormy or smoggy or foggy times during the day. As far as solar powered transportation services go, there are still some quirks that need to be fixed before mass production of such vehicles is rolled out.

The most noticeable difference is the speed. Solar powered cars are far slower that their counterparts. But again, due to the fast development of the solar car and the technologies that go with it, this drawback will soon disappear. When you look at the things that I mentioned about the disadvantages of solar energy, you will see that most of them have solutions while others you just need to compromise a bit. I still think that harnessing the power of the sun is the way to go, so these downsides of solar energy are just a small obstacle that we need to overcome.

The future of solar energy on transportation:

Are you familiar with the World Solar Challenge? It is a race specifically for solar cars. Solar cars basically have arrays of photovoltaic cells which converts the sun's rays into usable electrical energy. The purpose of the race is to raise awareness on the use of the sun's energy on transportation and the development of other alternative forms of energy particularly the solar cells. The future of using solar energy on transportation services may still be a little hazy given the practical difficulties involve in converting ordinary cars into solar cars but the idea is here to stay and hopefully develops into something promising and useful. At this point, solar cars have been built to join solar car races. Very few have been constructed for practical and commercial purposes.

There are several reasons why the solar car remains on the background. The design of a solar car relies on the electrical system of the vehicle. The system controls the electricity the flows from the photovoltaic cells to the batteries, to the wheels, and to the controls. The electric motor that moves the vehicle is powered purely by the electricity produced by the solar cells.

The solar cells, depending on the number installed on the vehicle, can produce more or less 1000 watts of power from the sun's rays. To give you an idea, 1000 watts is just enough electricity to power an electric iron or even a toaster. And since the sun will most likely be covered by clouds at one time or the other, or the car goes through a tunnel or something, solar cars are equipped with batteries to serve as backup power supply for the motor. The battery packs are charged by the solar cells. However, the batteries are not charge while driving the solar car unless you intend to go very slow. Just like a gas pedal in conventional motors, a motor controller regulates the amount of electricity that enters the motor to speed up or slow down the vehicle whenever needed. Solar cars are not that slow as perceived by almost everyone.

These cars can go to as fast as 80-85 mph. With this, you can see why solar cars are not yet into commercial production. Nowadays, solar cells can harness more than 21% of the sun's energy that hit the surface. If the time comes that the cells can actually get more energy from the sun then maybe we can see solar cars on the streets. But at this time, it is quite difficult to make a commercial production model of a solar car. Nevertheless, there are companies who have already created some concept solar cars and are testing how road worthy they are. There's even a scooter that is street legal and runs from batteries charged from photovoltaic cells. Other possible application of solar car technologies is on golf carts which runs pretty slow in the first place and can be appreciated by golfers as well.

The future of solar energy on transportation is still not that clear. The application of solar energy on homes and buildings has been moving forward in recent years so hopefully we can find new ways of converting the sun's energy into usable electricity. And this time something that can be economically and efficiently installed in conventional cars.

The Future of Solar Energy, How It Looks and How It Affects Nature:

The future of solar energy lies on the indigenous hands of people who never tire out from thinking of ways in order to make life easier to live. With the advancement in the technology, the boom of the Internet age and a lot of other things, there will come a time when people will turn their backs on whatever is conventional. This can be good and bad in many ways, depending on who is looking at it and from what perspective. But people's quest for the advancement and development of everything that surrounds them provides lots of negative effects as well.

Here are only some.

1. Sometimes, people neglect the environment and how to properly take care of it for the mere fact that they are greedy to get their ideas done no matter what the consequences to the nature will be. Such advancements create harmful effects in the whole state and balance of nature. How many times have you heard about forest denudation or grave floods that kill people? All these occurrences can also be rooted to the activities of men that suffice for their own good without so much consideration for their natural habitat and the nature.

2. With the continuing advancement of everything that surrounds people, the generational gap becomes wider and wider. Old folks will fight for the benefits of the conventional tools and mediums. The newer generations cannot afford to sit on those old ways to do things. They are a slave to the continuing technological developments. It is okay to initiate change. It is good to find better ways to do things. But people must be cautious in achieving this. They must think about everything around them before they even start on their venture to newer and better ways to achieve greatness. The Innovations As of today, solar energy is one of the best options that people have with regards to alternative power sources. This has already evolved. There was a time when you can only avail such power source when the sun is present and that is during daytime. With the genius of the people behind the development of this resource, they were able to create green gas that can produce electricity. This is done by splitting water properties into hydrogen and oxygen. Both gasses will then be grouped into a cell that will be the electricity source. The same geniuses estimated that the entire planet can rely to an hour of sunlight for its one year electricity consumption. Solar cells have been developed to produce electricity from the energy coming from the sun. The panels for such technology can also be used to heat water and cook food. There are now the solar heating, solar cookers and solar furnaces as add-ons to this innovative venture. There are now hydrogen based cars. These are fueled by the split hydrogen in water. The solar cells also power the satellites that orbit through the surface of the Earth. This is the reason why there are advancements that people benefit from such as satellite phones and TV, accurate weather forecasting, even the development of the GPS technology and a lot more. There are a lot of benefits that people can gain from the future of solar energy. You just have to think that whatever you do or however you use such technology for your own good, you must always think of ways to protect your environment first to be able to get the most out of such improvements.

The Benefits of Solar Energy:

Solar energy will benefit a lot of people and not only the rich. This is why some governments have increased funding for this type of technology because they are aware of its many benefits. For one, solar energy is very cheap compared to other technologies. It is also renewable unlike coal or the rest which are non-renewable and hard to maintain. It also improves the health of people since it does not produce any carbon dioxide emissions unlike kerosene lamps that give out fumes which are just as deadly as smoking 2 packs of cigarettes a day. It also reduces the incidents of fire that are often associated with the use of kerosene, candles, diesel fuel and gasoline for generators. Solar energy is almost maintenance free because the solar cells used will last for 20 years or more before it has to be replaced.

You just have to keep the panels clean so it is able to absorb sunlight and convert that into electricity. These are also very useful in remote locations where power lines are not yet available. Some examples of these include fish houses, highway signs, marine applications, remote lighting and telecommunication. If countries focus on solar energy and other renewable techniques, they will be able to conserve their foreign exchange because they no longer have to use it to pay for foreign oil. This money can then be used for other things such as health care, infrastructure projects and education.

Solar energy will also reduce your electricity bills because you are no longer dependent on electricity coming from the power company. The only downside to solar energy is the initial cost in setting it up. Yes you will have to buy a lot of solar panels which are quite expensive but in the long run, you will be able to save more because you don't have to pay for anything else to keep them running. Should the cost of solar cells be beyond your budget, you can probably invest in used systems first then try to acquire the brand new ones later on. Another benefit of using solar energy is that you get to conserve fossil fuels and other natural resources that are quickly diminishing as a direct result of an increase in the world's population which could compromise the needs of the future generations. So should people get into solar energy? The answer is yes because it is safe, cheap and good for the environment. You only have to worry when the sun isn't shining because when this happens, rays from the sun won't be able to produce electricity so you have to rely on other means to get power. The same also goes when there is a blackout or brownout because you will soon lose power from your solar system.

The demand for solar energy is increasing and you should join in. Aside from reducing your electric bill, homeowners who use solar energy may claim up to $2,000 in federal investment tax credit in the first year while businesses may claim a 30% federal investment tax credit.

Believe it or not, solar energy has one other benefit and that it increases the value of your home. According to home appraisers, a dollar decrease in your energy bill results in a $20 increase in its property value so do the match and you can easily figure out how much your home will be worth after you decide to invest in solar energy.

The History of Solar Energy:

Solar energy is for everyone simply because the sun shines in every corner of the planet. In fact, the history of solar energy can be traced back to the Greeks that were then passed on to the Romans which marked the first people to ever use the passive solar design. Passive solar design is a way to warm the home based on the dwelling's design. They may not have had glass windows back then but their architecture made it possible for the people to use the sun's rays to light and heat indoor spaces. As a result, there was no need to burn food that often which was in short supply. In 1861, Auguste Mouchout invented the first active solar motor. Unfortunately, its expensive price made it impossible to produce commercially. Less than 20 years later, Charles Fritts invented solar cells, which will later on be used to power homes, heaters, satellites and other devices today. Since what he invented was very primitive, other people experimented on solar energy. One such person was

Albert Einstein who won the Nobel Prize for physics in his research on the photoelectric effect which is a phenomenon associated with the generation of electricity through solar cells. In 1953, Bell Laboratories which we know today as AT&T labs developed the first silicon solar cell capable of generating a measurable electric current. Three years later, solar cells ran $300 per watt. With the Cold War and the Space Race on, this was used to power satellites and crafts. But the biggest event in the development of solar energy occurred during the oil crisis of 1973. This prompted the US government to invest heavily in the solar electric cell that was developed by Bell Laboratories 20 years ago.

By the 1990's, research towards solar energy came to a standstill as the price of oil dropped in the world market. Funds were diverted elsewhere and the United States which was probably the leader in this form of alternative energy was soon surpassed by other nations mainly Germany and Japan. In 2002 for example, Japan had installed 25,000 solar panels on rooftops. Because of that, the price of solar panels went down as the demand for it was on the rise.

To date, solar energy is growing at a modest 30% per year. Although there have been improvements in solar energy, its fundamentals are still the same. The sun's rays are collected and then converted into electricity. Aside from powering homes or office buildings, the technology has been used to power aircraft, cars and boats. Unfortunately, none of these have been made available yet for public use. We still rely heavily on oil for electricity, gasoline for our cars, fuel for planes and ships.

In fact, the US is one of the biggest oil users in the world. To prove a point, the department of Defense consumes 395,000 barrels per This has to change because our oil reserves are almost depleted and many experts believe that global supply for these non-renewable resources will be gone before the end of the century. We have to do our share to push for renewable energy and one of them happens to be solar energy.

The Pros and Cons of Solar Energy:

Solar energy is one of the best forms of renewable energy. But why don't we rely on it so much compared to other countries? The answer is simply that there are pros and cons with using this form of alternative energy. The pros of using solar energy is that the system is easy to install, there are no energy costs once it is set up, there are no emissions like air pollutants or greenhouse gas and the sun is widely available. The pros of using solar energy is that the system is easy to install, there are no energy costs once it is set up, there are no emissions like air pollutants or greenhouse gas and the sun is widely available. A solar energy system is composed of the solar panels, the inverter, battery, charge controller, wires and support structure. For you to produce a kilowatt of power, you will need 10 to 12 solar panels that will occupy an area of 100 square feet.

If you are worried that this will cause damage to your roof, don't because it is made of light weight materials. When you call a contractor, it will usually take a day or two to install and cost around $10,000. Not that many people will have cash on hand to pay for it so they can avail of a home equity loan to pay for it. If you use a kilowatt of solar energy, you can save 170 lbs. of coal from being burned, about 300lbs of carbon dioxide from being released into the atmosphere or 105 gallons of water that most homeowners use up every month.

The cons are solar cells are expensive, the rays can only be collected during the day time, the weather and where you are located will play a factor in how much sunlight you can get and you will need a big area to collect the power. But some experts believe that price of these cells and its ability to collect power will improve in the future. Right now, a kilowatt of solar energy can only produce 1,600 kilowatts of hours per year in sunny climate. That means you will receive 5.5 hours of electricity per day. If you produce about 750 kilowatts of power, you will only get 2.5 hours of power per day.

Solar panels come in various colors and usually have a 5 year warranty.Since manufacturers are aware that solar energy can only work when the sun is out, they have installed batteries so you get more than 5 hours of power even during cloudy days and nights. This is because the batteries are designed to absorb, insulate, transmit and reflect rays coming from the sun.

But solar energy can be applied to other things and not just powering our homes. It can be used to power small devices like calculators to bigger things like planes, satellites and cars. Since these are easy to maintain, you don't have to worry about anything. People should take this seriously especially when this is not a renewable source of energy.

Things We Should Know Before Investing in Solar Energy:

There is no doubt that there are a lot of benefits in using solar energy. Aside from protecting the environment, you get to save a great deal of money. But before you switch to solar energy, here are a few things you should consider. First, is your roof right for solar power? Most solar power systems can be installed as long as the roof is flat and made of material such as bitumen, composite shingle, cement tile, metal or tar and gravel. If this is how your roof is positioned, then there shouldn't be any problems. The solar panels will be installed parallel to the roof surface.

If you are concerned that the weight could be too heavy for your roof, don't be since this is very light and quite rare that you have to do some structural work before installing the system. When you are looking for a contractor, find out how much it will cost to install the system. You should compare these first before you decide in picking the best one. But you should know right now that installing solar powered cells are a bit expensive. There are also no financing programs you can avail of. Your best bet if you don't have enough money is to apply for a home equity loan. If you are planning to install this in a commercial establishment, the various loans you can avail of include the capital equipment loan, equipment secured loan, property secured loan or the SAFE-BIDCO energy efficiency loan.

Non-profit organizations may also avail of special loans for solar energy and the best one is through third party financing. In this case, the non-profit organization and the contractor will purchase the system and make use of the tax credits. The third party will then pass on the charges for the produced power to the non-profit and after the system has depreciated, this is sold to the non-profit at a discount. The end result is that you pay for less than what you are currently paying for because it is maintenance free. Will installing a solar system have any effect on your property? The answer is yes. In fact, it will increase the resale value of your property without having to pay much more in terms of property taxes. If you have a lot of space to spare, you may even be able to zero out your electric bill as long as the sun comes out so you can convert sunlight into electricity.

Aside from increasing the properly value, you will also be able to avail of tax credits from the government. Solar energy can power your home in the same way you get electricity from the grid. You won't be able to use it when there is a power outage or when the sun is shining but fortunately, this doesn't happen daily so it is still an alternative form of energy worth considering.

Using solar energy goes way back:
Recollecting the history of solar energy brings us back to the 1970s energy crisis and oil embargo which caused long lines in gasoline stations, high gasoline prices, and even caused panic among consumers and investors alike in the United States. Knowledge about oil being a non-renewable resource has been around since the 1800s.

But it was only during and after the 70s energy crisis that people really began to realize the consequences of depending too much on an already depleting energy resource. However, utilizing the sun's energy is not really a recent development. It has been used by ancient civilizations for warmth, for food and crop preparations and various agricultural purposes. What's new are the technologies involved in harnessing this energy and utilizing it for man's daily use. The technology began in the 1830's when Edmund Becquerel made public his studies on how solar light can be harnessed into usable energy. However, nobody followed up on this idea nor explore any practical use.

The next breakthrough on solar power came after thirty years Becquerel published his works. In 1860s, the French Monarch commissioned Augusted Mouchout to find other sources of energy. And Mouchout looked up in the sky for inspiration. His series of solar powered contractions were quite impressive back then. His inventions included a motor that run on solar energy, a steam engine that uses the sun's light, and an ice maker that fully rely on solar power. After Mouchout, there were several other notable achievements in the line of solar power. Among these is the works of William Adams in the 1870s which utilized mirrors to channel the power of the sun to make a steam engine run. Adams' power tower design concept is still in use today.

Another notable work is by Charles Fritz in the early 1880s. His studies were attuned on turning sunlight into electricity, which he later accomplished. But one of the most significant development in modern solar energy occurred in the 1950s. Early in the decade, R.S. Ohl discovered that sunlight produces large numbers of free electrons when it strikes silicon. Then in the mid-1950s Gerald Pearson, Calvin Fuller, and Daryl Chaplin was able to capture those free electrons and convert them in electricity.

Today, silicon cells are used to make solar cells and solar panels for harnessing the sun's energy. Immediately these solar cells were made into good use and the first among to use them was the field of space aeronautics. These silicon based solar cells were used to power satellites that orbit the earth. The satellite Vanguard I was the first one launched out to space which rely on solar cells for power. More satellites followed. Nowadays, more and more research and studies are being conducted on how best to utilize the sun's energy. Especially today where it is said that about 30-50 years from the now, the world oil reserves will be totally depleted. Thus, the search for alternative sources of energy continuous.

The sun is expected to die out in a couple of thousand of years, it's too long to worry about and man can have all the sun's energy until that day. The challenge today is creating solar energy power in more efficient and cost effective e way. Admittedly, the costs of those photo cells are not that cheap to be accessible by most of the ordinary consumers. The movement today in the science and technology committee is to be able to provide cheap alternative source of energy.

What is Solar Energy?
Solar energy is a form of renewable energy as it utilizes the radiant energy coming from the sun. This is done by converting sunlight into electricity using solar cells. Solar cells or photovoltaics were invented in the 1880's by Charles Fritts. Although it did not convert a lot of sunlight into electricity at the time, this started a revolution that

continued on to the 20th century. The greatest example is perhaps the Vanguard 1 which was a satellite fitted with solar cells that enabled it to transmit back to earth after its chemical battery was exhausted. Its success prompted NASA and its Russian counterpart to the same with other satellites including Telstar hich continues to serve as the backbone of the telecommunications structure today.The most significant event that stimulated the demand for solar energy was the 1973 oil crisis.

Early on, power companies would charge the consumer a hundred dollars per watt. In the 1980's, it became only $7 per watt. Unfortunately, the lack of government funding did not sustain its growth so the growth of solar energy was only 15% annually from 1984 to 1996. There have been a decline in the demand for solar energy in the US but this increased in Japan and Germany. From 31.2 megawatts of power in 1994, this increased to 318 megawatts in 1999 and world wide production growth increased by 30% towards the end of the 20th century.

Next to these two countries, Spain is the third largest user of solar energy followed by France, Italy and South Korea.

There are three basic approaches to get the most out of solar energy. It is namely passive, active and solar photovoltaic systems.

1.In passive, it has to do a lot with the building design. This will enable the building to avoid heat loss so people inside will feel a great degree of comfort with the help of controlled ventilation and day lighting. Homes that apply this will greatly reduce their heating requirements by as much as 80% with minimal cost.

2. Active solar heating is used to convert sunlight into heat which provides space or water heating. Used extensively in Europe, getting the right size will cover 50% to 60% of your hot water heating requirements.

3. Lastly is photovoltaic which converts solar radiation into electricity. This is done by installing solar cells in the ground and the greater the intensity of the light, the greater the flow of electricity. These are available in different sizes and some are installed in consumer devices like calculators and watches.

Some vehicles are now powered using solar energy. Cars although not yet produced commercially compete in the World Solar Challenge which invites competitors from around the world to compete in this annual event in Australia. There are also unmanned aerial vehicles and balloons. To date,solar energy has only been successful in passenger boats.

Many of us take the sun for granted and if we are really serious about preserving the environment and reducing our demand for oil, solar energy is just one of the options we have on the table. We have to lobby and convince our government leaders to do more because it is the cheapest means of providing our home with electricity compared to rechargeable batteries, kerosene or candles.

Wind power vs Solar energy an even match:

Today in center stage is a battle for the ages. On the right corner, packing a hurricane punch yet is known to move softly as a breeze is wind power. On the left corner, with a scorching hot aura, moves in a speed of light, is solar energy. Wind power versus solar energy, which one is going to be declared the champion of the alternative energy movement?! Let's get ready to rumble! Or something like that. I apologize for that intro but I just can't help. I figured that if I was going to match one alternative energy resource against the other, then I'll make some extravagant introduction. Just imagine the drum rolls. Actually, there is an existing debate among environmentalists and even scientists on which energy resource should be developed first given their advantages and drawbacks. Staying away from the personal biases, numerous studies have shown that overall, wind power is more cost effective than harnessing the sun's energy.

Let's see the reasons behind that conclusion. Harnessing the sun's energy can be done by a number of ways. But probably the simplest way which can be applied in a small home is by using photovoltaic cells or PV or solar cells. What happens is that sunlight hit the surface of a photovoltaic (PV) panel which responds by creating free electrons which is channelled to generate an electric current. Wind power on the other hand utilizes a propeller and a shaft system which has a magnet wrapped by a coil of wire inside. As the wind turns the propeller and the magnet inside, the electrons in the wire are forced to move along the wire producing an electrical current. Both ways are quite simple but the complexities now lies on the costs of producing the necessary equipment especially the mechanisms that will maximize the power output. When costs of production of photovoltaic cells and wind turbine are compared, the latter is much cheaper to produce. Although, manufacturers of photovoltaic cells stress that as the demand on PV cells increase, the costs of production decreases. So its just a matter of time before PV cells become price competitive.

Other problems include the logistics of placing the equipment. A solar panel requires quite a large space plus, your location on the globe will affect the amount of sunlight you receive and consequently the amount of power you produce. The further away from the equator you are, the less amount of sunlight you can harness. Also, on the average, the PV cells have a 15-20% efficiency rate. The problem with wind power on the other hand is that not all areas will have winds favorable for a turbine. And if you do locate a place where winds are strong and the turbine can be maximized, you'll find that the area (more often than not) is inhabited by various species of birds. You don't want to kill birds with your turbine, do you? Now going back to our wind power vs. solar energy match-up, indeed we do have to agree that wind power is more cost efficient. However, both alternative energy resource will play a big role in our future.

It is, therefore, in my humble opinion that we both develop the two technologies simultaneously for each one has their advantages and disadvantages and each one can be properly utilized for specific areas.

We Can Have a Home Powered By Solar Energy:

Do you like to live in a home that is energy efficient? The good news is you can given there are technologies these days that can make that happen and one good example happens to be solar energy. Solar energy is the process of using the sun's radiant rays to power your home. For this to work, you will need to get some solar panels and then have this install by a contractor. Ideally, you will need a flat area measuring about a hundred square feet. This is good to install between 10 to 12 solar panels that can produce about a kilowatt of power. If you think 1 kilowatt is small, think again because this is equivalent to 1,600 kilowatts of hours per year. That translates to 5.5 hours of electricity per day if you are using it to the max. Otherwise, excess power will be stored in the battery which will help bring electricity to the house during a blackout or at night.

Aside from the solar panels, you will also need the inverter, battery, charge controller, wires and support structure. Each of these parts are important since the system will not work without the other so whoever you choose as a contractor should have everything ready prior to installation. Once everything is set up, you can already enjoy your solar powered home.

Since it requires minimal maintenance, it can last up to 20 years before you have to replace anything. If you have a larger area to work with, why not invest in a solar thermal roof? The difference between this and the first one mentioned is that you convert the entire roof into a giant collector. It is quite expensive and takes a couple of days to complete but worth every penny. The only reason why not that many people invest in such a system is because most roofs are not oriented towards the south with the steep pitch needed to maximize solar energy especially during the winter.

You will have to do some major construction work to make this happen. Solar energy is just one way for you to stop relying on power coming from the grid. When the sun isn't shining, you have to be ready by preparing other ways to generate electricity. One example that can be used at home is wind energy. Here, you use fans to collect the wind's kinetic energy similar to windmills that you see in the farm. The only difference is that the blades are connected to a drive shaft that turns an electric generator to produce electricity.

You just have to do some research to find out if solar energy is feasible for your home. You should know how much power you consume on a monthly basis and also where exactly is your house located.

Should your study show it is possible to live on solar energy, it is best to apply for a home equity loan to pay for the installation costs because you will surely get a return on your investment later on in the form of tax credit and a utility bill that won't exceed $10. So what are you waiting for? If you don't want to rely on power from the electric company, go ahead and invest in solar energy.

Why Are Solar Panels So Popular?

Over the past 20 years solar panels have become extremely popular with homeowners, business and the agricultural industry.

There are many different reasons why people are interested in solar but we have narrowed them down to **3 main reasons.**

Money:

Firstly, the most common reason why solar is popular is because of money.

Solar panels can provide homeowners with a massive saving toward their energy bill (if not completely reduce it altogether).

When people catch wind of their neighbors slashing their energy bill in half, they simply want a piece of the pie. By having a reduced energy bill it means that you will free up your cash flow each month to spend on stuff that you like or your family.

The finance side of solar is the main reason why it has become so popular in today's age.

Environment:

The second most popular reason is because of the environment.

Solar panels are being installed to help take a stance against climate change. People are willing to invest their money into something that will not pollute the planet we live on. Installing solar panels will help by generating clean energy that can also be sold.

This is much better than burning fossil fuels and oils which has a negative effect on the planet. We are realising the sustainability of solar panels which is making them more popular.

Government Incentives :

Thirdly, solar panels are getting a name for themselves through government incentives.

It is pretty hard to resist when the government is offering to buy back any excess solar energy you produce...

Plus lets not forget the massive reduction in the upfront cost, an interest free loan to help reduce the cost even more and then a STC certificate that can be sold for money!

Even with commercial solar for businesses there are rebates and grants being offered as incentives to help with the move to solar.

We Need a PV System to Generate Solar Energy : Solar energy has been around for quite some time. In fact, now is the best time to get it if you want to cut your electric bill and do your share to protect the environment. For that to happen, you will need to buy a PV system. This is designed to reduce or eliminate the amount of electricity you purchase from the utility especially when there could be a price increase in the next few months. The best part about the PV system is that it generates clean electricity which is clean, reliable and renewable since it does not emit any harmful gases into the atmosphere. The PV system must be placed in an area that is free from any obstruction otherwise, it will not be able to capture the sun's rays. A lot of experts say that the south facing roof is best while the east and west is sufficient. If the roof is not available, it can be mounted on the ground. You should know that PV systems come in various sizes so you should get the one that matches our electrical needs. If you consume about 6,500 kilowatts a year, then a PV system within the 3 to 4 kilowatt range is right for your home. You can measure this by reviewing your past electric bills and making some projections Naturally, the size of the PV system will determine the amount of space needed. If you do not use that much electricity, 50 square feet may be sufficient. However, a larger system may require a little over 600 square feet. Just remember that a kilowatt of electricity requires an area of 100 square feet. Solar energy is converted with the help of an inverter since this is what changes direct current to alternating current. You will also need batteries so excess energy may be stored so you can still use solar energy during the evening or during a power outage. The size of the PV system is also in direct proportion with the cost. Most cost from $1 to $1.5 per watt and when you include installation, the bill may reach be from $1,500 to $2,500. The cost of the PV system should not discourage you from investing in solar energy. People who use it are able to get tax rebates and it will also increase the value of your home. With that, the only thing to do now is to call a reputable solar energy provider. One other thing you should know about the PV system is that this should also be connected to your grid. For this to work, you have to enter into an interconnection agreement with your utility. This agreement will address the issue with regards to the terms and conditions under which your system is tied up with them. This also includes what is known as net metering which allows you to bank any surplus electricity that your system generates on the electric grid in the same manner that you will be charged accordingly should you consume more electricity than what you have banked. You need a PV system to generate solar energy. You just need to know what size of a system you require so this can be installed by your solar provider.

An Overview on the Interesting Facts about Solar Energy:

There are lots of interesting facts about solar energy. Educating yourself about this will prove to be beneficial in the long run. You can share the information to your loved ones. You can teach them of ways on how they can help to conserve the energy. You can also do your share to help this method to advance if you are a genius in the field. But if you are an ordinary citizen who only wants to enjoy, then feast on. But remember that you also have responsibilities to the environment that you must accomplish in order to do your part in the whole scheme of things. The Facts that Matter

1. Solar radiation makes it possible for the energy coming from the sun to be used as power source and energy that can in turn be used for many purposes. The technology on this aspect is characterized in two ways. They can either be passive or active. This will depend on the methods that are used to get, convert and allocate sunlight. What are active solar techniques? These utilize pumps, photovoltaic panels and fans to renovate sunlight into useful resources. These aim to increase the energy supply that is why these can also be referred as supply side technologies. The passive solar techniques, on the other hand, use only selected resources with constructive thermal properties, utilize the kind of spaces that can circulate air naturally and apply the position of buildings and structures towards the sun. These will lessen the need for other sources and can also be referred as the demand side technology.

2. Solar energy has influenced many factors that surround people. This can be referred in planning and designing buildings. This process can be rooted back at the early days of the architectural history. The Greeks and the Chinese first used such factor in building and constructing their architectural pieces and on their planning methods.

3. Solar energy is also being utilized by the agricultural sector because they rely heavily on its benefits in order to gain more harvest. They developed ways in order to plant the kind of crops that will grow according to the amount of sun that they will be getting for the season. This can also be used to dry the crops, pump water, brooding of chicks and to dry animal manures that can later be used as fertilizers.

4. On seasons like the Little Ice Age, fruit walls were used by French and Chinese farmers to be able to collect and store solar energy to help them keep the plants warm and to speedy up the process of ripening of fruits. These walls serve as the thermal masses. The fruit walls that were first developed were perpendicular to the ground and faced the south direction. Over time, innovations were done and slopping walls were used to gain more advantage from the sun. 5. To convert the solar light into heat, people have developed green houses. These enable the production and cultivation of specialty crops all year round. Such innovation made it possible for crops to be produced in untimely seasons and in places where you think that those plants won't grow. And these are only some of the interesting facts about solar energy. These give you a good peek at how wonderful nature is and how people have developed ways to use it to advance in many aspects of their lives.

5. To convert the solar light into heat, people have developed green houses. These enable the production and cultivation of specialty crops all year round. Such innovation made it possible for crops to be produced in untimely seasons and in places where you think that those plants won't grow. And these are only some of the interesting facts about solar energy. These give you a good peek at how wonderful nature is and how people have developed ways to use it to advance in many aspects of their lives.

Analysing the benefits of solar energy:

We all know that using solar energy is a good thing to do. We have heard, and there are quite a number of them, all about the benefits of solar energy and we can't agree why we can't turn this alternative form of energy source to a primary one. But despite the advantages, solar power has yet to fully make it in the mainstream. Let's go back and discuss a couple of the advantages of solar energy and see why keep going back to fossil fuels for energy resource. In the long run, solar power saves money. Initial costs of installation and operations may be more expensive that other energy forms but after settling the expenses, you have an energy resource that is free. Nobody charges for using sunlight, right? The return of investment can also be shorter depending on how much energy you use. You won't spend too much on maintenance either plus those photovoltaic cells can last for 15 to 20 years. There are no mechanical or moving parts to oil and maintain nor are there parts that need to be replaced yearly. Of course solar power is environmental friendly. First its renewable not like fossil fuels which according to studies will be gone in four to five decades. The process of converting energy to usable electricity does not involve the release of toxic chemicals which can harm the environment. Carbon dioxide, nitrogen oxide, sulphur dioxide, lead, and mercury emissions will be a memory of the past when everyone goes solar. Relying on the sun for power also helps reduce global warming. Aside from the toxic wastes and pollutants, using solar power will limit other aspects of the energy industry like hazards of working with and transporting oil or natural gas. Also, other health risks are present in the use of other fuels like kerosene and candles which are still popular in third world countries. With solar energy, these risks will be minimized if not totally eliminated. The use of solar panels is also good for remote areas where providing basic electricity services is troublesome if not totally impossible at all. Solar energy can be transported to far flung villages and once installed they can be left alone for years with little or without maintenance. Communities in Asian countries have successfully installed solar panels in their community and have been enjoying the benefits of clean and reliable power for years.

For a poor country, producing electricity through solar energy can mean independence from oil producing countries which controls the supply and prices of oil. With such independence, new policies on energy can be created which will maximize the benefit for its citizens. Countries will also not be wary on natural disasters which hampers delivery of oil. With this new found independence, countries can invest its national budget on other programs aside from purchasing oil from foreign sources. There are several disadvantages of using solar power and one of which is the costs. But thinking about it in the long run, you'll see that the benefits of solar energy outweigh the disadvantages. Plus, with the current development in the field of science and technology, solar power is becoming more and more convenient and it would not be surprising to find solar energy as a primary source of power in the next few years

Arguments against solar energy:

We all know that solar energy is a good renewable energy resource and that we should start to utilize it more especially when the Earth's fossil fuel reserves are slowly dwindling and will run out in 30 to 50 years. We better look at the various alternative energies and begin a fast tracking of development to hasten our independence on non-renewable fossil fuels. And solar energy is as good as any other alternative energy resource out there. However, several arguments against solar energy have been raised through the years. But probably the most convincing argument is the high costs of solar energy utilization. The problem with solar energy is that you can only harness it during the daytime. And even when the sun is up, the sunlight will be interrupted by occasional cloud covers, rains, fog, and even smog. So in order to harness the sun's energy we need equipment that can get as much solar power as possible at a given time and we need some way of storing that energy so we can use them without any interruptions. We do have the technology to harness the sun's energy, convert it into usable electricity, and store them for future use. And that technology itself is the primary reason why solar power has not caught on even today.

The process of making solar panels as well as the technology for storing that harnessed power remains to be quite expensive. The good thing about this fact today is that due to the recent increase in the costs of fuel and gas, solar power is no longer a far fetched alternative. The gap between the costs has gone down considerably and hopefully in the near future, the costs of solar energy production will be quite competitive. Furthermore, the costs of photovoltaic cells are indeed quite expensive that contemporary oil and gas equipment. But one of the flaws of the argument of costs is that people tend to limit their perspective of solar energy as to only referring to photovoltaic cells. There are other means of harnessing solar energy and not all of them are as expensive as PV cell manufacturing. One way of getting the sun's energy and converting it into usable electricity is the concept of solar thermal plants. In solar thermal technology, various solar collectors are utilized to generate heat which can be applied from the simplest heating and ventilation of houses to the production of massive amounts of electricity.

The use of mirrors or lenses to reflect sunlight to towers equipped with liquids that heat up and produce steam. The steam then turns turbines which in turn generates the electricity needed. The process adds another step compared to photovoltaics which converts solar energy directly into electricity. Nevertheless, solar thermal systems of power production is cheaper that the production of PV cells. For a larger consumer market, it seems that solar thermal energy is the way to go. Regardless, the point here really is to emphasize that solar energy has more to offer. The cost of production is a valid argument against solar energy but still there are ways around it. Costs can be minimized by using other techniques of harnessing solar energy or future developments in the field of science and technology will produce products that are more cost efficient that what are available today.

Countries on the helm of solar energy technology:

The US is not a leading user of solar energy for a very obvious reason: they can still afford to buy fossil fuels from the international market. In other countries the oil prices are ten times higher in the US and sometimes going for the alternative is a lot better in the long run. Today, more and more countries are looking at solar energy as a primary source of power. There are several countries which can be considered as at the helm of solar energy technology.The number one use of solar energy is Germany. It captures almost 50% of the world market of photovoltaic cells. Nowhere else in the world can you find the most number of households with solar panels installed on their roof tops. Germany has this Renewable Energies Laws (EEG) which passed in 2000. The law certainly helped Germans feel the need to go renewable.

According to statistics, Germans invested nearly US$5 billion in solar photovoltaic systems and have contributed considerable in the growth of the solar energy market. Although most of the things that we see are solar panels, it doesn't mean that Germany's solar industry is not limited to the production of photovoltaic cells for electricity. Other notable usage in Germany includes solar panels for home water heating system. Some news indicate that the German solar hot water market earns U.S.$1.5 billion per year. The "solar park" in Arnstein, Bavaria, Germany is one of the biggest photovoltaic plants in the world. It became operational in 2006 and with more than 1,400 PV solar panels, it can produce 12 megawatts of energy.The next biggest country in terms of usage of solar energy is Spain. The solar energy usage in the country, more specifically the photovoltaic cells usage, has a world market share of 27%. Spain has no sign of slowing down its aggressive and pro-active approach in solar energy. Solar fields are being constructed one of the latest ones is the 60 MW solar field in Olmedilla de Alarcón, near Cuenca. There are other big solar plants in Spain and these include the solar park 12 miles outside of Salamanca, Salamanca, Spain which have 70,000 PV panels divided into three 36-hectare arrays. The arrays produce an output is 13.8 megawatts and has been powering roughly 5,000 homes since it opened in 2007. And the rest of the world follow Germany and Spain. Japan and the US still have a market share in the photovoltaic world market. The two countries both have an 8% market share, a far cry from Germany and Spain. Nevertheless, it is quite important that countries continue to improve their status in the world solar market. Other notable country that uses solar power includes Algeria, Australia, Italy, and Portugal. Aside from the rich European countries, people in Israel. and India are realizing the importance of having alternative sources of energy. These are the countries on the helm of solar energy technology. But, other countries are slowly catching up. The government of Israel, for example, required all residential buildings to install solar water heating systems in the early 90s. Today, business establishments like hotels and office buildings are trying to use solar power as an alternative from using fossil fuels whose prices continue to soar in the world market. India is facing a similar energy crisis and they are also looking at solar energy to get them through it.

Facts about Solar Energy, Some Things to Ponder and why?:

What are the facts about solar energy that we know? It is given that this comes from the sun. This was developed by people in order to take advantage and benefit from everything that the sun can provide. You can also easily guess the goals of these people why they opt to develop such technology. For one, they want to make lives easier to live. Second, they want to find other resources that people can use in their everyday lives. Maybe they also want to profit from the experience because if this will all be successful, people, businesses and industries will gain a lot from what is being developed. During the first years of its introduction, people deem that this technological advancement can only be used by wealthy people. It used to cater mostly for the can afford types of individuals. What if it can heat pool and can run spas? .But the evolution of the solar energy is just starting.

Nowadays, the benefits can be felt even by ordinary citizens. Researchers keep thinking of ways to arrive at this state. And this is proving to be good for everybody's sake. The scientists developed solar panels that can power up homes. They made this available not only for the rich and famous, but they sold the idea to governments. The latter used the innovation to bring electricity to people in their countries who still haven't experienced to live in the comfort of having this kind of power source. As a result, many people experience how it is like to have lights. They have also resorted to businesses that can be aided by such technology. The maintenance is still on-going while the technology is still being pursued. But the fact remains that this has been made available even for the ordinary Person. 2. Aside from electricity, solar energy can be used to heat water and cook food. Life is really becoming easier as people find ways to achieve such state. While the developments are still under way, people are finding ways to make such resource available for everybody.

Different organizations and government agencies help in making this product affordable for everyone no matter what your status in life is. As time passes by, people will be able to develop more and more gadgets and tools to make lives easier. There will come a time when almost everybody can benefit from this. The first notion that the solar energy is only for the wealthy will cease to be remembered. The responsibility now lies on to people's hands to take care of nature. They must give back to nature for everything that they have also gotten in the process. Technological advancements can be better achieved if people will consider how these can affect the natural habitat in general. It is okay to get what people want and what people need. But this must always be done with precaution and by thinking of the effects that these will have on everything. It is fun to learn some facts about solar energy every once in a while. These will excite you about the process. But more so, these must open your eyes to the whole scheme of nature and how important it is to take care of our surroundings to be able to benefit more in the long run.

How to Conserve Solar Energy through Your Little Ways:

As an ordinary person who lives according to what the day brings, have you ever thought about how to conserve solar energy? Do you even care? You may think you are an ordinary worker, or a simple wife or mother. Should you even care about such things? The answer is yes. You must bear in mind that you are part of a whole spectrum of nature. Whatever you do will affect all the things around you. Everything must be conserved, including solar energy. Here are some suggestions to throw in your little efforts to achieve this goal.

1. Plant trees. Nature works wonders. Every element around us affects everything else. By planting trees, you will be able to maximize the energy coming from the sun. This will be directed to help the plants grow and produce harvests. With healthy plants and trees rooted to the soil, the soil will be firm. This will be able to hold its structure even in times of natural disasters.

2. Limit your use of the energy coming from the sun. With today's innovations, there are lots of things that are being developed to use solar energy as a power source. The source may be free. But to be able to turn it to such power source, there are things that are utilized for this reason. If you will abuse the use of such technology, the crash of the materials used to put this up will be fast. This will take a toll on you especially if you rely a lot on this advancement.

3. Teach kids about the importance of solar energy. You can gain knowledge through research and through your everyday interaction with other people about this thing called the solar energy. You must tell your kids about its importance, they must be educated about it at an early age. They are the future of the nation. What you teach them now will be instilled to them until they grow old. At such a young age, they must know about how they can contribute to conserve energy.

4. Take good care of nature. This is the most important thing that you can do to help advance such cause. The sun can cause damage to people and nature if people won't do the necessary steps to care for nature in the first place. There are lots of things that you get from the environment. It wouldn't hurt to look back every now and then and see what you can do to give back to what it has already given to you. The idea here is that everything in this life must be conserved. You cannot abuse the power that you possess to gain so much without even thinking how your actions affect the world around you. It is all right to go with the flow of the continuing advancement of the technology. Look at the options available to you nowadays with regards to solar energy. This can be used to power homes and vehicles. This can give light, heat water and cook your food. This can give you satellite television and phones for supreme entertainment and communications enjoyment. This can give you luxuries like spas and warm water at pools. You must learn everything on how to conserve solar energy so that you can do your part in making sure that such resource will be available as long as you live.

How Does Solar Energy Work:

Ever wondered how solar energy is converted into electricity? Well, this will give you an idea how it works. First, solar panels are installed over a flat surface like the roof of your home. Once activated, it absorbs the sun's rays since the panels are made of semi-conducting materials such as silicon. Electrons are then knocked off loose from their atoms so it can produce electricity. This process by which light is converted into electricity is better known as the photovoltaic effect. From there, you now have direct current electricity and when this enters an inverter, it is converted into 220 volt AC which is the electricity needed to power the home. Of course this is connected to the utility panel in the house so the lights and the appliances will work when these are switched on. If you are not using that much electricity from the solar energy generated, it is stored in a battery so will be able to supply the house with power during a power outage or at night. Should the battery be full, the excess electricity is then exported to the utility grid if your system happens to be connected to it. When your solar energy runs out, utility supplied electricity kicks in.

If you are not using that much electricity from the solar energy generated, it is stored in a battery so will be able to supply the house with power during a power outage or at night. Should the battery be full, the excess electricity is then exported to the utility grid if your system happens to be connected to it.When your solar energy runs out, utility supplied electricity kicks in. The flow of electricity of solar energy is measured using a utility meter which spins backward and forward. It will go backward when you are producing more energy than you need and forward when you need additional power from the utility company. These two are only offset when you pay for the additional energy from the utility company. Any surplus is sold back to what is known as net metering

A smaller version of this is used to power a water heater inside the home. Using the same principles, homeowners get to convert sunlight into heat to get warm water. As you can see, transforming sunlight into solar energy is very easy. But why do countries like Germany and Japan use it more often than the US? The answer is because it is much cheaper for them to use this form of alternative energy compared to oil. Also, although the US initiated this during the 1973 oil crisis, it is not as popular as it was back then because the government neither increased the budget in research for alternative forms of energy nor gave incentives so people will be encourage into doing that again.

Most state regulations also prohibit individuals from installing their own devices even if this is used to give you warm water. Chances are, you won't even find anyone to do it so you will probably have to do it yourself. Just remember that if there is a problem with the plumbing, your insurance will not cover it. Should the state allow you to install such a system, you will not be entitled to the rebate. Using solar cells is just one way to make the most out of solar energy. Your other option is passive solar energy which helps avoid heat loss so those inside will not feel too cold or too hot throughout the day. This is used by a lot of homeowners living in the southwest since they do not need that much insulation compared to homeowners who live in other parts of the US.

Net Metering and Solar Energy:

You can't help but get into net metering when you decide to invest in solar energy because you sometimes consume more or less than what you actually generate. When you consume less energy, your electric meter spins backward, if you use more then it goes forward. Net metering is simply a special metering and billing agreement between you and the electric service provider. You are eligible for this if you reside in a residential area and generate some form of energy using solar, wind energy or a combination of both. It also has to be located on your premises and connected to the grid. For this to work, you need to have a meter capable of moving in both directions. Most meters these days can do that but if your provider wants to use two meters, they will have to pay for it.

However, if you enter into a time of use billing agreement, you will have to be one to buy the unit. The net metering agreement works by letting you use the electricity you generate first before you use what you normally get from your electric service provider. Your meter should show the net which is measured as the difference between the electricity you purchased and what you actually purchased. The benefit of the net metering system is that it allows you to store electricity when you are not there and then use it the moment you get home. Since there is a law that expands net metering, you can take advantage of it by generating electricity during peak hours and then using it during off peak periods. Another benefit is the fact that you only pay the net electricity that you use. If you consume below the baseline, you pay less and more if you go over it. If what you use offsets what you normally get from a provider, then you will most likely pay a lower rate. Since you entered into an agreement with your provider, you will still be billed monthly.

This will state the amount of power you generated and the amount you actually consumed. On the anniversary of your agreement, you will be billed for the previous 12 months but you can also request for this on a monthly basis. Keep in mind that you will not be paid for the excess generation of electricity in a given year although some do. If you want to use solar energy, you have to contact your electric service provider and ask if they offer net metering. When the papers are drawn up, remember that they cannot require you to pay for any meters beyond the bi-directional meter. They cannot conduct any tests or impose any requirements if it meets existing national standards for grid-interconnected systems. Lastly, you don't have to buy additional insurance or buy power from any of their affiliates.

Net metering is a policy and also an incentive when you decide to use solar energy. This is because you reduce the number of kilowatts used by your electric service provider which in turn decreases the emissions of carbon dioxide into the air.

Solar energy in households:

The sun is a great source of energy. It would be great to use solar energy in your homes especially nowadays when the prices of oil and gas continue to increase. Because of the high fuel and gas prices, more and more people are experimenting on the use of solar energy in their households in their attempts to minimize the costs of basic utilities. The sun's energy can be harnessed in different ways depending on how you would utilize the end product. There are so called solar collectors which are placed on the roof tops or used in buildings. The main purpose of these solar collectors is to provide heating and even ventilation for the houses and buildings.

These collectors harness the sun's energy by magnifying the sunlight several times and transferring that heat to air or water. That heated air or water is stored and will provide the building or home heating and hot water whenever needed. The only problem here is that not all places have equal amounts of sunlight.As you go farther from the equator, the strength of the sun is reduced. But still, this is a much better solution than relying on electric grids which do not reach remote areas. It is just a mater of storing the heat generated from the solar collector properly. For example, some buildings in Sweden utilized an underground storage facility where solar energy is stored resulting to savings from heating the building and their water. In areas where gas and fuel are out of reach of the pockets of poor communities, residents have to rely on solar cooking for their meals. They use this bowl shaped discs equipped with mirrors or reflectors which directs all the sunlight on the middle where a pot is placed.

The same technology is being used in India, Sri Lanka, and Nepal. This serves are a good alternative from conventional fuels like coal, firewood, and gas. They can use these solar stoves during a sunny day and use traditional fuels when the weather is not that good. This reliance by communities on solar cooking should encourage more studies on how to make photovoltaic cells cheaper for an ordinary household. At this time, the use of solar cells is not economically friendly for a single household. However, the approach here is to install a series of solar panels which would be shared by the whole community. This could be a good idea depending on your usage, but for basic lighting purposes these could work in small poor communities. In some areas, community cooperatives have found ways to bring electricity to households out of reach of power grids.

In the Philippines for example, a local cooperative provided households loans to enable them to install a basic solar power module which can produce enough electricity for three light bulbs. This ay be laughable in our standards but to these people who have been living all their lives with the flickering light of the candles, three electric light bulbs make a great deal of a difference.

The story is the same in other countries. In Israel, the high costs of photovoltaic cells have clamped down the growth of solar energy in the country. It if fortunate, therefore, that the Israeli government is now providing incentives for households that would use solar energy. However, according to industry analysts, the costs of solar cells production will go down as the demand increase.

Also, most are hopeful that recent discoveries and advancement in technologies will find a way to bring down costs of using solar energy. Ordinary households using solar energy is an ideal scenario that we should all strive to achieve.

Solar energy simplified:

The sun shines, we collect the sunlight, we convert the sunlight into usable forms, and we enjoy the benefits. You can't get any simpler than that. But okay, I know you need more explanations. You've been looking all over the web for information and you need, no you deserve, more than just a single sentence. The following would be my attempt in simplifying the concept of solar energy and I just hope you get something out of it. The sun produces huge amounts of energy. But what the earth gets is a pretty small share of that energy. However, even if we get only a miniscule amount, the energy we receive from the sun is more than enough for our needs. Believe it or not, a day's worth of sunlight when harnessed properly can power a big country like the US for more than a year.

So if that's how much energy we can get from the sun, why do we rely too much on fossil fuels which will disappear in 40 to 50 years time? The main problem is that the sun shines all throughout the world. That energy is so spread out that harnessing it is really a challenge. But still, there are other factors at work here, political, economical, and even cultural in nature which contributes to the slow progress of solar technologies. But that will need a whole chapter, nay, a whole book to discuss so let's leave that alone for a moment. There are various ways how we harness sunlight and the specific way may depend on how we plan to use that energy. But we can divide the usage into two general concepts, converting solar power into heat and the other one is converting it into electricity.

Using solar power to heat homes is a pretty good example of the first category. There are two ways that can be used, the first one relies on the positioning of the house's windows and the second one involves the use of some mechanical devices to distribute the heat throughout the house. Solar water heaters are also now available. What you do is provide a solar collector where the heat from the sun is trapped and collected. That heat is then transferred to the after that goes out of your faucets and showers. Converting solar power into electricity, however, needs a little bit more explanation. There are basically two ways we can get electricity out of solar power. The first one involves the use of photovoltaic cells and the second one is using various solar thermal systems. Photovoltaic cells are more commonly known as solar cells. These cells are made from silicon wafers and phosphorous.

When sunlight strikes the surface of the silicon wafers, free electrons are produced. The electrons are then harnessed via attaching a wire to the cells. As the electrons leave the cells and pass through the wire, an electronic current is produced. One major flaw of the photovoltaic cells is that they can be quite expensive plus they only convert a small amount of sunlight. Hopefully these cells can be cheaper, more efficient and more suitable to the needs of consumers in the future.

The great thing about solar energy is that it does not produce any kinds of pollution unlike fossil fuels which spit out substantive amounts of pollutants in the air and even in the water. Plus the sun is pretty much in good health aid it is still very far from dying. We can utilize more than enough energy from the sun that will last us for a lifetime.

Solar Energy, How Does It Benefit the Agricultural Sector:

What is solar energy? To put it simply, this is the energy coming from the sun. The heat and light that the sun provides are essential to life. Can you even imagine life without the sun? It will not be normal and there are lots of things and experiences that people can no longer indulge into if ever that will be the case. Everybody relies on the sun for its benefits. Did you know that the earth gets 1740 watts of insolation or the incoming radiation from the sun? This happens at the upper part of the atmosphere. Almost 30% gets reflected back to the space. The rest of the percentage is being absorbed by the clouds, land masses and oceans.

The Agricultural Sector :

If you can think of one industry that won't survive without the energy coming from the sun, what will be the first thing on your mind? There may be many sectors that must rely on the sun's benefits. But the agricultural and horticulture industry will not thrive without it. They have no other options. If the sun will be gone, these sectors will die. The sun is need by the agricultural and horticulture departments to be able to grow their produce. The latter is needed by people as well as animals. These sectors' productivity will depend on the amount of energy that they are getting from the sun. It must be balanced in all ways. It can never too little. And it must also not be so much. If it is too little, the plans may not be able to grow accordingly. The farmers won't achieve the required harvests in order to feed the population. And if it is too much, this will damage the crops. This will also cause bad effects on people's health. But if the latter is the case, people can think of ways in order to achieve the needed produce by manually trying to reduce the amount of heat that can be directed on the plants. But if the situation becomes unbearable, it might lead to drought and deaths. Farmers must know when the sun will be up, when sunny days will be long and factors like that so that they can settle for what kinds of plants they must plant to survive the kind of weather condition.

Here are only some of the things that they resort to in order to optimize the full benefits of the energy coming from the sun.

- Timed planting cycles
- Timed planting cycles

- Tailored row orientation
- Mixing different varieties of crops to improve the yields

Do you ever wonder what farmers did in times like the Little Ice Age? It is said that English and French farmers resorted to fruit walls. These fruit walls help in maximizing the collection of the energy from the sun. These serve as the thermal masses. These walls help in keeping the plants warm to speed up the process of growing and ripening of produce.

The sun's energy is also being utilized in these sectors in vital activities such as drying the crops, pumping of water, drying animals' manure, brooding of chicks and a lot more. It is hard to imagine the agriculture and horticulture sectors to survive without the solar energy. If there are anybody who knows the importance of the sun, these people are the first in line.

Solar Energy is the Future:

We consume fossil fuels at a greater rate than we have ever had over the past 50 years. That demand is fueled by the increase of cars on the street,the number of planes that take to the air and the number of homes that need electricity. Sadly, we will have depleted these resources by the end of this century which is why we have to come up with other ways to get power and solar energy may be the future. Solar energy is simply extracting the sun's energy for power. Just to tell you how powerful the sun is, it can burn scrub lands and give you sunburn if you are out in the sun without any protection. In fact, the Greeks and the Chinese used this to set fire until the 1880's by Charles Fritts made the first solar cell.

Instead of using a heater to warm up the home, sunlight can be used to control the temperature. You will just need large windows and shades to control the amount of sunlight that will go inside and keep the heat absorbed during the day to remain at night. Solar energy can also provide warm water as it warms up cold water that passes down through the closed flat panels called collectors. But solar energy does not only give warmth to the home.

It can also be used to help power it which reduces our dependence on non-renewable resources like oil or coal. This occurs when solar cells are installed on the roof so it will be able to capture as much solar rays as possible and then converts this into electricity. You will need 10 or 12 to capture at least a kilowatt of power and more if you are powering more than just your home. The only limitation which challenges the use of solar energy is that it can only generate power during the day. The answer to this is to put an auxiliary system in place that will store the energy and kick when the sun is not available. This comes in the form of batteries which will provide power in the evening or a brownout. Advances in technology have taken solar energy to the next level.

NASA uses it to power satellites in orbit, solar panels installed onboard aircraft allow it to fly across oceans while cars can travel speeds up to 40 miles per hour. It is used to power a lighthouse so seafarers will be able to find their way at sea while aircraft can land in an airport in the middle of the frozen desert. Solar energy is safe for the environment since it does not emit any harmful gases or chemicals into the air. It is a renewable resource that has not yet been fully tapped by a lot of countries which makes it very viable for the future.

But is it the only answer to reduce our dependence on oil? No because solar energy is just one of the options. We can also harness the power of the wind, the wave in the oceans, geothermal heat, hydroelectricity and a lot more instead of relying on coal or even nuclear energy that may harm the environment. It is something we have to push for the next generation.

Technologies for harnessing solar energy:

Harnessing the sun's energy efficiently is not an easy feat. The sunlight is so widespread that finding the most effective way of capturing it requires advanced knowledge and technology. There are several technologies for utilizing solar energy and all are unique and are dedicated for specific applications. First up are the photovoltaic cells or commonly known as solar cells. These are probably the best known way of harnessing the energy's sun. Whenever one talk about solar power, the first things that come to mind include having panels and panels of photovoltaic cells or PV. These cells contain semi-conductors, commonly are made from silicon, which absorbs the light from the sun. When sunlight hit the surface of the silicon, new free electrons are created. As the electrons are channeled out of the silicon, electric current is created. The second solar power technology is the concentrating solar power systems. This one involves using mirrors to reflect sunlight to one area. Some systems incorporate high tech devices to track the movement of the sun and adjust the mirrors to maximize the amount of sunlight the system receives. The sunlight reflected from the mirrors is used to heat or power a conventional power plant. Other systems channel the light from the mirrors to an area filled with photovoltaic cells. There are several kinds of concentrated solar power systems, the most popular ones are the solar trough, parabolic dish and solar power tower. The solar trough uses large, U-shaped (parabolic) reflectors to point the sunlight to a tower at the center of the mirrors. At the center tower, hot oil is heated by the sun's energy and help boil water to create steam which is then used to power convention plants. The power tower system uses the same concept as solar troughs.

Mirrors are used to reflect sunlight to a center tower where a liquid is heated and utilized for the creation of steam which will power a power. The parabolic dish system uses mirrored dishes to focus and concentrate sunlight onto a receiver. The size of the dish varies but it is commonly 10 times bigger than an ordinary cable satellite dish. Another solar power technology used today is the solar water heating systems. This is a simple one. The process involves collecting the energy directly from the sun to heat water or liquids which in turn heats up the water.

This is more common in households are ideal for family use. In order to capture the sunlight, solar panels have to be installed in your home or in the place where you will be needing hot water like a swimming pool area. You will need a big space for this but in the long run, you will be able to save lots of money from your electric bill. For commercial establishments, an ideal solar power technology is the transpired solar collector or otherwise known as the solar wall. It involves using perforated solar collectors where outside air passes before it enters the building.

These are but a few of the technologies around which can be used for utilizing the power of the sun. The technologies for harnessing solar energy continue to evolve as new technologies and discoveries are being accomplished. Everything might change in a few years time. Plus, the whole solar power technologies will become more price competitive which will benefit the general consumers.

The downsides of solar energy:

Not that I'm against using solar energy or anything but there are some downsides of using solar energy. My intention is to illustrate these disadvantages so that people can realize the other side of the coin to prepare them and not so much as to dissuade them from using solar energy. I am for everything that can save the planet. View this explanation as an introduction where we can still improve the current technologies involving solar energy. One of the first and major drawbacks of using solar power is the costs. The expense is considerably higher than the conventional electric installation. From the purchase to the initial installations of the solar panel unit, the cost is a significant factor to consider.

The high costs of solar power panels lie on the expensive semi-conductor materials that convert sunlight into electricity. However, as technology progresses and as the need slowly increases, the costs of solar panels are expected to go down, something on the level of being competitive with other energy resources. Another to consider is space. We're talking about installing a solar panel which is not small. It requires a significant amount of space which also helps maximize the amount of sunlight it can collect and convert into electricity. Some households will have the panels installed on their roof others will designate a place for it on the year or on top of a pole. The same space problems will need to be readdressed once you decide to add panels when your current setup is no longer enough for your family's needs. Positioning is also vital.

The solar panels will need to be facing a direction where it will receive the most amount of sunlight in a day. However, there is always a solution. If space does not permit such installations, there are some add-ons that can help maximize sun exposure. Positioning is also vital.

The solar panels will need to be facing a direction where it will receive the most amount of sunlight in a day. However, there is always a solution. If space does not permit such installations, there are some add-ons that can help maximize sun exposure. At night, you might encounter a problem with relying solely on solar power. Although the solution here is to purchase batteries which you can charge during the day and use at night. You will need a couple of batteries though to be able to sustain your electricity needs through cloudy, stormy or smoggy or foggy times during the day. As far as solar powered transportation services go, there are still some quirks that need to be fixed before mass production of such vehicles is rolled out.

The most noticeable difference is the speed. Solar powered cars are far slower that their counterparts. But again, due to the fast development of the solar car and the technologies that go with it, this drawback will soon disappear. When you look at the things that I mentioned about the disadvantages of solar energy, you will see that most of them have solutions while others you just need to compromise a bit. I still think that harnessing the power of the sun is the way to go, so these downsides of solar energy are just a small obstacle that we need to overcome.

The future of solar energy on transportation:

Are you familiar with the World Solar Challenge? It is a race specifically for solar cars. Solar cars basically have arrays of photovoltaic cells which converts the sun's rays into usable electrical energy. The purpose of the race is to raise awareness on the use of the sun's energy on transportation and the development of other alternative forms of energy particularly the solar cells. The future of using solar energy on transportation services may still be a little hazy given the practical difficulties involve in converting ordinary cars into solar cars but the idea is here to stay and hopefully develops into something promising and useful. At this point, solar cars have been built to join solar car races. Very few have been constructed for practical and commercial purposes.

There are several reasons why the solar car remains on the background. The design of a solar car relies on the electrical system of the vehicle. The system controls the electricity the flows from the photovoltaic cells to the batteries, to the wheels, and to the controls. The electric motor that moves the vehicle is powered purely by the electricity produced by the solar cells.

The solar cells, depending on the number installed on the vehicle, can produce more or less 1000 watts of power from the sun's rays. To give you an idea, 1000 watts is just enough electricity to power an electric iron or even a toaster. And since the sun will most likely be covered by clouds at one time or the other, or the car goes through a tunnel or something, solar cars are equipped with batteries to serve as backup power supply for the motor. The battery packs are charged by the solar cells. However, the batteries are not charge while driving the solar car unless you intend to go very slow. Just like a gas pedal in conventional motors, a motor controller regulates the amount of electricity that enters the motor to speed up or slow down the vehicle whenever needed. Solar cars are not that slow as perceived by almost everyone.

These cars can go to as fast as 80-85 mph. With this, you can see why solar cars are not yet into commercial production. Nowadays, solar cells can harness more than 21% of the sun's energy that hit the surface. If the time comes that the cells can actually get more energy from the sun then maybe we can see solar cars on the streets. But at this time, it is quite difficult to make a commercial production model of a solar car. Nevertheless, there are companies who have already created some concept solar cars and are testing how road worthy they are. There's even a scooter that is street legal and runs from batteries charged from photovoltaic cells. Other possible application of solar car technologies is on golf carts which runs pretty slow in the first place and can be appreciated by golfers as well.

The future of solar energy on transportation is still not that clear. The application of solar energy on homes and buildings has been moving forward in recent years so hopefully we can find new ways of converting the sun's energy into usable electricity. And this time something that can be economically and efficiently installed in conventional cars.

The Future of Solar Energy, How It Looks and How It Affects Nature:

The future of solar energy lies on the indigenous hands of people who never tire out from thinking of ways in order to make life easier to live. With the advancement in the technology, the boom of the Internet age and a lot of other things, there will come a time when people will turn their backs on whatever is conventional. This can be good and bad in many ways, depending on who is looking at it and from what perspective. But people's quest for the advancement and development of everything that surrounds them provides lots of negative effects as well.

Here are only some.

1.Sometimes, people neglect the environment and how to properly take care of it for the mere fact that they are greedy to get their ideas done no matter what the consequences to the nature will be. Such advancements create harmful effects in the whole state and balance of nature. How many times have you heard about forest denudation or grave floods that kill people? All these occurrences can also be rooted to the activities of men that suffice for their own good without so much consideration for their natural habitat and the nature.

2. With the continuing advancement of everything that surrounds people, the generational gap becomes wider and wider. Old folks will fight for the benefits of the conventional tools and mediums. The newer generations cannot afford to sit on those old ways to do things. They are a slave to the continuing technological developments. It is okay to initiate change. It is good to find better ways to do things. But people must be cautious in achieving this. They must think about everything around them before they even start on their venture to newer and better ways to achieve greatness. The Innovations As of today, solar energy is one of the best options that people have with regards to alternative power sources. This has already evolved. There was a time when you can only avail such power source when the sun is present and that is during daytime. With the genius of the people behind the development of this resource, they were able to create green gas that can produce electricity. This is done by splitting water properties into hydrogen and oxygen. Both gasses will then be grouped into a cell that will be the electricity source. The same geniuses estimated that the entire planet can rely to an hour of sunlight for its one year electricity consumption. Solar cells have been developed to produce electricity from the energy coming from the sun. The panels for such technology can also be used to heat water and cook food. There are now the solar heating, solar cookers and solar furnaces as add-ons to this innovative venture. There are now hydrogen based cars. These are fueled by the split hydrogen in water. The solar cells also power the satellites that orbit through the surface of the Earth. This is the reason why there are advancements that people benefit from such as satellite phones and TV, accurate weather forecasting, even the development of the GPS technology and a lot more. There are a lot of benefits that people can gain from the future of solar energy. You just have to think that whatever you do or however you use such technology for your own good, you must always think of ways to protect your environment first to be able to get the most out of such improvements.

The Benefits of Solar Energy:

Solar energy will benefit a lot of people and not only the rich. This is why some governments have increased funding for this type of technology because they are aware of its many benefits. For one, solar energy is very cheap compared to other technologies. It is also renewable unlike coal or the rest which are non-renewable and hard to maintain. It also improves the health of people since it does not produce any carbon dioxide emissions unlike kerosene lamps that give out fumes which are just as deadly as smoking 2 packs of cigarettes a day. It also reduces the incidents of fire that are often associated with the use of kerosene, candles,diesel fuel and gasoline for generators. Solar energy is almost maintenance free because the solar cells used will last for 20 years or more before it has to be replaced.

You just have to keep the panels clean so it is able to absorb sunlight and convert that into electricity. These are also very useful in remote locations where power lines are not yet available. Some examples of these include fish houses, highway signs,marine applications, remote lighting and telecommunication. If countries focus on solar energy and other renewable techniques, they will be able to conserve their foreign exchange because they no longer have to use it to pay for foreign oil. This money can then be used for other things such as health care, infrastructure projects and education.

Solar energy will also reduce your electricity bills because you are no longer dependent on electricity coming from the power company. The only downside to solar energy is the initial cost in setting it up. Yes you will have to buy a lot of solar panels which are quite expensive but in the long run, you will be able to save more because you don't have to pay for anything else to keep them running. Should the cost of solar cells be beyond your budget, you can probably invest in used systems first then try to acquire the brand new ones later on. Another benefit of using solar energy is that you get to conserve fossil fuels and other natural resources that are quickly diminishing as a direct result of an increase in the world's population which could compromise the needs of the future generations. So should people get into solar energy? The answer is yes because it is safe, cheap and good for the environment. You only have to worry when the sun isn't shining because when this happens, rays from the sun won't be able to produce electricity so you have to rely on other means to get power. The same also goes when there is a blackout or brownout because you will soon lose power from your solar system.

The demand for solar energy is increasing and you should join in. Aside from reducing your electric bill, homeowners who use solar energy may claim up to $2,000 in federal investment tax credit in the first year while businesses may claim a 30% federal investment tax credit.

Believe it or not, solar energy has one other benefit and that it increases the value of your home. According to home appraisers, a dollar decrease in your energy bill results in a $20 increase in its property value so do the match and you can easily figure out how much your home will be worth after you decide to invest in solar energy.

The History of Solar Energy:

Solar energy is for everyone simply because the sun shines in every corner of the planet. In fact, the history of solar energy can be traced back to the Greeks that were then passed on to the Romans which marked the first people to ever use the passive solar design. Passive solar design is a way to warm the home based on the dwelling's design. They may not have had glass windows back then but their architecture made it possible for the people to use the sun's rays to light and heat indoor spaces. As a result, there was no need to burn food that often which was in short supply. In 1861, Auguste Mouchout invented the first active solar motor. Unfortunately, its expensive price made it impossible to produce commercially. Less than 20 years later, Charles Fritts invented solar cells,which will later on be used to power homes, heaters, satellites and other devices today. Since what he invented was very primitive, other people experimented on solar energy. One such person was

Albert Einstein who won the Nobel Prize for physics in his research on the photoelectric effect which is a phenomenon associated with the generation of electricity through solar cells. In 1953, Bell Laboratories which we know today as AT&T labs developed the first silicon solar cell capable of generating a measurable electric current. Three years later, solar cells ran $300 per watt. With the Cold War and the Space Race on, this was used to power satellites and crafts. But the biggest event in the development of solar energy occurred during the oil crisis of 1973. This prompted the US government to invest heavily in the solar electric cell that was developed by Bell Laboratories 20 years ago.

By the 1990's, research towards solar energy came to a standstill as the price of oil dropped in the world market. Funds were diverted elsewhere and the United States which was probably the leader in this form of alternative energy was soon surpassed by other nations mainly Germany and Japan. In 2002 for example, Japan had installed 25,000 solar panels on rooftops. Because of that, the price of solar panels went down as the demand for it was on the rise.

To date, solar energy is growing at a modest 30% per year. Although there have been improvements in solar energy, its fundamentals are still the same. The sun's rays are collected and then converted into electricity. Aside from powering homes or office buildings, the technology has been used to power aircraft, cars and boats. Unfortunately, none of these have been made available yet for public use. We still rely heavily on oil for electricity, gasoline for our cars, fuel for planes and ships.

In fact, the US is one of the biggest oil users in the world. To prove a point, the department of Defense consumes 395,000 barrels per This has to change because our oil reserves are almost depleted and many experts believe that global supply for these non-renewable resources will be gone before the end of the century. We have to do our share to push for renewable energy and one of them happens to be solar energy.

The Pros and Cons of Solar Energy:

Solar energy is one of the best forms of renewable energy. But why don't we rely on it so much compared to other countries? The answer is simply that there are pros and cons with using this form of alternative energy. The pros of using solar energy is that the system is easy to install, there are no energy costs once it is set up, there are no emissions like air pollutants or greenhouse gas and the sun is widely available. The pros of using solar energy is that the system is easy to install, there are no energy costs once it is set up, there are no emissions like air pollutants or greenhouse gas and the sun is widely available. A solar energy system is composed of the solar panels, the inverter, battery, charge controller, wires and support structure. For you to produce a kilowatt of power, you will need 10 to 12 solar panels that will occupy an area of 100 square feet.

If you are worried that this will cause damage to your roof, don't because it is made of light weight materials. When you call a contractor, it will usually take a day or two to install and cost around $10,000. Not that many people will have cash on hand to pay for it so they can avail of a home equity loan to pay for it. If you use a kilowatt of solar energy, you can save 170 lbs. of coal from being burned, about 300lbs of carbon dioxide from being released into the atmosphere or 105 gallons of water that most homeowners use up every month.

The cons are solar cells are expensive, the rays can only be collected during the day time, the weather and where you are located will play a factor in how much sunlight you can get and you will need a big area to collect the power. But some experts believe that price of these cells and its ability to collect power will improve in the future. Right now, a kilowatt of solar energy can only produce 1,600 kilowatts of hours per year in sunny climate. That means you will receive 5.5 hours of electricity per day. If you produce about 750 kilowatts of power, you will only get 2.5 hours of power per day.

Solar panels come in various colors and usually have a 5 year warranty.Since manufacturers are aware that solar energy can only work when the sun is out, they have installed batteries so you get more than 5 hours of power even during cloudy days and nights. This is because the batteries are designed to absorb, insulate, transmit and reflect rays coming from the sun.

But solar energy can be applied to other things and not just powering our homes. It can be used to power small devices like calculators to bigger things like planes, satellites and cars. Since these are easy to maintain, you don't have to worry about anything. People should take this seriously especially when this is not a renewable source of energy.

Things We Should Know Before Investing in Solar Energy:

There is no doubt that there are a lot of benefits in using solar energy. Aside from protecting the environment, you get to save a great deal of money. But before you switch to solar energy, here are a few things you should consider. First, is your roof right for solar power? Most solar power systems can be installed as long as the roof is flat and made of material such as bitumen, composite shingle, cement tile, metal or tar and gravel. If this is how your roof is positioned, then there shouldn't be any problems. The solar panels will be installed parallel to the roof surface.

If you are concerned that the weight could be too heavy for your roof, don't be since this is very light and quite rare that you have to do some structural work before installing the system. When you are looking for a contractor, find out how much it will cost to install the system. You should compare these first before you decide in picking the best one. But you should know right now that installing solar powered cells are a bit expensive. There are also no financing programs you can avail of. Your best bet if you don't have enough money is to apply for a home equity loan. If you are planning to install this in a commercial establishment, the various loans you can avail of include the capital equipment loan, equipment secured loan, property secured loan or the SAFE-BIDCO energy efficiency loan.

Non-profit organizations may also avail of special loans for solar energy and the best one is through third party financing. In this case, the non-profit organization and the contractor will purchase the system and make use of the tax credits. The third party will then pass on the charges for the produced power to the non-profit and after the system has depreciated, this is sold to the non-profit at a discount. The end result is that you pay for less than what you are currently paying for because it is maintenance free. Will installing a solar system have any effect on your property? The answer is yes. In fact, it will increase the resale value of your property without having to pay much more in terms of property taxes. If you have a lot of space to spare, you may even be able to zero out your electric bill as long as the sun comes out so you can convert sunlight into electricity.

Aside from increasing the properly value, you will also be able to avail of tax credits from the government. Solar energy can power your home in the same way you get electricity from the grid. You won't be able to use it when there is a power outage or when the sun is shining but fortunately, this doesn't happen daily so it is still an alternative form of energy worth considering.

Using solar energy goes way back:

Recollecting the history of solar energy brings us back to the 1970s energy crisis and oil embargo which caused long lines in gasoline stations, high gasoline prices, and even caused panic among consumers and investors alike in the United States. Knowledge about oil being a non-renewable resource has been around since the 1800s.

But it was only during and after the 70s energy crisis that people really began to realize the consequences of depending too much on an already depleting energy resource. However, utilizing the sun's energy is not really a recent development. It has been used by ancient civilizations for warmth, for food and crop preparations and various agricultural purposes. What's new are the technologies involved in harnessing this energy and utilizing it for man's daily use. The technology began in the 1830's when Edmund Becquerel made public his studies on how solar light can be harnessed into usable energy. However, nobody followed up on this idea nor explore any practical use.

The next breakthrough on solar power came after thirty years Becquerel published his works. In 1860s, the French Monarch commissioned Augusted Mouchout to find other sources of energy. And Mouchout looked up in the sky for inspiration. His series of solar powered contractions were quite impressive back then. His inventions included a motor that run on solar energy, a steam engine that uses the sun's light, and an ice maker that fully rely on solar power. After Mouchout, there were several other notable achievements in the line of solar power. Among these is the works of William Adams in the 1870s which utilized mirrors to channel the power of the sun to make a steam engine run. Adams' power tower design concept is still in use today.

Another notable work is by Charles Fritz in the early 1880s. His studies were attuned on turning sunlight into electricity, which he later accomplished. But one of the most significant development in modern solar energy occurred in the 1950s. Early in the decade, R.S. Ohl discovered that sunlight produces large numbers of free electrons when it strikes silicon. Then in the mid-1950s Gerald Pearson, Calvin Fuller, and Daryl Chaplin was able to capture those free electrons and convert them in electricity.

Today, silicon cells are used to make solar cells and solar panels for harnessing the sun's energy. Immediately these solar cells were made into good use and the first among to use them was the field of space aeronautics. These silicon based solar cells were used to power satellites that orbit the earth. The satellite Vanguard I was the first one launched out to space which rely on solar cells for power. More satellites followed. Nowadays, more and more research and studies are being conducted on how best to utilize the sun's energy. Especially today where it is said that about 30-50 years from the now, the world oil reserves will be totally depleted. Thus, the search for alternative sources of energy continuous.

The sun is expected to die out in a couple of thousand of years, it's too long to worry about and man can have all the sun's energy until that day. The challenge today is creating solar energy power in more efficient and cost effective e way. Admittedly, the costs of those photo cells are not that cheap to be accessible by most of the ordinary consumers. The movement today in the science and technology committee is to be able to provide cheap alternative source of energy.

What is Solar Energy?

Solar energy is a form of renewable energy as it utilizes the radiant energy coming from the sun. This is done by converting sunlight into electricity using solar cells. Solar cells or photovoltaics were invented in the 1880's by Charles Fritts. Although it did not convert a lot of sunlight into electricity at the time, this started a revolution that continued on to the 20th century. The greatest example is perhaps the Vanguard 1 which was a satellite fitted with solar cells that enabled it to transmit back to earth after its chemical battery was exhausted. Its success prompted NASA and its Russian counterpart to the same with other satellites including Telstar hich continues to serve as the backbone of the telecommunications structure today.The most significant event that stimulated the demand for solar energy was the 1973 oil crisis.

Early on, power companies would charge the consumer a hundred dollars per watt. In the 1980's, it became only $7 per watt. Unfortunately, the lack of government funding did not sustain its growth so the growth of solar energy was only 15% annually from 1984 to 1996. There have been a decline in the demand for solar energy in the US but this increased in Japan and Germany. From 31.2 megawatts of power in 1994, this increased to 318 megawatts in 1999 and world wide production growth increased by 30% towards the end of the 20th century.

Next to these two countries, Spain is the third largest user of solar energy followed by France, Italy and South Korea.

There are three basic approaches to get the most out of solar energy. It is namely passive, active and solar photovoltaic systems.

1.In passive, it has to do a lot with the building design. This will enable the building to avoid heat loss so people inside will feel a great degree of comfort with the help of controlled ventilation and day lighting. Homes that apply this will greatly reduce their heating requirements by as much as 80% with minimal cost.

2. Active solar heating is used to convert sunlight into heat which provides space or water heating. Used extensively in Europe, getting the right size will cover 50% to 60% of your hot water heating requirements.

3. Lastly is photovoltaic which converts solar radiation into electricity. This is done by installing solar cells in the ground and the greater the intensity of the light, the greater the flow of electricity. These are available in different sizes and some are installed in consumer devices like calculators and watches.

Some vehicles are now powered using solar energy. Cars although not yet produced commercially compete in the World Solar Challenge which invites competitors from around the world to compete in this annual event in Australia. There are also unmanned aerial vehicles and balloons. To date, solar energy has only been successful in passenger boats.

Many of us take the sun for granted and if we are really serious about preserving the environment and reducing our demand for oil, solar energy is just one of the options we have on the table. We have to lobby and convince our government leaders to do more because it is the cheapest means of providing our home with electricity compared to rechargeable batteries, kerosene or candles.

Wind power vs Solar energy an even match:

Today in center stage is a battle for the ages. On the right corner, packing a hurricane punch yet is known to move softly as a breeze is wind power. On the left corner, with a scorching hot aura, moves in a speed of light, is solar energy. Wind power versus solar energy, which one is going to be declared the champion of the alternative energy movement?! Let's get ready to rumble! Or something like that. I apologize for that intro but I just can't help. I figured that if I was going to match one alternative energy resource against the other, then I'll make some extravagant introduction. Just imagine the drum rolls. Actually, there is an existing debate among environmentalists and even scientists on which energy resource should be developed first given their advantages and drawbacks. Staying away from the personal biases, numerous studies have shown that overall, wind power is more cost effective than harnessing the sun's energy.

Let's see the reasons behind that conclusion. Harnessing the sun's energy can be done by a number of ways. But probably the simplest way which can be applied in a small home is by using photovoltaic cells or PV or solar cells. What happens is that sunlight hit the surface of a photovoltaic (PV) panel which responds by creating free electrons which is channelled to generate an electric current. Wind power on the other hand utilizes a propeller and a shaft system which has a magnet wrapped by a coil of wire inside. As the wind turns the propeller and the magnet inside, the electrons in the wire are forced to move along the wire producing an electrical current. Both ways are quite simple but the complexities now lies on the costs of producing the necessary equipment especially the mechanisms that will maximize the power output. When costs of production of photovoltaic cells and wind turbine are compared, the latter is much cheaper to produce. Although, manufacturers of photovoltaic cells stress that as the demand on PV cells increase, the costs of production decreases. So its just a matter of time before PV cells become price competitive.

Other problems include the logistics of placing the equipment. A solar panel requires quite a large space plus, your location on the globe will affect the amount of sunlight you receive and consequently the amount of power you produce. The further away from the equator you are, the less amount of sunlight you can harness. Also, on the average, the PV cells have a 15-20% efficiency rate. The problem with wind power on the other hand is that not all areas will have winds favorable for a turbine. And if you do locate a place where winds are strong and the turbine can be maximized, you'll find that the area (more often than not) is inhabited by various species of birds. You don't want to kill birds with your turbine, do you? Now going back to our wind power vs. solar energy match-up, indeed we do have to agree that wind power is more cost efficient. However, both alternative energy resource will play a big role in our future.

It is, therefore, in my humble opinion that we both develop the two technologies simultaneously for each one has their advantages and disadvantages and each one can be properly utilized for specific areas.

We Can Have a Home Powered By Solar Energy:

Do you like to live in a home that is energy efficient? The good news is you can given there are technologies these days that can make that happen and one good example happens to be solar energy. Solar energy is the process of using the sun's radiant rays to power your home. For this to work, you will need to get some solar panels and then have this install by a contractor. Ideally, you will need a flat area measuring about a hundred square feet. This is good to install between 10 to 12 solar panels that can produce about a kilowatt of power. If you think 1 kilowatt is small, think again because this is equivalent to 1,600 kilowatts of hours per year. That translates to 5.5 hours of electricity per day if you are using it to the max. Otherwise, excess power will be stored in the battery which will help bring electricity to the house during a blackout or at night.

Aside from the solar panels, you will also need the inverter, battery, charge controller, wires and support structure. Each of these parts are important since the system will not work without the other so whoever you choose as a contractor should have everything ready prior to installation. Once everything is set up, you can already enjoy your solar powered home.

Since it requires minimal maintenance, it can last up to 20 years before you have to replace anything. If you have a larger area to work with, why not invest in a solar thermal roof? The difference between this and the first one mentioned is that you convert the entire roof into a giant collector. It is quite expensive and takes a couple of days to complete but worth every penny. The only reason why not that many people invest in such a system is because most roofs are not oriented towards the south with the steep pitch needed to maximize solar energy especially during the winter.

You will have to do some major construction work to make this happen. Solar energy is just one way for you to stop relying on power coming from the grid. When the sun isn't shining, you have to be ready by preparing other ways to generate electricity. One example that can be used at home is wind energy. Here, you use fans to collect the wind's kinetic energy similar to windmills that you see in the farm. The only difference is that the blades are connected to a drive shaft that turns an electric generator to produce electricity.

You just have to do some research to find out if solar energy is feasible for your home. You should know how much power you consume on a monthly basis and also where exactly is your house located.

Should your study show it is possible to live on solar energy, it is best to apply for a home equity loan to pay for the installation costs because you will surely get a return on your investment later on in the form of tax credit and a utility bill that won't exceed $10. So what are you waiting for? If you don't want to rely on power from the electric company, go ahead and invest in solar energy.

Why Are Solar Panels So Popular?

Over the past 20 years solar panels have become extremely popular with homeowners, business and the agricultural industry.

There are many different reasons why people are interested in solar but we have narrowed them down to **3 main reasons.**

Money:

Firstly, the most common reason why solar is popular is because of money.

Solar panels can provide homeowners with a massive saving toward their energy bill (if not completely reduce it altogether).

When people catch wind of their neighbors slashing their energy bill in half, they simply want a piece of the pie. By having a reduced energy bill it means that you will free up your cash flow each month to spend on stuff that you like or your family.

The finance side of solar is the main reason why it has become so popular in today's age.

Environment:

The second most popular reason is because of the environment.

Solar panels are being installed to help take a stance against climate change. People are willing to invest their money into something that will not pollute the planet we live on. Installing solar panels will help by generating clean energy that can also be sold.

This is much better than burning fossil fuels and oils which has a negative effect on the planet. We are realising the sustainability of solar panels which is making them more popular.

Government Incentives :

Thirdly, solar panels are getting a name for themselves through government incentives.

It is pretty hard to resist when the government is offering to buy back any excess solar energy you produce...

Plus lets not forget the massive reduction in the upfront cost, an interest free loan to help reduce the cost even more and then a STC certificate that can be sold for money!

Even with commercial solar for businesses there are rebates and grants being offered as incentives to help with the move to solar.

We Need a PV System to Generate Solar Energy : Solar energy has been around for quite some time. In fact, now is the best time to get it if you want to cut your electric bill and do your share to protect the environment. For that to happen, you will need to buy a PV system. This is designed to reduce or eliminate the amount of electricity you purchase from the utility especially when there could be a price increase in the next few months. The best part about the PV system is that it generates clean electricity which is clean, reliable and renewable since it does not emit any harmful gases into the atmosphere. The PV system must be placed in an area that is free from any obstruction otherwise, it will not be able to capture the sun's rays. A lot of experts say that the south facing roof is best while the east and west is sufficient. If the roof is not available, it can be mounted on the ground. You should know that PV systems come in various sizes so you should get the one that matches our electrical needs. If you consume about 6,500 kilowatts a year, then a PV system within the 3 to 4 kilowatt range is right for your home. You can measure this by reviewing your past electric bills and making some projections Naturally, the size of the PV system will determine the amount of space needed. If you do not use that much electricity, 50 square feet may be sufficient. However, a larger system may require a little over 600 square feet. Just remember that a kilowatt of electricity requires an area of 100 square feet. Solar energy is converted with the help of an inverter since this is what changes direct current to alternating current. You will also need batteries so excess energy may be stored so you can still use solar energy during the evening or during a power outage. The size of the PV system is also in direct proportion with the cost. Most cost from $1 to $1.5 per watt and when you include installation, the bill may reach be from $1,500 to $2,500. The cost of the PV system should not discourage you from investing in solar energy. People who use it are able to get tax rebates and it will also increase the value of your home. With that, the only thing to do now is to call a reputable solar energy provider. One other thing you should know about the PV system is that this should also be connected to your grid. For this to work, you have to enter into an interconnection agreement with your utility. This agreement will address the issue with regards to the terms and conditions under which your system is tied up with them. This also includes what is known as net metering which allows you to bank any surplus electricity that your system generates on the electric grid in the same manner that you will be charged accordingly should you consume more electricity than what you have banked. You need a PV system to generate solar energy. You just need to know what size of a system you require so this can be installed by your solar provider.

An Overview on the Interesting Facts about Solar Energy:

There are lots of interesting facts about solar energy. Educating yourself about this will prove to be beneficial in the long run. You can share the information to your loved ones. You can teach them of ways on how they can help to conserve the energy. You can also do your share to help this method to advance if you are a genius in the field. But if you are an ordinary citizen who only wants to enjoy, then feast on. But remember that you also have responsibilities to the environment that you must accomplish in order to do your part in the whole scheme of things. The Facts that Matter

1. Solar radiation makes it possible for the energy coming from the sun to be used as power source and energy that can in turn be used for many purposes. The technology on this aspect is characterized in two ways. They can either be passive or active. This will depend on the methods that are used to get, convert and allocate sunlight. What are active solar techniques? These utilize pumps, photovoltaic panels and fans to renovate sunlight into useful resources. These aim to increase the energy supply that is why these can also be referred as supply side technologies. The passive solar techniques, on the other hand, use only selected resources with constructive thermal properties, utilize the kind of spaces that can circulate air naturally and apply the position of buildings and structures towards the sun. These will lessen the need for other sources and can also be referred as the demand side technology.

2. Solar energy has influenced many factors that surround people. This can be referred in planning and designing buildings. This process can be rooted back at the early days of the architectural history. The Greeks and the Chinese first used such factor in building and constructing their architectural pieces and on their planning methods.

3. Solar energy is also being utilized by the agricultural sector because they rely heavily on its benefits in order to gain more harvest. They developed ways in order to plant the kind of crops that will grow according to the amount of sun that they will be getting for the season. This can also be used to dry the crops, pump water, brooding of chicks and to dry animal manures that can later be used as fertilizers.

4. On seasons like the Little Ice Age, fruit walls were used by French and Chinese farmers to be able to collect and store solar energy to help them keep the plants warm and to speedy up the process of ripening of fruits. These walls serve as the thermal masses. The fruit walls that were first developed were perpendicular to the ground and faced the south direction. Over time, innovations were done and slopping walls were used to gain more advantage from the sun. 5. To convert the solar light into heat, people have developed green houses. These enable the production and cultivation of specialty crops all year round. Such innovation made it possible for crops to be produced in untimely seasons and in places where you think that those plants won't grow. And these are only some of the interesting facts about solar energy. These give you a good peek at how wonderful nature is and how people have developed ways to use it to advance in many aspects of their lives.

5. To convert the solar light into heat, people have developed green houses. These enable the production and cultivation of specialty crops all year round. Such innovation made it possible for crops to be produced in untimely seasons and in places where you think that those plants won't grow. And these are only some of the interesting facts about solar energy. These give you a good peek at how wonderful nature is and how people have developed ways to use it to advance in many aspects of their lives.

Analysing the benefits of solar energy:

We all know that using solar energy is a good thing to do. We have heard, and there are quite a number of them, all about the benefits of solar energy and we can't agree why we can't turn this alternative form of energy source to a primary one. But despite the advantages, solar power has yet to fully make it in the mainstream. Let's go back and discuss a couple of the advantages of solar energy and see why keep going back to fossil fuels for energy resource. In the long run, solar power saves money. Initial costs of installation and operations may be more expensive that other energy forms but after settling the expenses, you have an energy resource that is free. Nobody charges for using sunlight, right? The return of investment can also be shorter depending on how much energy you use. You won't spend too much on maintenance either plus those photovoltaic cells can last for 15 to 20 years. There are no mechanical or moving parts to oil and maintain nor are there parts that need to be replaced yearly. Of course solar power is environmental friendly. First its renewable not like fossil fuels which according to studies will be gone in four to five decades. The process of converting energy to usable electricity does not involve the release of toxic chemicals which can harm the environment. Carbon dioxide, nitrogen oxide, sulphur dioxide, lead, and mercury emissions will be a memory of the past when everyone goes solar. Relying on the sun for power also helps reduce global warming. Aside from the toxic wastes and pollutants, using solar power will limit other aspects of the energy industry like hazards of working with and transporting oil or natural gas. Also, other health risks are present in the use of other fuels like kerosene and candles which are still popular in third world countries. With solar energy, these risks will be minimized if not totally eliminated. The use of solar panels is also good for remote areas where providing basic electricity services is troublesome if not totally impossible at all. Solar energy can be transported to far flung villages and once installed they can be left alone for years with little or without maintenance. Communities in Asian countries have successfully installed solar panels in their community and have been enjoying the benefits of clean and reliable power for years.

For a poor country, producing electricity through solar energy can mean independence from oil producing countries which controls the supply and prices of oil. With such independence, new policies on energy can be created which will maximize the benefit for its citizens. Countries will also not be wary on natural disasters which hampers delivery of oil. With this new found independence, countries can invest its national budget on other programs aside from purchasing oil from foreign sources. There are several disadvantages of using solar power and one of which is the costs. But thinking about it in the long run, you'll see that the benefits of solar energy outweigh the disadvantages. Plus, with the current development in the field of science and technology, solar power is becoming more and more convenient and it would not be surprising to find solar energy as a primary source of power in the next few years

Arguments against solar energy:

We all know that solar energy is a good renewable energy resource and that we should start to utilize it more especially when the Earth's fossil fuel reserves are slowly dwindling and will run out in 30 to 50 years. We better look at the various alternative energies and begin a fast tracking of development to hasten our independence on non-renewable fossil fuels. And solar energy is as good as any other alternative energy resource out there. However, several arguments against solar energy have been raised through the years. But probably the most convincing argument is the high costs of solar energy utilization. The problem with solar energy is that you can only harness it during the daytime. And even when the sun is up, the sunlight will be interrupted by occasional cloud covers, rains, fog, and even smog. So in order to harness the sun's energy we need equipment that can get as much solar power as possible at a given time and we need some way of storing that energy so we can use them without any interruptions. We do have the technology to harness the sun's energy, convert it into usable electricity, and store them for future use. And that technology itself is the primary reason why solar power has not caught on even today.

The process of making solar panels as well as the technology for storing that harnessed power remains to be quite expensive. The good thing about this fact today is that due to the recent increase in the costs of fuel and gas, solar power is no longer a far fetched alternative. The gap between the costs has gone down considerably and hopefully in the near future, the costs of solar energy production will be quite competitive. Furthermore, the costs of photovoltaic cells are indeed quite expensive that contemporary oil and gas equipment. But one of the flaws of the argument of costs is that people tend to limit their perspective of solar energy as to only referring to photovoltaic cells. There are other means of harnessing solar energy and not all of them are as expensive as PV cell manufacturing. One way of getting the sun's energy and converting it into usable electricity is the concept of solar thermal plants. In solar thermal technology, various solar collectors are utilized to generate heat which can be applied from the simplest heating and ventilation of houses to the production of massive amounts of electricity.

The use of mirrors or lenses to reflect sunlight to towers equipped with liquids that heat up and produce steam. The steam then turns turbines which in turn generates the electricity needed. The process adds another step compared to photovoltaics which converts solar energy directly into electricity. Nevertheless, solar thermal systems of power production is cheaper that the production of PV cells. For a larger consumer market, it seems that solar thermal energy is the way to go. Regardless, the point here really is to emphasize that solar energy has more to offer. The cost of production is a valid argument against solar energy but still there are ways around it. Costs can be minimized by using other techniques of harnessing solar energy or future developments in the field of science and technology will produce products that are more cost efficient that what are available today.

Countries on the helm of solar energy technology:

The US is not a leading user of solar energy for a very obvious reason: they can still afford to buy fossil fuels from the international market. In other countries the oil prices are ten times higher in the US and sometimes going for the alternative is a lot better in the long run. Today, more and more countries are looking at solar energy as a primary source of power. There are several countries which can be considered as at the helm of solar energy technology. The number one use of solar energy is Germany. It captures almost 50% of the world market of photovoltaic cells. Nowhere else in the world can you find the most number of households with solar panels installed on their roof tops. Germany has this Renewable Energies Laws (EEG) which passed in 2000. The law certainly helped Germans feel the need to go renewable.

According to statistics, Germans invested nearly US$5 billion in solar photovoltaic systems and have contributed considerable in the growth of the solar energy market. Although most of the things that we see are solar panels, it doesn't mean that Germany's solar industry is not limited to the production of photovoltaic cells for electricity. Other notable usage in Germany includes solar panels for home water heating system. Some news indicate that the German solar hot water market earns U.S.$1.5 billion per year. The "solar park" in Arnstein, Bavaria, Germany is one of the biggest photovoltaic plants in the world. It became operational in 2006 and with more than 1,400 PV solar panels, it can produce 12 megawatts of energy. The next biggest country in terms of usage of solar energy is Spain. The solar energy usage in the country, more specifically the photovoltaic cells usage, has a world market share of 27%. Spain has no sign of slowing down its aggressive and pro-active approach in solar energy. Solar fields are being constructed one of the latest ones is the 60 MW solar field in Olmedilla de Alarcón, near Cuenca. There are other big solar plants in Spain and these include the solar park 12 miles outside of Salamanca, Salamanca, Spain which have 70,000 PV panels divided into three 36-hectare arrays. The arrays produce an output is 13.8 megawatts and has been powering roughly 5,000 homes since it opened in 2007. And the rest of the world follow Germany and Spain. Japan and the US still have a market share in the photovoltaic world market. The two countries both have an 8% market share, a far cry from Germany and Spain. Nevertheless, it is quite important that countries continue to improve their status in the world solar market. Other notable country that uses solar power includes Algeria, Australia, Italy, and Portugal. Aside from the rich European countries, people in Israel. and India are realizing the importance of having alternative sources of energy. These are the countries on the helm of solar energy technology. But, other countries are slowly catching up. The government of Israel, for example, required all residential buildings to install solar water heating systems in the early 90s. Today, business establishments like hotels and office buildings are trying to use solar power as an alternative from using fossil fuels whose prices continue to soar in the world market. India is facing a similar energy crisis and they are also looking at solar energy to get them through it.

Facts about Solar Energy, Some Things to Ponder and why?:

What are the facts about solar energy that we know? It is given that this comes from the sun. This was developed by people in order to take advantage and benefit from everything that the sun can provide. You can also easily guess the goals of these people why they opt to develop such technology. For one, they want to make lives easier to live. Second, they want to find other resources that people can use in their everyday lives. Maybe they also want to profit from the experience because if this will all be successful, people, businesses and industries will gain a lot from what is being developed. During the first years of its introduction, people deem that this technological advancement can only be used by wealthy people. It used to cater mostly for the can afford types of individuals. What if it can heat pool and can run spas? .But the evolution of the solar energy is just starting.

Nowadays, the benefits can be felt even by ordinary citizens. Researchers keep thinking of ways to arrive at this state. And this is proving to be good for everybody's sake. The scientists developed solar panels that can power up homes. They made this available not only for the rich and famous, but they sold the idea to governments. The latter used the innovation to bring electricity to people in their countries who still haven't experienced to live in the comfort of having this kind of power source. As a result, many people experience how it is like to have lights. They have also resorted to businesses that can be aided by such technology. The maintenance is still on-going while the technology is still being pursued. But the fact remains that this has been made available even for the ordinary Person. 2. Aside from electricity, solar energy can be used to heat water and cook food. Life is really becoming easier as people find ways to achieve such state. While the developments are still under way, people are finding ways to make such resource available for everybody.

Different organizations and government agencies help in making this product affordable for everyone no matter what your status in life is. As time passes by, people will be able to develop more and more gadgets and tools to make lives easier. There will come a time when almost everybody can benefit from this. The first notion that the solar energy is only for the wealthy will cease to be remembered. The responsibility now lies on to people's hands to take care of nature. They must give back to nature for everything that they have also gotten in the process. Technological advancements can be better achieved if people will consider how these can affect the natural habitat in general. It is okay to get what people want and what people need. But this must always be done with precaution and by thinking of the effects that these will have on everything. It is fun to learn some facts about solar energy every once in a while. These will excite you about the process. But more so, these must open your eyes to the whole scheme of nature and how important it is to take care of our surroundings to be able to benefit more in the long run.

How to Conserve Solar Energy through Your Little Ways:

As an ordinary person who lives according to what the day brings, have you ever thought about how to conserve solar energy? Do you even care? You may think you are an ordinary worker, or a simple wife or mother. Should you even care about such things? The answer is yes.You must bear in mind that you are part of a whole spectrum of nature.Whatever you do will affect all the things around you. Everything must be conserved, including solar energy. Here are some suggestions to throw in your little efforts to achieve this goal.

1. Plant trees. Nature works wonders. Every element around us affects everything else. By planting trees, you will be able to maximize the energy coming from the sun. This will be directed to help the plants grow and produce harvests. With healthy plants and trees rooted to the soil, the soil will be firm. This will be able to hold its structure even in times of natural disasters.

2. Limit your use of the energy coming from the sun. With today's innovations, there are lots of things that are being developed to use solar energy as a power source. The source may be free. But to be able to turn it to such power source, there are things that are utilized for this reason. If you will abuse the use of such technology, the crash of the materials used to put this up will be fast. This will take a toll on you especially if you rely a lot on this advancement.

3. Teach kids about the importance of solar energy. You can gain knowledge through research and through your everyday interaction with other people about this thing called the solar energy. You must tell your kids about its importance, they must be educated about it at an early age. They are the future of the nation. What you teach them now will be instilled to them until they grow old. At such a young age, they must know about how they can contribute to conserve energy.

4. Take good care of nature. This is the most important thing that you can do to help advance such cause. The sun can cause damage to people and nature if people won't do the necessary steps to care for nature in the first place. There are lots of things that you get from the environment. It wouldn't hurt to look back every now and then and see what you can do to give back to what it has already given to you. The idea here is that everything in this life must be conserved. You cannot abuse the power that you possess to gain so much without even thinking how your actions affect the world around you. It is all right to go with the flow of the continuing advancement of the technology. Look at the options available to you nowadays with regards to solar energy. This can be used to power homes and vehicles. This can give light, heat water and cook your food. This can give you satellite television and phones for supreme entertainment and communications enjoyment. This can give you luxuries like spas and warm water at pools. You must learn everything on how to conserve solar energy so that you can do your part in making sure that such resource will be available as long as you live.

How Does Solar Energy Work:

Ever wondered how solar energy is converted into electricity? Well, this will give you an idea how it works. First, solar panels are installed over a flat surface like the roof of your home. Once activated, it absorbs the sun's rays since the panels are made of semi-conducting materials such as silicon. Electrons are then knocked off loose from their atoms so it can produce electricity. This process by which light is converted into electricity is better known as the photovoltaic effect. From there, you now have direct current electricity and when this enters an inverter, it is converted into 220 volt AC which is the electricity needed to power the home. Of course this is connected to the utility panel in the house so the lights and the appliances will work when these are switched on. If you are not using that much electricity from the solar energy generated, it is stored in a battery so will be able to supply the house with power during a power outage or at night. Should the battery be full, the excess electricity is then exported to the utility grid if your system happens to be connected to it. When your solar energy runs out, utility supplied electricity kicks in.

If you are not using that much electricity from the solar energy generated, it is stored in a battery so will be able to supply the house with power during a power outage or at night. Should the battery be full, the excess electricity is then exported to the utility grid if your system happens to be connected to it.When your solar energy runs out, utility supplied electricity kicks in. The flow of electricity of solar energy is measured using a utility meter which spins backward and forward. It will go backward when you are producing more energy than you need and forward when you need additional power from the utility company. These two are only offset when you pay for the additional energy from the utility company. Any surplus is sold back to what is known as net metering

A smaller version of this is used to power a water heater inside the home. Using the same principles, homeowners get to convert sunlight into heat to get warm water. As you can see, transforming sunlight into solar energy is very easy. But why do countries like Germany and Japan use it more often than the US? The answer is because it is much cheaper for them to use this form of alternative energy compared to oil. Also, although the US initiated this during the 1973 oil crisis, it is not as popular as it was back then because the government neither increased the budget in research for alternative forms of energy nor gave incentives so people will be encourage into doing that again.

Most state regulations also prohibit individuals from installing their own devices even if this is used to give you warm water. Chances are, you won't even find anyone to do it so you will probably have to do it yourself. Just remember that if there is a problem with the plumbing, your insurance will not cover it. Should the state allow you to install such a system, you will not be entitled to the rebate. Using solar cells is just one way to make the most out of solar energy. Your other option is passive solar energy which helps avoid heat loss so those inside will not feel too cold or too hot throughout the day. This is used by a lot of homeowners living in the southwest since they do not need that much insulation compared to homeowners who live in other parts of the US.

Net Metering and Solar Energy:

You can't help but get into net metering when you decide to invest in solar energy because you sometimes consume more or less than what you actually generate. When you consume less energy, your electric meter spins backward, if you use more then it goes forward. Net metering is simply a special metering and billing agreement between you and the electric service provider. You are eligible for this if you reside in a residential area and generate some form of energy using solar, wind energy or a combination of both. It also has to be located on your premises and connected to the grid. For this to work, you need to have a meter capable of moving in both directions. Most meters these days can do that but if your provider wants to use two meters, they will have to pay for it.

However, if you enter into a time of use billing agreement, you will have to be one to buy the unit. The net metering agreement works by letting you use the electricity you generate first before you use what you normally get from your electric service provider. Your meter should show the net which is measured as the difference between the electricity you purchased and what you actually purchased. The benefit of the net metering system is that it allows you to store electricity when you are not there and then use it the moment you get home. Since there is a law that expands net metering, you can take advantage of it by generating electricity during peak hours and then using it during off peak periods. Another benefit is the fact that you only pay the net electricity that you use. If you consume below the baseline, you pay less and more if you go over it. If what you use offsets what you normally get from a provider, then you will most likely pay a lower rate. Since you entered into an agreement with your provider, you will still be billed monthly.

This will state the amount of power you generated and the amount you actually consumed. On the anniversary of your agreement, you will be billed for the previous 12 months but you can also request for this on a monthly basis. Keep in mind that you will not be paid for the excess generation of electricity in a given year although some do. If you want to use solar energy, you have to contact your electric service provider and ask if they offer net metering. When the papers are drawn up, remember that they cannot require you to pay for any meters beyond the bi-directional meter. They cannot conduct any tests or impose any requirements if it meets existing national standards for grid-interconnected systems. Lastly, you don't have to buy additional insurance or buy power from any of their affiliates.

Net metering is a policy and also an incentive when you decide to use solar energy. This is because you reduce the number of kilowatts used by your electric service provider which in turn decreases the emissions of carbon dioxide into the air.

Solar energy in households:

The sun is a great source of energy. It would be great to use solar energy in your homes especially nowadays when the prices of oil and gas continue to increase. Because of the high fuel and gas prices, more and more people are experimenting on the use of solar energy in their households in their attempts to minimize the costs of basic utilities. The sun's energy can be harnessed in different ways depending on how you would utilize the end product. There are so called solar collectors which are placed on the roof tops or used in buildings. The main purpose of these solar collectors is to provide heating and even ventilation for the houses and buildings.

These collectors harness the sun's energy by magnifying the sunlight several times and transferring that heat to air or water. That heated air or water is stored and will provide the building or home heating and hot water whenever needed. The only problem here is that not all places have equal amounts of sunlight.As you go farther from the equator, the strength of the sun is reduced. But still, this is a much better solution than relying on electric grids which do not reach remote areas. It is just a mater of storing the heat generated from the solar collector properly. For example, some buildings in Sweden utilized an underground storage facility where solar energy is stored resulting to savings from heating the building and their water. In areas where gas and fuel are out of reach of the pockets of poor communities, residents have to rely on solar cooking for their meals. They use this bowl shaped discs equipped with mirrors or reflectors which directs all the sunlight on the middle where a pot is placed.

The same technology is being used in India, Sri Lanka, and Nepal. This serves are a good alternative from conventional fuels like coal, firewood, and gas. They can use these solar stoves during a sunny day and use traditional fuels when the weather is not that good. This reliance by communities on solar cooking should encourage more studies on how to make photovoltaic cells cheaper for an ordinary household. At this time, the use of solar cells is not economically friendly for a single household. However, the approach here is to install a series of solar panels which would be shared by the whole community. This could be a good idea depending on your usage, but for basic lighting purposes these could work in small poor communities. In some areas, community cooperatives have found ways to bring electricity to households out of reach of power grids.

In the Philippines for example, a local cooperative provided households loans to enable them to install a basic solar power module which can produce enough electricity for three light bulbs. This ay be laughable in our standards but to these people who have been living all their lives with the flickering light of the candles, three electric light bulbs make a great deal of a difference.

The story is the same in other countries. In Israel, the high costs of photovoltaic cells have clamped down the growth of solar energy in the country. It if fortunate, therefore, that the Israeli government is now providing incentives for households that would use solar energy. However, according to industry analysts, the costs of solar cells production will go down as the demand increase.

Also, most are hopeful that recent discoveries and advancement in technologies will find a way to bring down costs of using solar energy. Ordinary households using solar energy is an ideal scenario that we should all strive to achieve.

Solar energy simplified:

The sun shines, we collect the sunlight, we convert the sunlight into usable forms, and we enjoy the benefits. You can't get any simpler than that. But okay, I know you need more explanations. You've been looking all over the web for information and you need, no you deserve, more than just a single sentence. The following would be my attempt in simplifying the concept of solar energy and I just hope you get something out of it. The sun produces huge amounts of energy. But what the earth gets is a pretty small share of that energy. However, even if we get only a miniscule amount, the energy we receive from the sun is more than enough for our needs. Believe it or not, a day's worth of sunlight when harnessed properly can power a big country like the US for more than a year.

So if that's how much energy we can get from the sun, why do we rely too much on fossil fuels which will disappear in 40 to 50 years time? The main problem is that the sun shines all throughout the world. That energy is so spread out that harnessing it is really a challenge. But still, there are other factors at work here, political, economical, and even cultural in nature which contributes to the slow progress of solar technologies. But that will need a whole chapter, nay, a whole book to discuss so let's leave that alone for a moment. There are various ways how we harness sunlight and the specific way may depend on how we plan to use that energy. But we can divide the usage into two general concepts, converting solar power into heat and the other one is converting it into electricity.

Using solar power to heat homes is a pretty good example of the first category. There are two ways that can be used, the first one relies on the positioning of the house's windows and the second one involves the use of some mechanical devices to distribute the heat throughout the house. Solar water heaters are also now available. What you do is provide a solar collector where the heat from the sun is trapped and collected. That heat is then transferred to the after that goes out of your faucets and showers. Converting solar power into electricity, however, needs a little bit more explanation. There are basically two ways we can get electricity out of solar power. The first one involves the use of photovoltaic cells and the second one is using various solar thermal systems. Photovoltaic cells are more commonly known as solar cells. These cells are made from silicon wafers and phosphorous.

When sunlight strikes the surface of the silicon wafers, free electrons are produced. The electrons are then harnessed via attaching a wire to the cells. As the electrons leave the cells and pass through the wire, an electronic current is produced. One major flaw of the photovoltaic cells is that they can be quite expensive plus they only convert a small amount of sunlight. Hopefully these cells can be cheaper, more efficient and more suitable to the needs of consumers in the future.

The great thing about solar energy is that it does not produce any kinds of pollution unlike fossil fuels which spit out substantive amounts of pollutants in the air and even in the water. Plus the sun is pretty much in good health aid it is still very far from dying. We can utilize more than enough energy from the sun that will last us for a lifetime.

Solar Energy, How Does It Benefit the Agricultural Sector:

What is solar energy? To put it simply, this is the energy coming from the sun. The heat and light that the sun provides are essential to life. Can you even imagine life without the sun? It will not be normal and there are lots of things and experiences that people can no longer indulge into if ever that will be the case. Everybody relies on the sun for its benefits. Did you know that the earth gets 1740 watts of insolation or the incoming radiation from the sun? This happens at the upper part of the atmosphere. Almost 30% gets reflected back to the space. The rest of the percentage is being absorbed by the clouds, land masses and oceans.

The Agricultural Sector :

If you can think of one industry that won't survive without the energy coming from the sun, what will be the first thing on your mind? There may be many sectors that must rely on the sun's benefits. But the agricultural and horticulture industry will not thrive without it. They have no other options. If the sun will be gone, these sectors will die. The sun is need by the agricultural and horticulture departments to be able to grow their produce. The latter is needed by people as well as animals. These sectors' productivity will depend on the amount of energy that they are getting from the sun. It must be balanced in all ways. It can never too little. And it must also not be so much. If it is too little, the plans may not be able to grow accordingly. The farmers won't achieve the required harvests in order to feed the population. And if it is too much, this will damage the crops. This will also cause bad effects on people's health. But if the latter is the case, people can think of ways in order to achieve the needed produce by manually trying to reduce the amount of heat that can be directed on the plants. But if the situation becomes unbearable, it might lead to drought and deaths. Farmers must know when the sun will be up, when sunny days will be long and factors like that so that they can settle for what kinds of plants they must plant to survive the kind of weather condition.

Here are only some of the things that they resort to in order to optimize the full benefits of the energy coming from the sun.

• Timed planting cycles
• Timed planting cycles
• Tailored row orientation
• Mixing different varieties of crops to improve the yields

Do you ever wonder what farmers did in times like the Little Ice Age? It is said that English and French farmers resorted to fruit walls. These fruit walls help in maximizing the collection of the energy from the sun. These serve as the thermal masses. These walls help in keeping the plants warm to speed up the process of growing and ripening of produce.

The sun's energy is also being utilized in these sectors in vital activities such as drying the crops, pumping of water, drying animals' manure, brooding of chicks and a lot more. It is hard to imagine the agriculture and horticulture sectors to survive without the solar energy. If there are anybody who knows the importance of the sun, these people are the first in line.

Solar Energy is the Future:

We consume fossil fuels at a greater rate than we have ever had over the past 50 years. That demand is fueled by the increase of cars on the street,the number of planes that take to the air and the number of homes that need electricity. Sadly, we will have depleted these resources by the end of this century which is why we have to come up with other ways to get power and solar energy may be the future. Solar energy is simply extracting the sun's energy for power. Just to tell you how powerful the sun is, it can burn scrub lands and give you sunburn if you are out in the sun without any protection. In fact, the Greeks and the Chinese used this to set fire until the 1880's by Charles Fritts made the first solar cell.

Instead of using a heater to warm up the home, sunlight can be used to control the temperature. You will just need large windows and shades to control the amount of sunlight that will go inside and keep the heat absorbed during the day to remain at night. Solar energy can also provide warm water as it warms up cold water that passes down through the closed flat panels called collectors. But solar energy does not only give warmth to the home.

It can also be used to help power it which reduces our dependence on non-renewable resources like oil or coal. This occurs when solar cells are installed on the roof so it will be able to capture as much solar rays as possible and then converts this into electricity. You will need 10 or 12 to capture at least a kilowatt of power and more if you are powering more than just your home. The only limitation which challenges the use of solar energy is that it can only generate power during the day. The answer to this is to put an auxiliary system in place that will store the energy and kick when the sun is not available. This comes in the form of batteries which will provide power in the evening or a brownout. Advances in technology have taken solar energy to the next level.

NASA uses it to power satellites in orbit, solar panels installed onboard aircraft allow it to fly across oceans while cars can travel speeds up to 40 miles per hour. It is used to power a lighthouse so seafarers will be able to find their way at sea while aircraft can land in an airport in the middle of the frozen desert. Solar energy is safe for the environment since it does not emit any harmful gases or chemicals into the air. It is a renewable resource that has not yet been fully tapped by a lot of countries which makes it very viable for the future.

But is it the only answer to reduce our dependence on oil? No because solar energy is just one of the options. We can also harness the power of the wind, the wave in the oceans, geothermal heat, hydroelectricity and a lot more instead of relying on coal or even nuclear energy that may harm the environment. It is something we have to push for the next generation.

Technologies for harnessing solar energy:

Harnessing the sun's energy efficiently is not an easy feat. The sunlight is so widespread that finding the most effective way of capturing it requires advanced knowledge and technology. There are several technologies for utilizing solar energy and all are unique and are dedicated for specific applications. First up are the photovoltaic cells or commonly known as solar cells. These are probably the best known way of harnessing the energy's sun. Whenever one talk about solar power, the first things that come to mind include having panels and panels of photovoltaic cells or PV. These cells contain semi-conductors, commonly are made from silicon, which absorbs the light from the sun. When sunlight hit the surface of the silicon, new free electrons are created. As the electrons are channeled out of the silicon, electric current is created. The second solar power technology is the concentrating solar power systems. This one involves using mirrors to reflect sunlight to one area. Some systems incorporate high tech devices to track the movement of the sun and adjust the mirrors to maximize the amount of sunlight the system receives. The sunlight reflected from the mirrors is used to heat or power a conventional power plant. Other systems channel the light from the mirrors to an area filled with photovoltaic cells. There are several kinds of concentrated solar power systems, the most popular ones are the solar trough, parabolic dish and solar power tower. The solar trough uses large, U-shaped (parabolic) reflectors to point the sunlight to a tower at the center of the mirrors. At the center tower, hot oil is heated by the sun's energy and help boil water to create steam which is then used to power convention plants. The power tower system uses the same concept as solar troughs.

Mirrors are used to reflect sunlight to a center tower where a liquid is heated and utilized for the creation of steam which will power a power. The parabolic dish system uses mirrored dishes to focus and concentrate sunlight onto a receiver. The size of the dish varies but it is commonly 10 times bigger than an ordinary cable satellite dish. Another solar power technology used today is the solar water heating systems. This is a simple one. The process involves collecting the energy directly from the sun to heat water or liquids which in turn heats up the water.

This is more common in households are ideal for family use. In order to capture the sunlight, solar panels have to be installed in your home or in the place where you will be needing hot water like a swimming pool area. You will need a big space for this but in the long run, you will be able to save lots of money from your electric bill. For commercial establishments, an ideal solar power technology is the transpired solar collector or otherwise known as the solar wall. It involves using perforated solar collectors where outside air passes before it enters the building.

These are but a few of the technologies around which can be used for utilizing the power of the sun. The technologies for harnessing solar energy continue to evolve as new technologies and discoveries are being accomplished. Everything might change in a few years time. Plus, the whole solar power technologies will become more price competitive which will benefit the general consumers.

The downsides of solar energy:

Not that I'm against using solar energy or anything but there are some downsides of using solar energy. My intention is to illustrate these disadvantages so that people can realize the other side of the coin to prepare them and not so much as to dissuade them from using solar energy. I am for everything that can save the planet. View this explanation as an introduction where we can still improve the current technologies involving solar energy. One of the first and major drawbacks of using solar power is the costs. The expense is considerably higher than the conventional electric installation. From the purchase to the initial installations of the solar panel unit, the cost is a significant factor to consider.

The high costs of solar power panels lie on the expensive semi-conductor materials that convert sunlight into electricity. However, as technology progresses and as the need slowly increases, the costs of solar panels are expected to go down, something on the level of being competitive with other energy resources. Another to consider is space. We're talking about installing a solar panel which is not small. It requires a significant amount of space which also helps maximize the amount of sunlight it can collect and convert into electricity. Some households will have the panels installed on their roof others will designate a place for it on the year or on top of a pole. The same space problems will need to be readdressed once you decide to add panels when your current setup is no longer enough for your family's needs. Positioning is also vital.

The solar panels will need to be facing a direction where it will receive the most amount of sunlight in a day. However, there is always a solution. If space does not permit such installations, there are some add-ons that can help maximize sun exposure. Positioning is also vital.

The solar panels will need to be facing a direction where it will receive the most amount of sunlight in a day. However, there is always a solution. If space does not permit such installations, there are some add-ons that can help maximize sun exposure. At night, you might encounter a problem with relying solely on solar power. Although the solution here is to purchase batteries which you can charge during the day and use at night. You will need a couple of batteries though to be able to sustain your electricity needs through cloudy, stormy or smoggy or foggy times during the day. As far as solar powered transportation services go, there are still some quirks that need to be fixed before mass production of such vehicles is rolled out.

The most noticeable difference is the speed. Solar powered cars are far slower that their counterparts. But again, due to the fast development of the solar car and the technologies that go with it, this drawback will soon disappear. When you look at the things that I mentioned about the disadvantages of solar energy, you will see that most of them have solutions while others you just need to compromise a bit. I still think that harnessing the power of the sun is the way to go, so these downsides of solar energy are just a small obstacle that we need to overcome.

The future of solar energy on transportation:

Are you familiar with the World Solar Challenge? It is a race specifically for solar cars. Solar cars basically have arrays of photovoltaic cells which converts the sun's rays into usable electrical energy. The purpose of the race is to raise awareness on the use of the sun's energy on transportation and the development of other alternative forms of energy particularly the solar cells. The future of using solar energy on transportation services may still be a little hazy given the practical difficulties involve in converting ordinary cars into solar cars but the idea is here to stay and hopefully develops into something promising and useful. At this point, solar cars have been built to join solar car races. Very few have been constructed for practical and commercial purposes.

There are several reasons why the solar car remains on the background. The design of a solar car relies on the electrical system of the vehicle. The system controls the electricity the flows from the photovoltaic cells to the batteries, to the wheels, and to the controls. The electric motor that moves the vehicle is powered purely by the electricity produced by the solar cells.

The solar cells, depending on the number installed on the vehicle, can produce more or less 1000 watts of power from the sun's rays. To give you an idea, 1000 watts is just enough electricity to power an electric iron or even a toaster. And since the sun will most likely be covered by clouds at one time or the other, or the car goes through a tunnel or something, solar cars are equipped with batteries to serve as backup power supply for the motor. The battery packs are charged by the solar cells. However, the batteries are not charge while driving the solar car unless you intend to go very slow. Just like a gas pedal in conventional motors, a motor controller regulates the amount of electricity that enters the motor to speed up or slow down the vehicle whenever needed. Solar cars are not that slow as perceived by almost everyone.

These cars can go to as fast as 80-85 mph. With this, you can see why solar cars are not yet into commercial production. Nowadays, solar cells can harness more than 21% of the sun's energy that hit the surface. If the time comes that the cells can actually get more energy from the sun then maybe we can see solar cars on the streets. But at this time, it is quite difficult to make a commercial production model of a solar car. Nevertheless, there are companies who have already created some concept solar cars and are testing how road worthy they are. There's even a scooter that is street legal and runs from batteries charged from photovoltaic cells. Other possible application of solar car technologies is on golf carts which runs pretty slow in the first place and can be appreciated by golfers as well.

The future of solar energy on transportation is still not that clear. The application of solar energy on homes and buildings has been moving forward in recent years so hopefully we can find new ways of converting the sun's energy into usable electricity. And this time something that can be economically and efficiently installed in conventional cars.

The Future of Solar Energy, How It Looks and How It Affects Nature:
The future of solar energy lies on the indigenous hands of people who never tire out from thinking of ways in order to make life easier to live. With the advancement in the technology, the boom of the Internet age and a lot of other things, there will come a time when people will turn their backs on whatever is conventional. This can be good and bad in many ways, depending on who is looking at it and from what perspective. But people's quest for the advancement and development of everything that surrounds them provides lots of negative effects as well.

Here are only some.

1.Sometimes, people neglect the environment and how to properly take care of it for the mere fact that they are greedy to get their ideas done no matter what the consequences to the nature will be. Such advancements create harmful effects in the whole state and balance of nature. How many times have you heard about forest denudation or grave floods that kill people? All these occurrences can also be rooted to the activities of men that suffice for their own good without so much consideration for their natural habitat and the nature.

2. With the continuing advancement of everything that surrounds people, the generational gap becomes wider and wider. Old folks will fight for the benefits of the conventional tools and mediums. The newer generations cannot afford to sit on those old ways to do things. They are a slave to the continuing technological developments. It is okay to initiate change. It is good to find better ways to do things. But people must be cautious in achieving this. They must think about everything around them before they even start on their venture to newer and better ways to achieve greatness. The Innovations As of today, solar energy is one of the best options that people have with regards to alternative power sources. This has already evolved. There was a time when you can only avail such power source when the sun is present and that is during daytime. With the genius of the people behind the development of this resource, they were able to create green gas that can produce electricity. This is done by splitting water properties into hydrogen and oxygen. Both gasses will then be grouped into a cell that will be the electricity source. The same geniuses estimated that the entire planet can rely to an hour of sunlight for its one year electricity consumption. Solar cells have been developed to produce electricity from the energy coming from the sun. The panels for such technology can also be used to heat water and cook food. There are now the solar heating, solar cookers and solar furnaces as add-ons to this innovative venture. There are now hydrogen based cars. These are fueled by the split hydrogen in water. The solar cells also power the satellites that orbit through the surface of the Earth. This is the reason why there are advancements that people benefit from such as satellite phones and TV, accurate weather forecasting, even the development of the GPS technology and a lot more. There are a lot of benefits that people can

gain from the future of solar energy. You just have to think that whatever you do or however you use such technology for your own good, you must always think of ways to protect your environment first to be able to get the most out of such improvements.

The Benefits of Solar Energy:

Solar energy will benefit a lot of people and not only the rich. This is why some governments have increased funding for this type of technology because they are aware of its many benefits. For one, solar energy is very cheap compared to other technologies. It is also renewable unlike coal or the rest which are non-renewable and hard to maintain. It also improves the health of people since it does not produce any carbon dioxide emissions unlike kerosene lamps that give out fumes which are just as deadly as smoking 2 packs of cigarettes a day. It also reduces the incidents of fire that are often associated with the use of kerosene, candles, diesel fuel and gasoline for generators. Solar energy is almost maintenance free because the solar cells used will last for 20 years or more before it has to be replaced.

You just have to keep the panels clean so it is able to absorb sunlight and convert that into electricity. These are also very useful in remote locations where power lines are not yet available. Some examples of these include fish houses, highway signs, marine applications, remote lighting and telecommunication. If countries focus on solar energy and other renewable techniques, they will be able to conserve their foreign exchange because they no longer have to use it to pay for foreign oil. This money can then be used for other things such as health care, infrastructure projects and education.

Solar energy will also reduce your electricity bills because you are no longer dependent on electricity coming from the power company. The only downside to solar energy is the initial cost in setting it up. Yes you will have to buy a lot of solar panels which are quite expensive but in the long run, you will be able to save more because you don't have to pay for anything else to keep them running. Should the cost of solar cells be beyond your budget, you can probably invest in used systems first then try to acquire the brand new ones later on. Another benefit of using solar energy is that you get to conserve fossil fuels and other natural resources that are quickly diminishing as a direct result of an increase in the world's population which could compromise the needs of the future generations. So should people get into solar energy? The answer is yes because it is safe, cheap and good for the environment. You only have to worry when the sun isn't shining because when this happens, rays from the sun won't be able to produce electricity so you have to rely on other means to get power. The same also goes when there is a blackout or brownout because you will soon lose power from your solar system.

The demand for solar energy is increasing and you should join in. Aside from reducing your electric bill, homeowners who use solar energy may claim up to $2,000 in federal investment tax credit in the first year while businesses may claim a 30% federal investment tax credit.

Believe it or not, solar energy has one other benefit and that it increases the value of your home. According to home appraisers, a dollar decrease in your energy bill results in a $20 increase in its property value so do the match and you can easily figure out how much your home will be worth after you decide to invest in solar energy.

The History of Solar Energy:

Solar energy is for everyone simply because the sun shines in every corner of the planet. In fact, the history of solar energy can be traced back to the Greeks that were then passed on to the Romans which marked the first people to ever use the passive solar design. Passive solar design is a way to warm the home based on the dwelling's design. They may not have had glass windows back then but their architecture made it possible for the people to use the sun's rays to light and heat indoor spaces. As a result, there was no need to burn food that often which was in short supply. In 1861, Auguste Mouchout invented the first active solar motor. Unfortunately, its expensive price made it impossible to produce commercially. Less than 20 years later, Charles Fritts invented solar cells, which will later on be used to power homes, heaters, satellites and other devices today. Since what he invented was very primitive, other people experimented on solar energy. One such person was

Albert Einstein who won the Nobel Prize for physics in his research on the photoelectric effect which is a phenomenon associated with the generation of electricity through solar cells. In 1953, Bell Laboratories which we know today as AT&T labs developed the first silicon solar cell capable of generating a measurable electric current.

Three years later, solar cells ran $300 per watt. With the Cold War and the Space Race on, this was used to power satellites and crafts. But the biggest event in the development of solar energy occurred during the oil crisis of 1973. This prompted the US government to invest heavily in the solar electric cell that was developed by Bell Laboratories 20 years ago.

By the 1990's, research towards solar energy came to a standstill as the price of oil dropped in the world market. Funds were diverted elsewhere and the United States which was probably the leader in this form of alternative energy was soon surpassed by other nations mainly Germany and Japan. In 2002 for example, Japan had installed 25,000 solar panels on rooftops. Because of that, the price of solar panels went down as the demand for it was on the rise.

To date, solar energy is growing at a modest 30% per year. Although there have been improvements in solar energy, its fundamentals are still the same. The sun's rays are collected and then converted into electricity. Aside from powering homes or office buildings, the technology has been used to power aircraft, cars and boats. Unfortunately, none of these have been made available yet for public use. We still rely heavily on oil for electricity, gasoline for our cars, fuel for planes and ships.

In fact, the US is one of the biggest oil users in the world. To prove a point, the department of Defense consumes 395,000 barrels per This has to change because our oil reserves are almost depleted and many experts believe that global supply for these non-renewable resources will be gone before the end of the century. We have to do our share to push for renewable energy and one of them happens to be solar energy.

The Pros and Cons of Solar Energy:

Solar energy is one of the best forms of renewable energy. But why don't we rely on it so much compared to other countries? The answer is simply that there are pros and cons with using this form of alternative energy. The pros of using solar energy is that the system is easy to install, there are no energy costs once it is set up, there are no emissions like air pollutants or greenhouse gas and the sun is widely available. The pros of using solar energy is that the system is easy to install, there are no energy costs once it is set up, there are no emissions like air pollutants or greenhouse gas and the sun is widely available. A solar energy system is composed of the solar panels, the inverter, battery, charge controller, wires and support structure. For you to produce a kilowatt of power, you will need 10 to 12 solar panels that will occupy an area of 100 square feet.

If you are worried that this will cause damage to your roof, don't because it is made of light weight materials. When you call a contractor, it will usually take a day or two to install and cost around $10,000. Not that many people will have cash on hand to pay for it so they can avail of a home equity loan to pay for it. If you use a kilowatt of solar energy, you can save 170 lbs. of coal from being burned, about 300lbs of carbon dioxide from being released into the atmosphere or 105 gallons of water that most homeowners use up every month.

The cons are solar cells are expensive, the rays can only be collected during the day time, the weather and where you are located will play a factor in how much sunlight you can get and you will need a big area to collect the power. But some experts believe that price of these cells and its ability to collect power will improve in the future. Right now, a kilowatt of solar energy can only produce 1,600 kilowatts of hours per year in sunny climate. That means you will receive 5.5 hours of electricity per day. If you produce about 750 kilowatts of power, you will only get 2.5 hours of power per day.

Solar panels come in various colors and usually have a 5 year warranty.Since manufacturers are aware that solar energy can only work when the sun is out, they have installed batteries so you get more than 5 hours of power even during cloudy days and nights. This is because the batteries are designed to absorb, insulate, transmit and reflect rays coming from the sun.

But solar energy can be applied to other things and not just powering our homes. It can be used to power small devices like calculators to bigger things like planes, satellites and cars. Since these are easy to maintain, you don't have to worry about anything. People should take this seriously especially when this is not a renewable source of energy.

Things We Should Know Before Investing in Solar Energy:

There is no doubt that there are a lot of benefits in using solar energy. Aside from protecting the environment, you get to save a great deal of money. But before you switch to solar energy, here are a few things you should consider.

First, is your roof right for solar power? Most solar power systems can be installed as long as the roof is flat and made of material such as bitumen, composite shingle, cement tile, metal or tar and gravel. If this is how your roof is positioned, then there shouldn't be any problems. The solar panels will be installed parallel to the roof surface.

If you are concerned that the weight could be too heavy for your roof, don't be since this is very light and quite rare that you have to do some structural work before installing the system. When you are looking for a contractor, find out how much it will cost to install the system. You should compare these first before you decide in picking the best one. But you should know right now that installing solar powered cells are a bit expensive. There are also no financing programs you can avail of. Your best bet if you don't have enough money is to apply for a home equity loan. If you are planning to install this in a commercial establishment, the various loans you can avail of include the capital equipment loan, equipment secured loan, property secured loan or the SAFE-BIDCO energy efficiency loan.

Non-profit organizations may also avail of special loans for solar energy and the best one is through third party financing. In this case, the non-profit organization and the contractor will purchase the system and make use of the tax credits. The third party will then pass on the charges for the produced power to the non-profit and after the system has depreciated, this is sold to the non-profit at a discount. The end result is that you pay for less than what you are currently paying for because it is maintenance free. Will installing a solar system have any effect on your property? The answer is yes. In fact, it will increase the resale value of your property without having to pay much more in terms of property taxes. If you have a lot of space to spare, you may even be able to zero out your electric bill as long as the sun comes out so you can convert sunlight into electricity.

Aside from increasing the properly value, you will also be able to avail of tax credits from the government. Solar energy can power your home in the same way you get electricity from the grid. You won't be able to use it when there is a power outage or when the sun is shining but fortunately, this doesn't happen daily so it is still an alternative form of energy worth considering.

Using solar energy goes way back:
Recollecting the history of solar energy brings us back to the 1970s energy crisis and oil embargo which caused long lines in gasoline stations, high gasoline prices, and even caused panic among consumers and investors alike in the United States. Knowledge about oil being a non-renewable resource has been around since the 1800s.

But it was only during and after the 70s energy crisis that people really began to realize the consequences of depending too much on an already depleting energy resource. However, utilizing the sun's energy is not really a recent development. It has been used by ancient civilizations for warmth, for food and crop preparations and various agricultural purposes. What's new are the technologies involved in harnessing this energy and utilizing it for man's daily use. The technology began in the 1830's when Edmund Becquerel made public his studies on how solar light can be harnessed into usable energy. However, nobody followed up on this idea nor explore any practical use.

The next breakthrough on solar power came after thirty years Becquerel published his works. In 1860s, the French Monarch commissioned Augusted Mouchout to find other sources of energy. And Mouchout looked up in the sky for inspiration. His series of solar powered contractions were quite impressive back then. His inventions included a motor that run on solar energy, a steam engine that uses the sun's light, and an ice maker that fully rely on solar power. After Mouchout, there were several other notable achievements in the line of solar power. Among these is the works of William Adams in the 1870s which utilized mirrors to channel the power of the sun to make a steam engine run. Adams' power tower design concept is still in use today.

Another notable work is by Charles Fritz in the early 1880s. His studies were attuned on turning sunlight into electricity, which he later accomplished. But one of the most significant development in modern solar energy occurred in the 1950s. Early in the decade, R.S. Ohl discovered that sunlight produces large numbers of free electrons when it strikes silicon. Then in the mid-1950s Gerald Pearson, Calvin Fuller, and Daryl Chaplin was able to capture those free electrons and convert them in electricity.

Today, silicon cells are used to make solar cells and solar panels for harnessing the sun's energy. Immediately these solar cells were made into good use and the first among to use them was the field of space aeronautics. These silicon based solar cells were used to power satellites that orbit the earth. The satellite Vanguard I was the first one launched out to space which rely on solar cells for power. More satellites followed. Nowadays, more and more research and studies are being conducted on how best to utilize the sun's energy. Especially today where it is said that about 30-50 years from the now, the world oil reserves will be totally depleted. Thus, the search for alternative sources of energy continuous.

The sun is expected to die out in a couple of thousand of years, it's too long to worry about and man can have all the sun's energy until that day. The challenge today is creating solar energy power in more efficient and cost effective e way. Admittedly, the costs of those photo cells are not that cheap to be accessible by most of the ordinary consumers. The movement today in the science and technology committee is to be able to provide cheap alternative source of energy.

What is Solar Energy?

Solar energy is a form of renewable energy as it utilizes the radiant energy coming from the sun. This is done by converting sunlight into electricity using solar cells. Solar cells or photovoltaics were invented in the 1880's by Charles Fritts. Although it did not convert a lot of sunlight into electricity at the time, this started a revolution that continued on to the 20th century. The greatest example is perhaps the Vanguard 1 which was a satellite fitted with solar cells that enabled it to transmit back to earth after its chemical battery was exhausted. Its success prompted NASA and its Russian counterpart to the same with other satellites including Telstar hich continues to serve as the backbone of the telecommunications structure today.The most significant event that stimulated the demand for solar energy was the 1973 oil crisis.

Early on, power companies would charge the consumer a hundred dollars per watt. In the 1980's, it became only $7 per watt. Unfortunately, the lack of government funding did not sustain its growth so the growth of solar energy was only 15% annually from 1984 to 1996. There have been a decline in the demand for solar energy in the US but this increased in Japan and Germany. From 31.2 megawatts of power in 1994, this increased to 318 megawatts in 1999 and world wide production growth increased by 30% towards the end of the 20th century.

Next to these two countries, Spain is the third largest user of solar energy followed by France, Italy and South Korea.

There are three basic approaches to get the most out of solar energy. It is namely passive, active and solar photovoltaic systems.

1.In passive, it has to do a lot with the building design. This will enable the building to avoid heat loss so people inside will feel a great degree of comfort with the help of controlled ventilation and day lighting. Homes that apply this will greatly reduce their heating requirements by as much as 80% with minimal cost.

2. Active solar heating is used to convert sunlight into heat which provides space or water heating. Used extensively in Europe, getting the right size will cover 50% to 60% of your hot water heating requirements.

3. Lastly is photovoltaic which converts solar radiation into electricity. This is done by installing solar cells in the ground and the greater the intensity of the light, the greater the flow of electricity. These are available in different sizes and some are installed in consumer devices like calculators and watches.

Some vehicles are now powered using solar energy. Cars although not yet produced commercially compete in the World Solar Challenge which invites competitors from around the world to compete in this annual event in Australia. There are also unmanned aerial vehicles and balloons. To date,solar energy has only been successful in passenger boats.

Many of us take the sun for granted and if we are really serious about preserving the environment and reducing our demand for oil, solar energy is just one of the options we have on the table. We have to lobby and convince our government leaders to do more because it is the cheapest means of providing our home with electricity compared to rechargeable batteries, kerosene or candles.

Wind power vs Solar energy an even match:

Today in center stage is a battle for the ages. On the right corner, packing a hurricane punch yet is known to move softly as a breeze is wind power. On the left corner, with a scorching hot aura, moves in a speed of light, is solar energy. Wind power versus solar energy, which one is going to be declared the champion of the alternative energy movement?! Let's get ready to rumble! Or something like that. I apologize for that intro but I just can't help. I figured that if I was going to match one alternative energy resource against the other, then I'll make some extravagant introduction. Just imagine the drum rolls. Actually, there is an existing debate among environmentalists and even scientists on which energy resource should be developed first given their advantages and drawbacks. Staying away from the personal biases, numerous studies have shown that overall, wind power is more cost effective than harnessing the sun's energy.

Let's see the reasons behind that conclusion. Harnessing the sun's energy can be done by a number of ways. But probably the simplest way which can be applied in a small home is by using photovoltaic cells or PV or solar cells. What happens is that sunlight hit the surface of a photovoltaic (PV) panel which responds by creating free electrons which is channelled to generate an electric current. Wind power on the other hand utilizes a propeller and a shaft system which has a magnet wrapped by a coil of wire inside. As the wind turns the propeller and the magnet inside, the electrons in the wire are forced to move along the wire producing an electrical current. Both ways are quite simple but the complexities now lies on the costs of producing the necessary equipment especially the mechanisms that will maximize the power output. When costs of production of photovoltaic cells and wind turbine are compared, the latter is much cheaper to produce. Although, manufacturers of photovoltaic cells stress that as the demand on PV cells increase, the costs of production decreases. So its just a matter of time before PV cells become price competitive.

Other problems include the logistics of placing the equipment. A solar panel requires quite a large space plus, your location on the globe will affect the amount of sunlight you receive and consequently the amount of power you produce. The further away from the equator you are, the less amount of sunlight you can harness. Also, on the average, the PV cells have a 15-20% efficiency rate. The problem with wind power on the other hand is that not all areas will have winds favorable for a turbine. And if you do locate a place where winds are strong and the turbine can be maximized, you'll find that the area (more often than not) is inhabited by various species of birds. You don't want to kill birds with your turbine, do you? Now going back to our wind power vs. solar energy match-up, indeed we do have to agree that wind power is more cost efficient. However, both alternative energy resource will play a big role in our future.

It is, therefore, in my humble opinion that we both develop the two technologies simultaneously for each one has their advantages and disadvantages and each one can be properly utilized for specific areas.

We Can Have a Home Powered By Solar Energy:

Do you like to live in a home that is energy efficient? The good news is you can given there are technologies these days that can make that happen and one good example happens to be solar energy. Solar energy is the process of using the sun's radiant rays to power your home. For this to work, you will need to get some solar panels and then have this install by a contractor. Ideally, you will need a flat area measuring about a hundred square feet. This is good to install between 10 to 12 solar panels that can produce about a kilowatt of power. If you think 1 kilowatt is small, think again because this is equivalent to 1,600 kilowatts of hours per year. That translates to 5.5 hours of electricity per day if you are using it to the max. Otherwise, excess power will be stored in the battery which will help bring electricity to the house during a blackout or at night.

Aside from the solar panels, you will also need the inverter, battery, charge controller, wires and support structure. Each of these parts are important since the system will not work without the other so whoever you choose as a contractor should have everything ready prior to installation. Once everything is set up, you can already enjoy your solar powered home.

Since it requires minimal maintenance, it can last up to 20 years before you have to replace anything. If you have a larger area to work with, why not invest in a solar thermal roof? The difference between this and the first one mentioned is that you convert the entire roof into a giant collector. It is quite expensive and takes a couple of days to complete but worth every penny. The only reason why not that many people invest in such a system is because most roofs are not oriented towards the south with the steep pitch needed to maximize solar energy especially during the winter.

You will have to do some major construction work to make this happen. Solar energy is just one way for you to stop relying on power coming from the grid. When the sun isn't shining, you have to be ready by preparing other ways to generate electricity. One example that can be used at home is wind energy. Here, you use fans to collect the wind's kinetic energy similar to windmills that you see in the farm. The only difference is that the blades are connected to a drive shaft that turns an electric generator to produce electricity.

You just have to do some research to find out if solar energy is feasible for your home. You should know how much power you consume on a monthly basis and also where exactly is your house located.

Should your study show it is possible to live on solar energy, it is best to apply for a home equity loan to pay for the installation costs because you will surely get a return on your investment later on in the form of tax credit and a utility bill that won't exceed $10. So what are you waiting for? If you don't want to rely on power from the electric company, go ahead and invest in solar energy.

Why Are Solar Panels So Popular?

Over the past 20 years solar panels have become extremely popular with homeowners, business and the agricultural industry.

There are many different reasons why people are interested in solar but we have narrowed them down to **3 main reasons**.

Money:

Firstly, the most common reason why solar is popular is because of money.

Solar panels can provide homeowners with a massive saving toward their energy bill (if not completely reduce it altogether).

When people catch wind of their neighbors slashing their energy bill in half, they simply want a piece of the pie. By having a reduced energy bill it means that you will free up your cash flow each month to spend on stuff that you like or your family.

The finance side of solar is the main reason why it has become so popular in today's age.

Environment:

The second most popular reason is because of the environment.

Solar panels are being installed to help take a stance against climate change. People are willing to invest their money into something that will not pollute the planet we live on. Installing solar panels will help by generating clean energy that can also be sold.

This is much better than burning fossil fuels and oils which has a negative effect on the planet. We are realising the sustainability of solar panels which is making them more popular.

Government Incentives :

Thirdly, solar panels are getting a name for themselves through government incentives.

It is pretty hard to resist when the government is offering to buy back any excess solar energy you produce…

Plus lets not forget the massive reduction in the upfront cost, an interest free loan to help reduce the cost even more and then a STC certificate that can be sold for money!

Even with commercial solar for businesses there are rebates and grants being offered as incentives to help with the move to solar.

We Need a PV System to Generate Solar Energy : Solar energy has been around for quite some time. In fact, now is the best time to get it if you want to cut your electric bill and do your share to protect the environment. For that to happen, you will need to buy a PV system. This is designed to reduce or eliminate the amount of electricity you purchase from the utility especially when there could be a price increase in the next few months. The best part about the PV system is that it generates clean electricity which is clean, reliable and renewable since it does not emit any harmful gases into the atmosphere. The PV system must be placed in an area that is free from any obstruction otherwise, it will not be able to capture the sun's rays. A lot of experts say that the south facing roof is best while the east and west is sufficient. If the roof is not available, it can be mounted on the ground. You should know that PV systems come in various sizes so you should get the one that matches our electrical needs. If you consume about 6,500 kilowatts a year, then a PV system within the 3 to 4 kilowatt range is right for your home. You can measure this by reviewing your past electric bills and making some projections Naturally, the size of the PV system will determine the amount of space needed. If you do not use that much electricity, 50 square feet may be sufficient. However, a larger system may require a little over 600 square feet. Just remember that a kilowatt of electricity requires an area of 100 square feet. Solar energy is converted with the help of an inverter since this is what changes direct current to alternating current. You will also need batteries so excess energy may be stored so you can still use solar energy during the evening or during a power outage. The size of the PV system is also in direct proportion with the cost. Most cost from $1 to $1.5 per watt and when you include installation, the bill may reach be from $1,500 to $2,500. The cost of the PV system should not discourage you from investing in solar energy. People who use it are able to get tax rebates and it will also increase the value of your home. With that, the only thing to do now is to call a reputable solar energy provider. One other thing you should know about the PV system is that this should also be connected to your grid. For this to work, you have to enter into an interconnection agreement with your utility. This agreement will address the issue with regards to the terms and conditions under which your system is tied up with them. This also includes what is known as net metering which allows you to bank any surplus electricity that your system generates on the electric grid in the same manner that you will be charged accordingly should you consume more electricity than what you have banked. You need a PV system to generate solar energy. You just need to know what size of a system you require so this can be installed by your solar provider.

An Overview on the Interesting Facts about Solar Energy:

There are lots of interesting facts about solar energy. Educating yourself about this will prove to be beneficial in the long run. You can share the information to your loved ones. You can teach them of ways on how they can help to conserve the energy. You can also do your share to help this method to advance if you are a genius in the field. But if you are an ordinary citizen who only wants to enjoy, then feast on. But remember that you also have responsibilities to the environment that you must accomplish in order to do your part in the whole scheme of things. The Facts that Matter

1. Solar radiation makes it possible for the energy coming from the sun to be used as power source and energy that can in turn be used for many purposes. The technology on this aspect is characterized in two ways. They can either be passive or active. This will depend on the methods that are used to get, convert and allocate sunlight. What are active solar techniques? These utilize pumps, photovoltaic panels and fans to renovate sunlight into useful resources. These aim to increase the energy supply that is why these can also be referred as supply side technologies. The passive solar techniques, on the other hand, use only selected resources with constructive thermal properties, utilize the kind of spaces that can circulate air naturally and apply the position of buildings and structures towards the sun. These will lessen the need for other sources and can also be referred as the demand side technology.

2. Solar energy has influenced many factors that surround people. This can be referred in planning and designing buildings. This process can be rooted back at the early days of the architectural history. The Greeks and the Chinese first used such factor in building and constructing their architectural pieces and on their planning methods.

3. Solar energy is also being utilized by the agricultural sector because they rely heavily on its benefits in order to gain more harvest. They developed ways in order to plant the kind of crops that will grow according to the amount of sun that they will be getting for the season. This can also be used to dry the crops, pump water, brooding of chicks and to dry animal manures that can later be used as fertilizers.

4. On seasons like the Little Ice Age, fruit walls were used by French and Chinese farmers to be able to collect and store solar energy to help them keep the plants warm and to speedy up the process of ripening of fruits. These walls serve as the thermal masses. The fruit walls that were first developed were perpendicular to the ground and faced the south direction. Over time, innovations were done and slopping walls were used to gain more advantage from the sun. 5. To convert the solar light into heat, people have developed green houses. These enable the production and cultivation of specialty crops all year round. Such innovation made it possible for crops to be produced in untimely seasons and in places where you think that those plants won't grow. And these are only some of the interesting facts about solar energy. These give you a good peek at how wonderful nature is and how people have developed ways to use it to advance in many aspects of their lives.

5. To convert the solar light into heat, people have developed green houses. These enable the production and cultivation of specialty crops all year round. Such innovation made it possible for crops to be produced in untimely seasons and in places where you think that those plants won't grow. And these are only some of the interesting facts about solar energy. These give you a good peek at how wonderful nature is and how people have developed ways to use it to advance in many aspects of their lives.

Analysing the benefits of solar energy:

We all know that using solar energy is a good thing to do. We have heard, and there are quite a number of them, all about the benefits of solar energy and we can't agree why we can't turn this alternative form of energy source to a primary one. But despite the advantages, solar power has yet to fully make it in the mainstream. Let's go back and discuss a couple of the advantages of solar energy and see why keep going back to fossil fuels for energy resource. In the long run, solar power saves money. Initial costs of installation and operations may be more expensive that other energy forms but after settling the expenses, you have an energy resource that is free. Nobody charges for using sunlight, right? The return of investment can also be shorter depending on how much energy you use. You won't spend too much on maintenance either plus those photovoltaic cells can last for 15 to 20 years. There are no mechanical or moving parts to oil and maintain nor are there parts that need to be replaced yearly. Of course solar power is environmental friendly. First its renewable not like fossil fuels which according to studies will be gone in four to five decades. The process of converting energy to usable electricity does not involve the release of toxic chemicals which can harm the environment. Carbon dioxide, nitrogen oxide, sulphur dioxide, lead, and mercury emissions will be a memory of the past when everyone goes solar. Relying on the sun for power also helps reduce global warming. Aside from the toxic wastes and pollutants, using solar power will limit other aspects of the energy industry like hazards of working with and transporting oil or natural gas. Also, other health risks are present in the use of other fuels like kerosene and candles which are still popular in third world countries. With solar energy, these risks will be minimized if not totally eliminated. The use of solar panels is also good for remote areas where providing basic electricity services is troublesome if not totally impossible at all. Solar energy can be transported to far flung villages and once installed they can be left alone for years with little or without maintenance. Communities in Asian countries have successfully installed solar panels in their community and have been enjoying the benefits of clean and reliable power for years.

For a poor country, producing electricity through solar energy can mean independence from oil producing countries which controls the supply and prices of oil. With such independence, new policies on energy can be created which will maximize the benefit for its citizens. Countries will also not be wary on natural disasters which hampers delivery of oil. With this new found independence, countries can invest its national budget on other programs aside from purchasing oil from foreign sources. There are several disadvantages of using solar power and one of which is the costs. But thinking about it in the long run, you'll see that the benefits of solar energy outweigh the disadvantages. Plus, with the current development in the field of science and technology, solar power is becoming more and more convenient and it would not be surprising to find solar energy as a primary source of power in the next few years

Arguments against solar energy:

We all know that solar energy is a good renewable energy resource and that we should start to utilize it more especially when the Earth's fossil fuel reserves are slowly dwindling and will run out in 30 to 50 years. We better look at the various alternative energies and begin a fast tracking of development to hasten our independence on non-renewable fossil fuels. And solar energy is as good as any other alternative energy resource out there. However, several arguments against solar energy have been raised through the years. But probably the most convincing argument is the high costs of solar energy utilization. The problem with solar energy is that you can only harness it during the daytime. And even when the sun is up, the sunlight will be interrupted by occasional cloud covers, rains, fog, and even smog. So in order to harness the sun's energy we need equipment that can get as much solar power as possible at a given time and we need some way of storing that energy so we can use them without any interruptions. We do have the technology to harness the sun's energy, convert it into usable electricity, and store them for future use. And that technology itself is the primary reason why solar power has not caught on even today.

The process of making solar panels as well as the technology for storing that harnessed power remains to be quite expensive. The good thing about this fact today is that due to the recent increase in the costs of fuel and gas, solar power is no longer a far fetched alternative. The gap between the costs has gone down considerably and hopefully in the near future, the costs of solar energy production will be quite competitive. Furthermore, the costs of photovoltaic cells are indeed quite expensive that contemporary oil and gas equipment. But one of the flaws of the argument of costs is that people tend to limit their perspective of solar energy as to only referring to photovoltaic cells. There are other means of harnessing solar energy and not all of them are as expensive as PV cell manufacturing. One way of getting the sun's energy and converting it into usable electricity is the concept of solar thermal plants. In solar thermal technology, various solar collectors are utilized to generate heat which can be applied from the simplest heating and ventilation of houses to the production of massive amounts of electricity.

The use of mirrors or lenses to reflect sunlight to towers equipped with liquids that heat up and produce steam. The steam then turns turbines which in turn generates the electricity needed. The process adds another step compared to photovoltaics which converts solar energy directly into electricity. Nevertheless, solar thermal systems of power production is cheaper that the production of PV cells. For a larger consumer market, it seems that solar thermal energy is the way to go. Regardless, the point here really is to emphasize that solar energy has more to offer. The cost of production is a valid argument against solar energy but still there are ways around it. Costs can be minimized by using other techniques of harnessing solar energy or future developments in the field of science and technology will produce products that are more cost efficient that what are available today.

Countries on the helm of solar energy technology:

The US is not a leading user of solar energy for a very obvious reason: they can still afford to buy fossil fuels from the international market. In other countries the oil prices are ten times higher in the US and sometimes going for the alternative is a lot better in the long run. Today, more and more countries are looking at solar energy as a primary source of power. There are several countries which can be considered as at the helm of solar energy technology.The number one use of solar energy is Germany. It captures almost 50% of the world market of photovoltaic cells. Nowhere else in the world can you find the most number of households with solar panels installed on their roof tops. Germany has this Renewable Energies Laws (EEG) which passed in 2000. The law certainly helped Germans feel the need to go renewable.

According to statistics, Germans invested nearly US$5 billion in solar photovoltaic systems and have contributed considerable in the growth of the solar energy market. Although most of the things that we see are solar panels, it doesn't mean that Germany's solar industry is not limited to the production of photovoltaic cells for electricity. Other notable usage in Germany includes solar panels for home water heating system. Some news indicate that the German solar hot water market earns U.S.$1.5 billion per year. The "solar park" in Arnstein, Bavaria, Germany is one of the biggest photovoltaic plants in the world. It became operational in 2006 and with more than 1,400 PV solar panels, it can produce 12 megawatts of energy.The next biggest country in terms of usage of solar energy is Spain. The solar energy usage in the country, more specifically the photovoltaic cells usage, has a world market share of 27%. Spain has no sign of slowing down its aggressive and pro-active approach in solar energy. Solar fields are being constructed one of the latest ones is the 60 MW solar field in Olmedilla de Alarcón, near Cuenca. There are other big solar plants in Spain and these include the solar park 12 miles outside of Salamanca, Salamanca, Spain which have 70,000 PV panels divided into three 36-hectare arrays. The arrays produce an output is 13.8 megawatts and has been powering roughly 5,000 homes since it opened in 2007. And the rest of the world follow Germany and Spain. Japan and the US still have a market share in the photovoltaic world market. The two countries both have an 8% market share, a far cry from Germany and Spain. Nevertheless, it is quite important that countries continue to improve their status in the world solar market. Other notable country that uses solar power includes Algeria, Australia, Italy, and Portugal. Aside from the rich European countries, people in Israel. and India are realizing the importance of having alternative sources of energy. These are the countries on the helm of solar energy technology. But, other countries are slowly catching up. The government of Israel, for example, required all residential buildings to install solar water heating systems in the early 90s. Today, business establishments like hotels and office buildings are trying to use solar power as an alternative from using fossil fuels whose prices continue to soar in the world market. India is facing a similar energy crisis and they are also looking at solar energy to get them through it.

Facts about Solar Energy, Some Things to Ponder and why?:

What are the facts about solar energy that we know? It is given that this comes from the sun. This was developed by people in order to take advantage and benefit from everything that the sun can provide. You can also easily guess the goals of these people why they opt to develop such technology. For one, they want to make lives easier to live. Second, they want to find other resources that people can use in their everyday lives. Maybe they also want to profit from the experience because if this will all be successful, people, businesses and industries will gain a lot from what is being developed. During the first years of its introduction, people deem that this technological advancement can only be used by wealthy people. It used to cater mostly for the can afford types of individuals. What if it can heat pool and can run spas? .But the evolution of the solar energy is just starting.

Nowadays, the benefits can be felt even by ordinary citizens. Researchers keep thinking of ways to arrive at this state. And this is proving to be good for everybody's sake. The scientists developed solar panels that can power up homes. They made this available not only for the rich and famous, but they sold the idea to governments. The latter used the innovation to bring electricity to people in their countries who still haven't experienced to live in the comfort of having this kind of power source. As a result, many people experience how it is like to have lights. They have also resorted to businesses that can be aided by such technology. The maintenance is still on-going while the technology is still being pursued. But the fact remains that this has been made available even for the ordinary Person.
2. Aside from electricity, solar energy can be used to heat water and cook food. Life is really becoming easier as people find ways to achieve such state. While the developments are still under way, people are finding ways to make such resource available for everybody.

Different organizations and government agencies help in making this product affordable for everyone no matter what your status in life is. As time passes by, people will be able to develop more and more gadgets and tools to make lives easier. There will come a time when almost everybody can benefit from this. The first notion that the solar energy is only for the wealthy will cease to be remembered. The responsibility now lies on to people's hands to take care of nature. They must give back to nature for everything that they have also gotten in the process. Technological advancements can be better achieved if people will consider how these can affect the natural habitat in general. It is okay to get what people want and what people need. But this must always be done with precaution and by thinking of the effects that these will have on everything. It is fun to learn some facts about solar energy every once in a while. These will excite you about the process. But more so, these must open your eyes to the whole scheme of nature and how important it is to take care of our surroundings to be able to benefit more in the long run.

How to Conserve Solar Energy through Your Little Ways:

As an ordinary person who lives according to what the day brings, have you ever thought about how to conserve solar energy? Do you even care? You may think you are an ordinary worker, or a simple wife or mother. Should you even care about such things? The answer is yes.You must bear in mind that you are part of a whole spectrum of nature.Whatever you do will affect all the things around you. Everything must be conserved, including solar energy. Here are some suggestions to throw in your little efforts to achieve this goal.

1. Plant trees. Nature works wonders. Every element around us affects everything else. By planting trees, you will be able to maximize the energy coming from the sun. This will be directed to help the plants grow and produce harvests. With healthy plants and trees rooted to the soil, the soil will be firm. This will be able to hold its structure even in times of natural disasters.

2. Limit your use of the energy coming from the sun. With today's innovations, there are lots of things that are being developed to use solar energy as a power source. The source may be free. But to be able to turn it to such power source, there are things that are utilized for this reason. If you will abuse the use of such technology, the crash of the materials used to put this up will be fast. This will take a toll on you especially if you rely a lot on this advancement.

3. Teach kids about the importance of solar energy. You can gain knowledge through research and through your everyday interaction with other people about this thing called the solar energy. You must tell your kids about its importance, they must be educated about it at an early age. They are the future of the nation. What you teach them now will be instilled to them until they grow old. At such a young age, they must know about how they can contribute to conserve energy.

4. Take good care of nature. This is the most important thing that you can do to help advance such cause. The sun can cause damage to people and nature if people won't do the necessary steps to care for nature in the first place. There are lots of things that you get from the environment. It wouldn't hurt to look back every now and then and see what you can do to give back to what it has already given to you. The idea here is that everything in this life must be conserved. You cannot abuse the power that you possess to gain so much without even thinking how

your actions affect the world around you. It is all right to go with the flow of the continuing advancement of the technology. Look at the options available to you nowadays with regards to solar energy. This can be used to power homes and vehicles. This can give light, heat water and cook your food. This can give you satellite television and phones for supreme entertainment and communications enjoyment. This can give you luxuries like spas and warm water at pools. You must learn everything on how to conserve solar energy so that you can do your part in making sure that such resource will be available as long as you live.

How Does Solar Energy Work:

Ever wondered how solar energy is converted into electricity? Well, this will give you an idea how it works. First, solar panels are installed over a flat surface like the roof of your home. Once activated, it absorbs the sun's rays since the panels are made of semi-conducting materials such as silicon. Electrons are then knocked off loose from their atoms so it can produce electricity. This process by which light is converted into electricity is better known as the photovoltaic effect. From there, you now have direct current electricity and when this enters an inverter, it is converted into 220 volt AC which is the electricity needed to power the home. Of course this is connected to the utility panel in the house so the lights and the appliances will work when these are switched on. If you are not using that much electricity from the solar energy generated, it is stored in a battery so will be able to supply the house with power during a power outage or at night. Should the battery be full, the excess electricity is then exported to the utility grid if your system happens to be connected to it. When your solar energy runs out, utility supplied electricity kicks in.

If you are not using that much electricity from the solar energy generated, it is stored in a battery so will be able to supply the house with power during a power outage or at night. Should the battery be full, the excess electricity is then exported to the utility grid if your system happens to be connected to it.When your solar energy runs out, utility supplied electricity kicks in. The flow of electricity of solar energy is measured using a utility meter which spins backward and forward. It will go backward when you are producing more energy than you need and forward when you need additional power from the utility company. These two are only offset when you pay for the additional energy from the utility company. Any surplus is sold back to what is known as net metering

A smaller version of this is used to power a water heater inside the home. Using the same principles, homeowners get to convert sunlight into heat to get warm water. As you can see, transforming sunlight into solar energy is very easy. But why do countries like Germany and Japan use it more often than the US? The answer is because it is much cheaper for them to use this form of alternative energy compared to oil. Also, although the US initiated this during the 1973 oil crisis, it is not as popular as it was back then because the government neither increased the budget in research for alternative forms of energy nor gave incentives so people will be encourage into doing that again.

Most state regulations also prohibit individuals from installing their own devices even if this is used to give you warm water. Chances are, you won't even find anyone to do it so you will probably have to do it yourself. Just remember that if there is a problem with the plumbing, your insurance will not cover it. Should the state allow you to install such a system, you will not be entitled to the rebate. Using solar cells is just one way to make the most out of solar energy. Your other option is passive solar energy which helps avoid heat loss so those inside will not feel too cold or too hot throughout the day. This is used by a lot of homeowners living in the southwest since they do not need that much insulation compared to homeowners who live in other parts of the US.

Net Metering and Solar Energy:

You can't help but get into net metering when you decide to invest in solar energy because you sometimes consume more or less than what you actually generate. When you consume less energy, your electric meter spins backward, if you use more then it goes forward. Net metering is simply a special metering and billing agreement between you and the electric service provider. You are eligible for this if you reside in a residential area and generate some form of energy using solar, wind energy or a combination of both. It also has to be located on your premises and connected to the grid. For this to work, you need to have a meter capable of moving in both directions. Most meters these days can do that but if your provider wants to use two meters, they will have to pay for it.

However, if you enter into a time of use billing agreement, you will have to be one to buy the unit. The net metering agreement works by letting you use the electricity you generate first before you use what you normally get from your electric service provider. Your meter should show the net which is measured as the difference between the electricity you purchased and what you actually purchased. The benefit of the net metering system is that it allows you to store electricity when you are not there and then use it the moment you get home. Since there is a law that expands net metering, you can take advantage of it by generating electricity during peak hours and then using it during off peak periods. Another benefit is the fact that you only pay the net electricity that you use. If you consume below the baseline, you pay less and more if you go over it. If what you use offsets what you normally get from a provider, then you will most likely pay a lower rate. Since you entered into an agreement with your provider, you will still be billed monthly.

This will state the amount of power you generated and the amount you actually consumed. On the anniversary of your agreement, you will be billed for the previous 12 months but you can also request for this on a monthly basis. Keep in mind that you will not be paid for the excess generation of electricity in a given year although some do. If you want to use solar energy, you have to contact your electric service provider and ask if they offer net metering. When the papers are drawn up, remember that they cannot require you to pay for any meters beyond the bi-directional meter. They cannot conduct any tests or impose any requirements if it meets existing national standards for grid-interconnected systems. Lastly, you don't have to buy additional insurance or buy power from any of their affiliates.

Net metering is a policy and also an incentive when you decide to use solar energy. This is because you reduce the number of kilowatts used by your electric service provider which in turn decreases the emissions of carbon dioxide into the air.

Solar energy in households:
The sun is a great source of energy. It would be great to use solar energy in your homes especially nowadays when the prices of oil and gas continue to increase. Because of the high fuel and gas prices, more and more people are experimenting on the use of solar energy in their households in their attempts to minimize the costs of basic utilities. The sun's energy can be harnessed in different ways depending on how you would utilize the end product. There are so called solar collectors which are placed on the roof tops or used in buildings. The main purpose of these solar collectors is to provide heating and even ventilation for the houses and buildings.

These collectors harness the sun's energy by magnifying the sunlight several times and transferring that heat to air or water. That heated air or water is stored and will provide the building or home heating and hot water whenever needed. The only problem here is that not all places have equal amounts of sunlight.As you go farther from the equator, the strength of the sun is reduced. But still, this is a much better solution than relying on electric grids which do not reach remote areas. It is just a mater of storing the heat generated from the solar collector properly. For example, some buildings in Sweden utilized an underground storage facility where solar energy is stored resulting to savings from heating the building and their water. In areas where gas and fuel are out of reach of the pockets of poor communities, residents have to rely on solar cooking for their meals. They use this bowl shaped discs equipped with mirrors or reflectors which directs all the sunlight on the middle where a pot is placed.

The same technology is being used in India, Sri Lanka, and Nepal. This serves are a good alternative from conventional fuels like coal, firewood, and gas. They can use these solar stoves during a sunny day and use traditional fuels when the weather is not that good. This reliance by communities on solar cooking should encourage more studies on how to make photovoltaic cells cheaper for an ordinary household. At this time, the use of solar cells is not economically friendly for a single household. However, the approach here is to install a series of solar panels which would be shared by the whole community. This could be a good idea depending on your usage, but for basic lighting purposes these could work in small poor communities. In some areas, community cooperatives have found ways to bring electricity to households out of reach of power grids.

In the Philippines for example, a local cooperative provided households loans to enable them to install a basic solar power module which can produce enough electricity for three light bulbs. This ay be laughable in our standards but to these people who have been living all their lives with the flickering light of the candles, three electric light bulbs make a great deal of a difference.

The story is the same in other countries. In Israel, the high costs of photovoltaic cells have clamped down the growth of solar energy in the country. It if fortunate, therefore, that the Israeli government is now providing incentives for households that would use solar energy. However, according to industry analysts, the costs of solar cells production will go down as the demand increase.

Also, most are hopeful that recent discoveries and advancement in technologies will find a way to bring down costs of using solar energy. Ordinary households using solar energy is an ideal scenario that we should all strive to achieve.

Solar energy simplified:

The sun shines, we collect the sunlight, we convert the sunlight into usable forms, and we enjoy the benefits. You can't get any simpler than that. But okay, I know you need more explanations. You've been looking all over the web for information and you need, no you deserve, more than just a single sentence. The following would be my attempt in simplifying the concept of solar energy and I just hope you get something out of it. The sun produces huge amounts of energy. But what the earth gets is a pretty small share of that energy. However, even if we get only a miniscule amount, the energy we receive from the sun is more than enough for our needs. Believe it or not, a day's worth of sunlight when harnessed properly can power a big country like the US for more than a year.

So if that's how much energy we can get from the sun, why do we rely too much on fossil fuels which will disappear in 40 to 50 years time? The main problem is that the sun shines all throughout the world. That energy is so spread out that harnessing it is really a challenge. But still, there are other factors at work here, political, economical, and even cultural in nature which contributes to the slow progress of solar technologies. But that will need a whole chapter, nay, a whole book to discuss so let's leave that alone for a moment. There are various ways how we harness sunlight and the specific way may depend on how we plan to use that energy. But we can divide the usage into two general concepts, converting solar power into heat and the other one is converting it into electricity.

Using solar power to heat homes is a pretty good example of the first category. There are two ways that can be used, the first one relies on the positioning of the house's windows and the second one involves the use of some mechanical devices to distribute the heat throughout the house. Solar water heaters are also now available. What you do is provide a solar collector where the heat from the sun is trapped and collected. That heat is then transferred to the after that goes out of your faucets and showers. Converting solar power into electricity, however, needs a little bit more explanation. There are basically two ways we can get electricity out of solar power. The first one involves the use of photovoltaic cells and the second one is using various solar thermal systems. Photovoltaic cells are more commonly known as solar cells. These cells are made from silicon wafers and phosphorous.

When sunlight strikes the surface of the silicon wafers, free electrons are produced. The electrons are then harnessed via attaching a wire to the cells. As the electrons leave the cells and pass through the wire, an electronic current is produced. One major flaw of the photovoltaic cells is that they can be quite expensive plus they only convert a small amount of sunlight. Hopefully these cells can be cheaper, more efficient and more suitable to the needs of consumers in the future.

The great thing about solar energy is that it does not produce any kinds of pollution unlike fossil fuels which spit out substantive amounts of pollutants in the air and even in the water. Plus the sun is pretty much in good health aid it is still very far from dying. We can utilize more than enough energy from the sun that will last us for a lifetime.

Solar Energy, How Does It Benefit the Agricultural Sector:

What is solar energy? To put it simply, this is the energy coming from the sun. The heat and light that the sun provides are essential to life. Can you even imagine life without the sun? It will not be normal and there are lots of things and experiences that people can no longer indulge into if ever that will be the case. Everybody relies on the sun for its benefits. Did you know that the earth gets 1740 watts of insolation or the incoming radiation from the sun? This happens at the upper part of the atmosphere. Almost 30% gets reflected back to the space. The rest of the percentage is being absorbed by the clouds, land masses and oceans.

The Agricultural Sector :

If you can think of one industry that won't survive without the energy coming from the sun, what will be the first thing on your mind? There may be many sectors that must rely on the sun's benefits. But the agricultural and horticulture industry will not thrive without it. They have no other options. If the sun will be gone, these sectors will die. The sun is need by the agricultural and horticulture departments to be able to grow their produce. The latter is needed by people as well as animals. These sectors' productivity will depend on the amount of energy that they are getting from the sun. It must be balanced in all ways. It can never too little. And it must also not be so much. If it is too little, the plans may not be able to grow accordingly. The farmers won't achieve the required harvests in order to feed the population. And if it is too much, this will damage the crops. This will also cause bad effects on people's health. But if the latter is the case, people can think of ways in order to achieve the needed produce by manually trying to reduce the amount of heat that can be directed on the plants. But if the situation becomes unbearable, it might lead to drought and deaths. Farmers must know when the sun will be up, when sunny days will be long and factors like that so that they can settle for what kinds of plants they must plant to survive the kind of weather condition.

Here are only some of the things that they resort to in order to optimize the full benefits of the energy coming from the sun.
- Timed planting cycles
- Timed planting cycles
- Tailored row orientation
- Mixing different varieties of crops to improve the yields

Do you ever wonder what farmers did in times like the Little Ice Age? It is said that English and French farmers resorted to fruit walls. These fruit walls help in maximizing the collection of the energy from the sun. These serve as the thermal masses. These walls help in keeping the plants warm to speed up the process of growing and ripening of produce.

The sun's energy is also being utilized in these sectors in vital activities such as drying the crops, pumping of water, drying animals' manure, brooding of chicks and a lot more. It is hard to imagine the agriculture and horticulture sectors to survive without the solar energy. If there are anybody who knows the importance of the sun, these people are the first in line.

Solar Energy is the Future:

We consume fossil fuels at a greater rate than we have ever had over the past 50 years. That demand is fueled by the increase of cars on the street,the number of planes that take to the air and the number of homes that need electricity. Sadly, we will have depleted these resources by the end of this century which is why we have to come up with other ways to get power and solar energy may be the future. Solar energy is simply extracting the sun's energy for power. Just to tell you how powerful the sun is, it can burn scrub lands and give you sunburn if you are out in the sun without any protection. In fact, the Greeks and the Chinese used this to set fire until the 1880's by Charles Fritts made the first solar cell.

Instead of using a heater to warm up the home, sunlight can be used to control the temperature. You will just need large windows and shades to control the amount of sunlight that will go inside and keep the heat absorbed during the day to remain at night. Solar energy can also provide warm water as it warms up cold water that passes down through the closed flat panels called collectors. But solar energy does not only give warmth to the home.

It can also be used to help power it which reduces our dependence on non-renewable resources like oil or coal. This occurs when solar cells are installed on the roof so it will be able to capture as much solar rays as possible and then converts this into electricity. You will need 10 or 12 to capture at least a kilowatt of power and more if you are powering more than just your home. The only limitation which challenges the use of solar energy is that it can only generate power during the day. The answer to this is to put an auxiliary system in place that will store the energy and kick when the sun is not available. This comes in the form of batteries which will provide power in the evening or a brownout. Advances in technology have taken solar energy to the next level.

NASA uses it to power satellites in orbit, solar panels installed onboard aircraft allow it to fly across oceans while cars can travel speeds up to 40 miles per hour. It is used to power a lighthouse so seafarers will be able to find their way at sea while aircraft can land in an airport in the middle of the frozen desert. Solar energy is safe for the environment since it does not emit any harmful gases or chemicals into the air. It is a renewable resource that has not yet been fully tapped by a lot of countries which makes it very viable for the future.

But is it the only answer to reduce our dependence on oil? No because solar energy is just one of the options. We can also harness the power of the wind, the wave in the oceans, geothermal heat, hydroelectricity and a lot more instead of relying on coal or even nuclear energy that may harm the environment. It is something we have to push for the next generation.

Technologies for harnessing solar energy:

Harnessing the sun's energy efficiently is not an easy feat. The sunlight is so widespread that finding the most effective way of capturing it requires advanced knowledge and technology. There are several technologies for utilizing solar energy and all are unique and are dedicated for specific applications. First up are the photovoltaic cells or commonly known as solar cells. These are probably the best known way of harnessing the energy's sun. Whenever one talk about solar power, the first things that come to mind include having panels and panels of photovoltaic cells or PV. These cells contain semi-conductors, commonly are made from silicon, which absorbs the light from the sun. When sunlight hit the surface of the silicon, new free electrons are created. As the electrons are channeled out of the silicon, electric current is created. The second solar power technology is the concentrating solar power systems. This one involves using mirrors to reflect sunlight to one area. Some systems incorporate high tech devices to track the movement of the sun and adjust the mirrors to maximize the amount of sunlight the system receives. The sunlight reflected from the mirrors is used to heat or power a conventional power plant. Other systems channel the light from the mirrors to an area filled with photovoltaic cells. There are several kinds of concentrated solar power systems, the most popular ones are the solar trough, parabolic dish and solar power tower. The solar trough uses large, U-shaped (parabolic) reflectors to point the sunlight to a tower at the center of the mirrors. At the center tower, hot oil is heated by the sun's energy and help boil water to create steam which is then used to power convention plants. The power tower system uses the same concept as solar troughs.

Mirrors are used to reflect sunlight to a center tower where a liquid is heated and utilized for the creation of steam which will power a power. The parabolic dish system uses mirrored dishes to focus and concentrate sunlight onto a receiver. The size of the dish varies but it is commonly 10 times bigger than an ordinary cable satellite dish. Another solar power technology used today is the solar water heating systems. This is a simple one. The process involves collecting the energy directly from the sun to heat water or liquids which in turn heats up the water.

This is more common in households are ideal for family use. In order to capture the sunlight, solar panels have to be installed in your home or in the place where you will be needing hot water like a swimming pool area. You will need a big space for this but in the long run, you will be able to save lots of money from your electric bill. For commercial establishments, an ideal solar power technology is the transpired solar collector or otherwise known as the solar wall. It involves using perforated solar collectors where outside air passes before it enters the building.

These are but a few of the technologies around which can be used for utilizing the power of the sun. The technologies for harnessing solar energy continue to evolve as new technologies and discoveries are being accomplished. Everything might change in a few years time. Plus, the whole solar power technologies will become more price competitive which will benefit the general consumers.

The downsides of solar energy:

Not that I'm against using solar energy or anything but there are some downsides of using solar energy. My intention is to illustrate these disadvantages so that people can realize the other side of the coin to prepare them and not so much as to dissuade them from using solar energy. I am for everything that can save the planet. View this explanation as an introduction where we can still improve the current technologies involving solar energy. One of the first and major drawbacks of using solar power is the costs. The expense is considerably higher than the conventional electric installation. From the purchase to the initial installations of the solar panel unit, the cost is a significant factor to consider.

The high costs of solar power panels lie on the expensive semi-conductor materials that convert sunlight into electricity. However, as technology progresses and as the need slowly increases, the costs of solar panels are expected to go down, something on the level of being competitive with other energy resources. Another to consider is space. We're talking about installing a solar panel which is not small. It requires a significant amount of space which also helps maximize the amount of sunlight it can collect and convert into electricity. Some households will have the panels installed on their roof others will designate a place for it on the year or on top of a pole. The same space problems will need to be readdressed once you decide to add panels when your current setup is no longer enough for your family's needs. Positioning is also vital.

The solar panels will need to be facing a direction where it will receive the most amount of sunlight in a day. However, there is always a solution. If space does not permit such installations, there are some add-ons that can help maximize sun exposure. Positioning is also vital.

The solar panels will need to be facing a direction where it will receive the most amount of sunlight in a day. However, there is always a solution. If space does not permit such installations, there are some add-ons that can help maximize sun exposure. At night, you might encounter a problem with relying solely on solar power. Although the solution here is to purchase batteries which you can charge during the day and use at night. You will need a couple of batteries though to be able to sustain your electricity needs through cloudy, stormy or smoggy or foggy times during the day. As far as solar powered transportation services go, there are still some quirks that need to be fixed before mass production of such vehicles is rolled out.

The most noticeable difference is the speed. Solar powered cars are far slower that their counterparts. But again, due to the fast development of the solar car and the technologies that go with it, this drawback will soon disappear. When you look at the things that I mentioned about the disadvantages of solar energy, you will see that most of them have solutions while others you just need to compromise a bit. I still think that harnessing the power of the sun is the way to go, so these downsides of solar energy are just a small obstacle that we need to overcome.

The future of solar energy on transportation:

Are you familiar with the World Solar Challenge? It is a race specifically for solar cars. Solar cars basically have arrays of photovoltaic cells which converts the sun's rays into usable electrical energy. The purpose of the race is to raise awareness on the use of the sun's energy on transportation and the development of other alternative forms of energy particularly the solar cells. The future of using solar energy on transportation services may still be a little hazy given the practical difficulties involve in converting ordinary cars into solar cars but the idea is here to stay and hopefully develops into something promising and useful. At this point, solar cars have been built to join solar car races. Very few have been constructed for practical and commercial purposes.

There are several reasons why the solar car remains on the background. The design of a solar car relies on the electrical system of the vehicle. The system controls the electricity the flows from the photovoltaic cells to the batteries, to the wheels, and to the controls. The electric motor that moves the vehicle is powered purely by the electricity produced by the solar cells.

The solar cells, depending on the number installed on the vehicle, can produce more or less 1000 watts of power from the sun's rays. To give you an idea, 1000 watts is just enough electricity to power an electric iron or even a toaster. And since the sun will most likely be covered by clouds at one time or the other, or the car goes through a tunnel or something, solar cars are equipped with batteries to serve as backup power supply for the motor. The battery packs are charged by the solar cells. However, the batteries are not charge while driving the solar car unless you intend to go very slow. Just like a gas pedal in conventional motors, a motor controller regulates the amount of electricity that enters the motor to speed up or slow down the vehicle whenever needed. Solar cars are not that slow as perceived by almost everyone.

These cars can go to as fast as 80-85 mph. With this, you can see why solar cars are not yet into commercial production. Nowadays, solar cells can harness more than 21% of the sun's energy that hit the surface. If the time comes that the cells can actually get more energy from the sun then maybe we can see solar cars on the streets. But at this time, it is quite difficult to make a commercial production model of a solar car. Nevertheless, there are companies who have already created some concept solar cars and are testing how road worthy they are. There's even a scooter that is street legal and runs from batteries charged from photovoltaic cells. Other possible application of solar car technologies is on golf carts which runs pretty slow in the first place and can be appreciated by golfers as well.

The future of solar energy on transportation is still not that clear. The application of solar energy on homes and buildings has been moving forward in recent years so hopefully we can find new ways of converting the sun's energy into usable electricity. And this time something that can be economically and efficiently installed in conventional cars.

The Future of Solar Energy, How It Looks and How It Affects Nature:

The future of solar energy lies on the indigenous hands of people who never tire out from thinking of ways in order to make life easier to live. With the advancement in the technology, the boom of the Internet age and a lot of other things, there will come a time when people will turn their backs on whatever is conventional. This can be good and bad in many ways, depending on who is looking at it and from what perspective. But people's quest for the advancement and development of everything that surrounds them provides lots of negative effects as well.

Here are only some.

1. Sometimes, people neglect the environment and how to properly take care of it for the mere fact that they are greedy to get their ideas done no matter what the consequences to the nature will be. Such advancements create harmful effects in the whole state and balance of nature. How many times have you heard about forest denudation or grave floods that kill people? All these occurrences can also be rooted to the activities of men that suffice for their own good without so much consideration for their natural habitat and the nature.

2. With the continuing advancement of everything that surrounds people, the generational gap becomes wider and wider. Old folks will fight for the benefits of the conventional tools and mediums. The newer generations cannot afford to sit on those old ways to do things. They are a slave to the continuing technological developments. It is okay to initiate change. It is good to find better ways to do things. But people must be cautious in achieving this. They must think about everything around them before they even start on their venture to newer and better ways to achieve greatness. The Innovations As of today, solar energy is one of the best options that people have with regards to alternative power sources. This has already evolved. There was a time when you can only avail such power source when the sun is present and that is during daytime. With the genius of the people behind the development of this resource, they were able to create green gas that can produce electricity. This is done by splitting water properties into hydrogen and oxygen. Both gasses will then be grouped into a cell that will be the electricity source. The same geniuses estimated that the entire planet can rely to an hour of sunlight for its one year electricity consumption. Solar cells have been developed to produce electricity from the energy coming from the sun. The panels for such technology can also be used to heat water and cook food. There are now the solar heating, solar cookers and solar furnaces as add-ons to this innovative venture. There are now hydrogen based cars. These are fueled by the split hydrogen in water. The solar cells also power the satellites that orbit through the surface of the Earth. This is the reason why there are advancements that people benefit from such as satellite phones and TV, accurate weather forecasting, even the development of the GPS technology and a lot more. There are a lot of benefits that people can gain from the future of solar energy. You just have to think that whatever you do or however you use such technology for your own good, you must always think of ways to protect your environment first to be able to get the most out of such improvements.

The Benefits of Solar Energy:

Solar energy will benefit a lot of people and not only the rich. This is why some governments have increased funding for this type of technology because they are aware of its many benefits. For one, solar energy is very cheap compared to other technologies. It is also renewable unlike coal or the rest which are non-renewable and hard to maintain. It also improves the health of people since it does not produce any carbon dioxide emissions unlike kerosene lamps that give out fumes which are just as deadly as smoking 2 packs of cigarettes a day. It also reduces the incidents of fire that are often associated with the use of kerosene, candles,diesel fuel and gasoline for generators. Solar energy is almost maintenance free because the solar cells used will last for 20 years or more before it has to be replaced.

You just have to keep the panels clean so it is able to absorb sunlight and convert that into electricity. These are also very useful in remote locations where power lines are not yet available. Some examples of these include fish houses, highway signs,marine applications, remote lighting and telecommunication. If countries focus on solar energy and other renewable techniques, they will be able to conserve their foreign exchange because they no longer have to use it to pay for foreign oil. This money can then be used for other things such as health care, infrastructure projects and education.

Solar energy will also reduce your electricity bills because you are no longer dependent on electricity coming from the power company. The only downside to solar energy is the initial cost in setting it up. Yes you will have to buy a lot of solar panels which are quite expensive but in the long run, you will be able to save more because you don't have to pay for anything else to keep them running. Should the cost of solar cells be beyond your budget, you can probably invest in used systems first then try to acquire the brand new ones later on. Another benefit of using solar energy is that you get to conserve fossil fuels and other natural resources that are quickly diminishing as a direct result of an increase in the world's population which could compromise the needs of the future generations. So should people get into solar energy? The answer is yes because it is safe, cheap and good for the environment. You only have to worry when the sun isn't shining because when this happens, rays from the sun won't be able to produce electricity so you have to rely on other means to get power. The same also goes when there is a blackout or brownout because you will soon lose power from your solar system.

The demand for solar energy is increasing and you should join in. Aside from reducing your electric bill, homeowners who use solar energy may claim up to $2,000 in federal investment tax credit in the first year while businesses may claim a 30% federal investment tax credit.

Believe it or not, solar energy has one other benefit and that it increases the value of your home. According to home appraisers, a dollar decrease in your energy bill results in a $20 increase in its property value so do the match and you can easily figure out how much your home will be worth after you decide to invest in solar energy.

The History of Solar Energy:

Solar energy is for everyone simply because the sun shines in every corner of the planet. In fact, the history of solar energy can be traced back to the Greeks that were then passed on to the Romans which marked the first people to ever use the passive solar design. Passive solar design is a way to warm the home based on the dwelling's design. They may not have had glass windows back then but their architecture made it possible for the people to use the sun's rays to light and heat indoor spaces. As a result, there was no need to burn food that often which was in short supply. In 1861, Auguste Mouchout invented the first active solar motor. Unfortunately, its expensive price made it impossible to produce commercially. Less than 20 years later, Charles Fritts invented solar cells,which will later on be used to power homes, heaters, satellites and other devices today. Since what he invented was very primitive, other people experimented on solar energy. One such person was

Albert Einstein who won the Nobel Prize for physics in his research on the photoelectric effect which is a phenomenon associated with the generation of electricity through solar cells. In 1953, Bell Laboratories which we know today as AT&T labs developed the first silicon solar cell capable of generating a measurable electric current. Three years later, solar cells ran $300 per watt. With the Cold War and the Space Race on, this was used to power satellites and crafts. But the biggest event in the development of solar energy occurred during the oil crisis of 1973. This prompted the US government to invest heavily in the solar electric cell that was developed by Bell Laboratories 20 years ago.

By the 1990's, research towards solar energy came to a standstill as the price of oil dropped in the world market. Funds were diverted elsewhere and the United States which was probably the leader in this form of alternative energy was soon surpassed by other nations mainly Germany and Japan. In 2002 for example, Japan had installed 25,000 solar panels on rooftops. Because of that, the price of solar panels went down as the demand for it was on the rise.

To date, solar energy is growing at a modest 30% per year. Although there have been improvements in solar energy, its fundamentals are still the same. The sun's rays are collected and then converted into electricity. Aside from powering homes or office buildings, the technology has been used to power aircraft, cars and boats. Unfortunately, none of these have been made available yet for public use. We still rely heavily on oil for electricity, gasoline for our cars, fuel for planes and ships.

In fact, the US is one of the biggest oil users in the world. To prove a point, the department of Defense consumes 395,000 barrels per This has to change because our oil reserves are almost depleted and many experts believe that global supply for these non-renewable resources will be gone before the end of the century. We have to do our share to push for renewable energy and one of them happens to be solar energy.

The Pros and Cons of Solar Energy:

Solar energy is one of the best forms of renewable energy. But why don't we rely on it so much compared to other countries? The answer is simply that there are pros and cons with using this form of alternative energy. The pros of using solar energy is that the system is easy to install, there are no energy costs once it is set up, there are no emissions like air pollutants or greenhouse gas and the sun is widely available. The pros of using solar energy is that the system is easy to install, there are no energy costs once it is set up, there are no emissions like air pollutants or greenhouse gas and the sun is widely available. A solar energy system is composed of the solar panels, the inverter, battery, charge controller, wires and support structure. For you to produce a kilowatt of power, you will need 10 to 12 solar panels that will occupy an area of 100 square feet.

If you are worried that this will cause damage to your roof, don't because it is made of light weight materials. When you call a contractor, it will usually take a day or two to install and cost around $10,000. Not that many people will have cash on hand to pay for it so they can avail of a home equity loan to pay for it. If you use a kilowatt of solar energy, you can save 170 lbs. of coal from being burned, about 300lbs of carbon dioxide from being released into the atmosphere or 105 gallons of water that most homeowners use up every month.

The cons are solar cells are expensive, the rays can only be collected during the day time, the weather and where you are located will play a factor in how much sunlight you can get and you will need a big area to collect the power. But some experts believe that price of these cells and its ability to collect power will improve in the future. Right now, a kilowatt of solar energy can only produce 1,600 kilowatts of hours per year in sunny climate. That means you will receive 5.5 hours of electricity per day. If you produce about 750 kilowatts of power, you will only get 2.5 hours of power per day.

Solar panels come in various colors and usually have a 5 year warranty.Since manufacturers are aware that solar energy can only work when the sun is out, they have installed batteries so you get more than 5 hours of power even during cloudy days and nights. This is because the batteries are designed to absorb, insulate, transmit and reflect rays coming from the sun.

But solar energy can be applied to other things and not just powering our homes. It can be used to power small devices like calculators to bigger things like planes, satellites and cars. Since these are easy to maintain, you don't have to worry about anything. People should take this seriously especially when this is not a renewable source of energy.

Things We Should Know Before Investing in Solar Energy:

There is no doubt that there are a lot of benefits in using solar energy. Aside from protecting the environment, you get to save a great deal of money. But before you switch to solar energy, here are a few things you should consider. First, is your roof right for solar power? Most solar power systems can be installed as long as the roof is flat and made of material such as bitumen, composite shingle, cement tile, metal or tar and gravel. If this is how your roof is positioned, then there shouldn't be any problems. The solar panels will be installed parallel to the roof surface.

If you are concerned that the weight could be too heavy for your roof, don't be since this is very light and quite rare that you have to do some structural work before installing the system. When you are looking for a contractor, find out how much it will cost to install the system. You should compare these first before you decide in picking the best one. But you should know right now that installing solar powered cells are a bit expensive. There are also no financing programs you can avail of. Your best bet if you don't have enough money is to apply for a home equity loan. If you are planning to install this in a commercial establishment, the various loans you can avail of include the capital equipment loan, equipment secured loan, property secured loan or the SAFE-BIDCO energy efficiency loan.

Non-profit organizations may also avail of special loans for solar energy and the best one is through third party financing. In this case, the non-profit organization and the contractor will purchase the system and make use of the tax credits. The third party will then pass on the charges for the produced power to the non-profit and after the system has depreciated, this is sold to the non-profit at a discount. The end result is that you pay for less than what you are currently paying for because it is maintenance free. Will installing a solar system have any effect on your property? The answer is yes. In fact, it will increase the resale value of your property without having to pay much more in terms of property taxes. If you have a lot of space to spare, you may even be able to zero out your electric bill as long as the sun comes out so you can convert sunlight into electricity.

Aside from increasing the properly value, you will also be able to avail of tax credits from the government. Solar energy can power your home in the same way you get electricity from the grid. You won't be able to use it when there is a power outage or when the sun is shining but fortunately, this doesn't happen daily so it is still an alternative form of energy worth considering.

Using solar energy goes way back:

Recollecting the history of solar energy brings us back to the 1970s energy crisis and oil embargo which caused long lines in gasoline stations, high gasoline prices, and even caused panic among consumers and investors alike in the United States. Knowledge about oil being a non-renewable resource has been around since the 1800s.

But it was only during and after the 70s energy crisis that people really began to realize the consequences of depending too much on an already depleting energy resource. However, utilizing the sun's energy is not really a recent development. It has been used by ancient civilizations for warmth, for food and crop preparations and various agricultural purposes. What's new are the technologies involved in harnessing this energy and utilizing it for man's daily use. The technology began in the 1830's when Edmund Becquerel made public his studies on how solar light can be harnessed into usable energy. However, nobody followed up on this idea nor explore any practical use.

The next breakthrough on solar power came after thirty years Becquerel published his works. In 1860s, the French Monarch commissioned Augusted Mouchout to find other sources of energy. And Mouchout looked up in the sky for inspiration. His series of solar powered contractions were quite impressive back then. His inventions included a motor that run on solar energy, a steam engine that uses the sun's light, and an ice maker that fully rely on solar power. After Mouchout, there were several other notable achievements in the line of solar power. Among these is the works of William Adams in the 1870s which utilized mirrors to channel the power of the sun to make a steam engine run. Adams' power tower design concept is still in use today.

Another notable work is by Charles Fritz in the early 1880s. His studies were attuned on turning sunlight into electricity, which he later accomplished. But one of the most significant development in modern solar energy occurred in the 1950s. Early in the decade, R.S. Ohl discovered that sunlight produces large numbers of free electrons when it strikes silicon. Then in the mid-1950s Gerald Pearson, Calvin Fuller, and Daryl Chaplin was able to capture those free electrons and convert them in electricity.

Today, silicon cells are used to make solar cells and solar panels for harnessing the sun's energy. Immediately these solar cells were made into good use and the first among to use them was the field of space aeronautics. These silicon based solar cells were used to power satellites that orbit the earth. The satellite Vanguard I was the first one launched out to space which rely on solar cells for power. More satellites followed. Nowadays, more and more research and studies are being conducted on how best to utilize the sun's energy. Especially today where it is said that about 30-50 years from the now, the world oil reserves will be totally depleted. Thus, the search for alternative sources of energy continuous.

The sun is expected to die out in a couple of thousand of years, it's too long to worry about and man can have all the sun's energy until that day. The challenge today is creating solar energy power in more efficient and cost effective e way. Admittedly, the costs of those photo cells are not that cheap to be accessible by most of the ordinary consumers. The movement today in the science and technology committee is to be able to provide cheap alternative source of energy.

What is Solar Energy?

Solar energy is a form of renewable energy as it utilizes the radiant energy coming from the sun. This is done by converting sunlight into electricity using solar cells. Solar cells or photovoltaics were invented in the 1880's by Charles Fritts. Although it did not convert a lot of sunlight into electricity at the time, this started a revolution that continued on to the 20th century. The greatest example is perhaps the Vanguard 1 which was a satellite fitted with solar cells that enabled it to transmit back to earth after its chemical battery was exhausted. Its success prompted NASA and its Russian counterpart to the same with other satellites including Telstar hich continues to serve as the backbone of the telecommunications structure today.The most significant event that stimulated the demand for solar energy was the 1973 oil crisis.

Early on, power companies would charge the consumer a hundred dollars per watt. In the 1980's, it became only $7 per watt. Unfortunately, the lack of government funding did not sustain its growth so the growth of solar energy was only 15% annually from 1984 to 1996. There have been a decline in the demand for solar energy in the US but this increased in Japan and Germany. From 31.2 megawatts of power in 1994, this increased to 318 megawatts in 1999 and world wide production growth increased by 30% towards the end of the 20th century.

Next to these two countries, Spain is the third largest user of solar energy followed by France, Italy and South Korea.

There are three basic approaches to get the most out of solar energy. It is namely passive, active and solar photovoltaic systems.

1.In passive, it has to do a lot with the building design. This will enable the building to avoid heat loss so people inside will feel a great degree of comfort with the help of controlled ventilation and day lighting. Homes that apply this will greatly reduce their heating requirements by as much as 80% with minimal cost.

2. Active solar heating is used to convert sunlight into heat which provides space or water heating. Used extensively in Europe, getting the right size will cover 50% to 60% of your hot water heating requirements.

3. Lastly is photovoltaic which converts solar radiation into electricity. This is done by installing solar cells in the ground and the greater the intensity of the light, the greater the flow of electricity. These are available in different sizes and some are installed in consumer devices like calculators and watches.

Some vehicles are now powered using solar energy. Cars although not yet produced commercially compete in the World Solar Challenge which invites competitors from around the world to compete in this annual event in Australia. There are also unmanned aerial vehicles and balloons. To date,solar energy has only been successful in passenger boats.

Many of us take the sun for granted and if we are really serious about preserving the environment and reducing our demand for oil, solar energy is just one of the options we have on the table. We have to lobby and convince our government leaders to do more because it is the cheapest means of providing our home with electricity compared to rechargeable batteries, kerosene or candles.

Wind power vs Solar energy an even match:

Today in center stage is a battle for the ages. On the right corner, packing a hurricane punch yet is known to move softly as a breeze is wind power. On the left corner, with a scorching hot aura, moves in a speed of light, is solar energy. Wind power versus solar energy, which one is going to be declared the champion of the alternative energy movement?! Let's get ready to rumble! Or something like that. I apologize for that intro but I just can't help. I figured that if I was going to match one alternative energy resource against the other, then I'll make some extravagant introduction. Just imagine the drum rolls. Actually, there is an existing debate among environmentalists and even scientists on which energy resource should be developed first given their advantages and drawbacks. Staying away from the personal biases, numerous studies have shown that overall, wind power is more cost effective than harnessing the sun's energy.

Let's see the reasons behind that conclusion. Harnessing the sun's energy can be done by a number of ways. But probably the simplest way which can be applied in a small home is by using photovoltaic cells or PV or solar cells. What happens is that sunlight hit the surface of a photovoltaic (PV) panel which responds by creating free electrons which is channelled to generate an electric current. Wind power on the other hand utilizes a propeller and a shaft system which has a magnet wrapped by a coil of wire inside. As the wind turns the propeller and the magnet inside, the electrons in the wire are forced to move along the wire producing an electrical current. Both ways are quite simple but the complexities now lies on the costs of producing the necessary equipment especially the mechanisms that will maximize the power output. When costs of production of photovoltaic cells and wind turbine are compared, the latter is much cheaper to produce. Although, manufacturers of photovoltaic cells stress that as the demand on PV cells increase, the costs of production decreases. So its just a matter of time before PV cells become price competitive.

Other problems include the logistics of placing the equipment. A solar panel requires quite a large space plus, your location on the globe will affect the amount of sunlight you receive and consequently the amount of power you produce. The further away from the equator you are, the less amount of sunlight you can harness. Also, on the average, the PV cells have a 15-20% efficiency rate. The problem with wind power on the other hand is that not all areas will have winds favorable for a turbine. And if you do locate a place where winds are strong and the turbine can be maximized, you'll find that the area (more often than not) is inhabited by various species of birds. You don't want to kill birds with your turbine, do you? Now going back to our wind power vs. solar energy match-up, indeed we do have to agree that wind power is more cost efficient. However, both alternative energy resource will play a big role in our future.

It is, therefore, in my humble opinion that we both develop the two technologies simultaneously for each one has their advantages and disadvantages and each one can be properly utilized for specific areas.

We Can Have a Home Powered By Solar Energy:

Do you like to live in a home that is energy efficient? The good news is you can given there are technologies these days that can make that happen and one good example happens to be solar energy. Solar energy is the process of using the sun's radiant rays to power your home. For this to work, you will need to get some solar panels and then have this install by a contractor. Ideally, you will need a flat area measuring about a hundred square feet. This is good to install between 10 to 12 solar panels that can produce about a kilowatt of power. If you think 1 kilowatt is small, think again because this is equivalent to 1,600 kilowatts of hours per year. That translates to 5.5 hours of electricity per day if you are using it to the max. Otherwise, excess power will be stored in the battery which will help bring electricity to the house during a blackout or at night.

Aside from the solar panels, you will also need the inverter, battery, charge controller, wires and support structure. Each of these parts are important since the system will not work without the other so whoever you choose as a contractor should have everything ready prior to installation. Once everything is set up, you can already enjoy your solar powered home.

Since it requires minimal maintenance, it can last up to 20 years before you have to replace anything. If you have a larger area to work with, why not invest in a solar thermal roof? The difference between this and the first one mentioned is that you convert the entire roof into a giant collector. It is quite expensive and takes a couple of days to complete but worth every penny. The only reason why not that many people invest in such a system is because most roofs are not oriented towards the south with the steep pitch needed to maximize solar energy especially during the winter.

You will have to do some major construction work to make this happen. Solar energy is just one way for you to stop relying on power coming from the grid. When the sun isn't shining, you have to be ready by preparing other ways to generate electricity. One example that can be used at home is wind energy. Here, you use fans to collect the wind's kinetic energy similar to windmills that you see in the farm. The only difference is that the blades are connected to a drive shaft that turns an electric generator to produce electricity.

You just have to do some research to find out if solar energy is feasible for your home. You should know how much power you consume on a monthly basis and also where exactly is your house located.

Should your study show it is possible to live on solar energy, it is best to apply for a home equity loan to pay for the installation costs because you will surely get a return on your investment later on in the form of tax credit and a utility bill that won't exceed $10. So what are you waiting for? If you don't want to rely on power from the electric company, go ahead and invest in solar energy.

Why Are Solar Panels So Popular?

Over the past 20 years solar panels have become extremely popular with homeowners, business and the agricultural industry.

There are many different reasons why people are interested in solar but we have narrowed them down to **3 main reasons**.

Money:

Firstly, the most common reason why solar is popular is because of money.

Solar panels can provide homeowners with a massive saving toward their energy bill (if not completely reduce it altogether).

When people catch wind of their neighbors slashing their energy bill in half, they simply want a piece of the pie. By having a reduced energy bill it means that you will free up your cash flow each month to spend on stuff that you like or your family.

The finance side of solar is the main reason why it has become so popular in today's age.

Environment:

The second most popular reason is because of the environment.

Solar panels are being installed to help take a stance against climate change. People are willing to invest their money into something that will not pollute the planet we live on. Installing solar panels will help by generating clean energy that can also be sold.

This is much better than burning fossil fuels and oils which has a negative effect on the planet. We are realising the sustainability of solar panels which is making them more popular.

Government Incentives :

Thirdly, solar panels are getting a name for themselves through government incentives.

It is pretty hard to resist when the government is offering to buy back any excess solar energy you produce...

Plus lets not forget the massive reduction in the upfront cost, an interest free loan to help reduce the cost even more and then a STC certificate that can be sold for money!

Even with commercial solar for businesses there are rebates and grants being offered as incentives to help with the move to solar.

We Need a PV System to Generate Solar Energy : Solar energy has been around for quite some time. In fact, now is the best time to get it if you want to cut your electric bill and do your share to protect the environment. For that to happen, you will need to buy a PV system. This is designed to reduce or eliminate the amount of electricity you purchase from the utility especially when there could be a price increase in the next few months. The best part about the PV system is that it generates clean electricity which is clean, reliable and renewable since it does not emit any harmful gases into the atmosphere. The PV system must be placed in an area that is free from any obstruction otherwise, it will not be able to capture the sun's rays. A lot of experts say that the south facing roof is best while the east and west is sufficient. If the roof is not available, it can be mounted on the ground. You should know that PV systems come in various sizes so you should get the one that matches our electrical needs. If you consume about 6,500 kilowatts a year, then a PV system within the 3 to 4 kilowatt range is right for your home. You can measure this by reviewing your past electric bills and making some projections Naturally, the size of the PV system will determine the amount of space needed. If you do not use that much electricity, 50 square feet may be sufficient. However, a larger system may require a little over 600 square feet. Just remember that a kilowatt of electricity requires an area of 100 square feet. Solar energy is converted with the help of an inverter since this is what changes direct current to alternating current. You will also need batteries so excess energy may be stored so you can still use solar energy during the evening or during a power outage. The size of the PV system is also in direct proportion with the cost. Most cost from $1 to $1.5 per watt and when you include installation, the bill may reach be from $1,500 to $2,500. The cost of the PV system should not discourage you from investing in solar energy. People who use it are able to get tax rebates and it will also increase the value of your home. With that, the only thing to do now is to call a reputable solar energy provider. One other thing you should know about the PV system is that this should also be connected to your grid. For this to work, you have to enter into an interconnection agreement with your utility. This agreement will address the issue with regards to the terms and conditions under which your system is tied up with them. This also includes what is known as net metering which allows you to bank any surplus electricity that your system generates on the electric grid in the same manner that you will be charged accordingly should you consume more electricity than what you have banked. You need a PV system to generate solar energy. You just need to know what size of a system you require so this can be installed by your solar provider.

An Overview on the Interesting Facts about Solar Energy:

There are lots of interesting facts about solar energy. Educating yourself about this will prove to be beneficial in the long run. You can share the information to your loved ones. You can teach them of ways on how they can help to conserve the energy. You can also do your share to help this method to advance if you are a genius in the field. But if you are an ordinary citizen who only wants to enjoy, then feast on. But remember that you also have responsibilities to the environment that you must accomplish in order to do your part in the whole scheme of things. The Facts that Matter

1. Solar radiation makes it possible for the energy coming from the sun to be used as power source and energy that can in turn be used for many purposes. The technology on this aspect is characterized in two ways. They can either be passive or active. This will depend on the methods that are used to get, convert and allocate sunlight. What are active solar techniques? These utilize pumps, photovoltaic panels and fans to renovate sunlight into useful resources. These aim to increase the energy supply that is why these can also be referred as supply side technologies. The passive solar techniques, on the other hand, use only selected resources with constructive thermal properties, utilize the kind of spaces that can circulate air naturally and apply the position of buildings and structures towards the sun. These will lessen the need for other sources and can also be referred as the demand side technology.

2. Solar energy has influenced many factors that surround people. This can be referred in planning and designing buildings. This process can be rooted back at the early days of the architectural history. The Greeks and the Chinese first used such factor in building and constructing their architectural pieces and on their planning methods.

3. Solar energy is also being utilized by the agricultural sector because they rely heavily on its benefits in order to gain more harvest. They developed ways in order to plant the kind of crops that will grow according to the amount of sun that they will be getting for the season. This can also be used to dry the crops, pump water, brooding of chicks and to dry animal manures that can later be used as fertilizers.

4. On seasons like the Little Ice Age, fruit walls were used by French and Chinese farmers to be able to collect and store solar energy to help them keep the plants warm and to speedy up the process of ripening of fruits. These walls serve as the thermal masses. The fruit walls that were first developed were perpendicular to the ground and faced the south direction. Over time, innovations were done and slopping walls were used to gain more advantage from the sun. 5. To convert the solar light into heat, people have developed green houses. These enable the production and cultivation of specialty crops all year round. Such innovation made it possible for crops to be produced in untimely seasons and in places where you think that those plants won't grow. And these are only some of the interesting facts about solar energy. These give you a good peek at how wonderful nature is and how people have developed ways to use it to advance in many aspects of their lives.

5. To convert the solar light into heat, people have developed green houses. These enable the production and cultivation of specialty crops all year round. Such innovation made it possible for crops to be produced in untimely seasons and in places where you think that those plants won't grow. And these are only some of the interesting facts about solar energy. These give you a good peek at how wonderful nature is and how people have developed ways to use it to advance in many aspects of their lives.

Analysing the benefits of solar energy:

We all know that using solar energy is a good thing to do. We have heard, and there are quite a number of them, all about the benefits of solar energy and we can't agree why we can't turn this alternative form of energy source to a primary one. But despite the advantages, solar power has yet to fully make it in the mainstream. Let's go back and discuss a couple of the advantages of solar energy and see why keep going back to fossil fuels for energy resource. In the long run, solar power saves money. Initial costs of installation and operations may be more expensive that other energy forms but after settling the expenses, you have an energy resource that is free. Nobody charges for using sunlight, right? The return of investment can also be shorter depending on how much energy you use. You won't spend too much on maintenance either plus those photovoltaic cells can last for 15 to 20 years. There are no mechanical or moving parts to oil and maintain nor are there parts that need to be replaced yearly. Of course solar power is environmental friendly. First its renewable not like fossil fuels which according to studies will be gone in four to five decades. The process of converting energy to usable electricity does not involve the release of toxic chemicals which can harm the environment. Carbon dioxide, nitrogen oxide, sulphur dioxide, lead, and mercury emissions will be a memory of the past when everyone goes solar. Relying on the sun for power also helps reduce global warming. Aside from the toxic wastes and pollutants, using solar power will limit other aspects of the energy industry like hazards of working with and transporting oil or natural gas. Also, other health risks are present in the use of other fuels like kerosene and candles which are still popular in third world countries. With solar energy, these risks will be minimized if not totally eliminated. The use of solar panels is also good for remote areas where providing basic electricity services is troublesome if not totally impossible at all. Solar energy can be transported to far flung villages and once installed they can be left alone for years with little or without maintenance. Communities in Asian countries have successfully installed solar panels in their community and have been enjoying the benefits of clean and reliable power for years.

For a poor country, producing electricity through solar energy can mean independence from oil producing countries which controls the supply and prices of oil. With such independence, new policies on energy can be created which will maximize the benefit for its citizens. Countries will also not be wary on natural disasters which hampers delivery of oil. With this new found independence, countries can invest its national budget on other programs aside from purchasing oil from foreign sources. There are several disadvantages of using solar power and one of which is the costs. But thinking about it in the long run, you'll see that the benefits of solar energy outweigh the disadvantages. Plus, with the current development in the field of science and technology, solar power is becoming more and more convenient and it would not be surprising to find solar energy as a primary source of power in the next few years

Arguments against solar energy:

We all know that solar energy is a good renewable energy resource and that we should start to utilize it more especially when the Earth's fossil fuel reserves are slowly dwindling and will run out in 30 to 50 years. We better look at the various alternative energies and begin a fast tracking of development to hasten our independence on non-renewable fossil fuels. And solar energy is as good as any other alternative energy resource out there. However, several arguments against solar energy have been raised through the years. But probably the most convincing argument is the high costs of solar energy utilization. The problem with solar energy is that you can only harness it during the daytime. And even when the sun is up, the sunlight will be interrupted by occasional cloud covers, rains, fog, and even smog. So in order to harness the sun's energy we need equipment that can get as much solar power as possible at a given time and we need some way of storing that energy so we can use them without any interruptions. We do have the technology to harness the sun's energy, convert it into usable electricity, and store them for future use. And that technology itself is the primary reason why solar power has not caught on even today.

The process of making solar panels as well as the technology for storing that harnessed power remains to be quite expensive. The good thing about this fact today is that due to the recent increase in the costs of fuel and gas, solar power is no longer a far fetched alternative. The gap between the costs has gone down considerably and hopefully in the near future, the costs of solar energy production will be quite competitive. Furthermore, the costs of photovoltaic cells are indeed quite expensive that contemporary oil and gas equipment. But one of the flaws of the argument of costs is that people tend to limit their perspective of solar energy as to only referring to photovoltaic cells. There are other means of harnessing solar energy and not all of them are as expensive as PV cell manufacturing. One way of getting the sun's energy and converting it into usable electricity is the concept of solar thermal plants. In solar thermal technology, various solar collectors are utilized to generate heat which can be applied from the simplest heating and ventilation of houses to the production of massive amounts of electricity.

The use of mirrors or lenses to reflect sunlight to towers equipped with liquids that heat up and produce steam. The steam then turns turbines which in turn generates the electricity needed. The process adds another step compared to photovoltaics which converts solar energy directly into electricity. Nevertheless, solar thermal systems of power production is cheaper that the production of PV cells. For a larger consumer market, it seems that solar thermal energy is the way to go. Regardless, the point here really is to emphasize that solar energy has more to offer. The cost of production is a valid argument against solar energy but still there are ways around it. Costs can be minimized by using other techniques of harnessing solar energy or future developments in the field of science and technology will produce products that are more cost efficient that what are available today.

Countries on the helm of solar energy technology:

The US is not a leading user of solar energy for a very obvious reason: they can still afford to buy fossil fuels from the international market. In other countries the oil prices are ten times higher in the US and sometimes going for the alternative is a lot better in the long run. Today, more and more countries are looking at solar energy as a primary source of power. There are several countries which can be considered as at the helm of solar energy technology.The number one use of solar energy is Germany. It captures almost 50% of the world market of photovoltaic cells. Nowhere else in the world can you find the most number of households with solar panels installed on their roof tops.

Germany has this Renewable Energies Laws (EEG) which passed in 2000. The law certainly helped Germans feel the need to go renewable.

According to statistics, Germans invested nearly US$5 billion in solar photovoltaic systems and have contributed considerable in the growth of the solar energy market. Although most of the things that we see are solar panels, it doesn't mean that Germany's solar industry is not limited to the production of photovoltaic cells for electricity. Other notable usage in Germany includes solar panels for home water heating system. Some news indicate that the German solar hot water market earns U.S.$1.5 billion per year. The "solar park" in Arnstein, Bavaria, Germany is one of the biggest photovoltaic plants in the world. It became operational in 2006 and with more than 1,400 PV solar panels, it can produce 12 megawatts of energy.The next biggest country in terms of usage of solar energy is Spain. The solar energy usage in the country, more specifically the photovoltaic cells usage, has a world market share of 27%. Spain has no sign of slowing down its aggressive and pro-active approach in solar energy. Solar fields are being constructed one of the latest ones is the 60 MW solar field in Olmedilla de Alarcón, near Cuenca. There are other big solar plants in Spain and these include the solar park 12 miles outside of Salamanca, Salamanca, Spain which have 70,000 PV panels divided into three 36-hectare arrays. The arrays produce an output is 13.8 megawatts and has been powering roughly 5,000 homes since it opened in 2007. And the rest of the world follow Germany and Spain. Japan and the US still have a market share in the photovoltaic world market. The two countries both have an 8% market share, a far cry from Germany and Spain. Nevertheless, it is quite important that countries continue to improve their status in the world solar market. Other notable country that uses solar power includes Algeria, Australia, Italy, and Portugal. Aside from the rich European countries, people in Israel. and India are realizing the importance of having alternative sources of energy. These are the countries on the helm of solar energy technology. But, other countries are slowly catching up. The government of Israel, for example, required all residential buildings to install solar water heating systems in the early 90s. Today, business establishments like hotels and office buildings are trying to use solar power as an alternative from using fossil fuels whose prices continue to soar in the world market. India is facing a similar energy crisis and they are also looking at solar energy to get them through it.

Facts about Solar Energy, Some Things to Ponder and why?:

What are the facts about solar energy that we know? It is given that this comes from the sun. This was developed by people in order to take advantage and benefit from everything that the sun can provide. You can also easily guess the goals of these people why they opt to develop such technology. For one, they want to make lives easier to live. Second, they want to find other resources that people can use in their everyday lives. Maybe they also want to profit from the experience because if this will all be successful, people, businesses and industries will gain a lot from what is being developed. During the first years of its introduction, people deem that this technological advancement can only be used by wealthy people. It used to cater mostly for the can afford types of individuals. What if it can heat pool and can run spas? .But the evolution of the solar energy is just starting.

Nowadays, the benefits can be felt even by ordinary citizens. Researchers keep thinking of ways to arrive at this state. And this is proving to be good for everybody's sake. The scientists developed solar panels that can power up homes. They made this available not only for the rich and famous, but they sold the idea to governments. The latter used the innovation to bring electricity to people in their countries who still haven't experienced to live in the comfort of having this kind of power source. As a result, many people experience how it is like to have lights. They have also resorted to businesses that can be aided by such technology. The maintenance is still on-going while the technology is still being pursued. But the fact remains that this has been made available even for the ordinary Person. 2. Aside from electricity, solar energy can be used to heat water and cook food. Life is really becoming easier as people find ways to achieve such state. While the developments are still under way, people are finding ways to make such resource available for everybody.

Different organizations and government agencies help in making this product affordable for everyone no matter what your status in life is. As time passes by, people will be able to develop more and more gadgets and tools to make lives easier. There will come a time when almost everybody can benefit from this. The first notion that the solar energy is only for the wealthy will cease to be remembered. The responsibility now lies on to people's hands to take care of nature. They must give back to nature for everything that they have also gotten in the process. Technological advancements can be better achieved if people will consider how these can affect the natural habitat in general. It is okay to get what people want and what people need. But this must always be done with precaution and by thinking of the effects that these will have on everything. It is fun to learn some facts about solar energy every once in a while. These will excite you about the process. But more so, these must open your eyes to the whole scheme of nature and how important it is to take care of our surroundings to be able to benefit more in the long run.

How to Conserve Solar Energy through Your Little Ways:

As an ordinary person who lives according to what the day brings, have you ever thought about how to conserve solar energy? Do you even care? You may think you are an ordinary worker, or a simple wife or mother. Should you even care about such things? The answer is yes.You must bear in mind that you are part of a whole spectrum of nature.Whatever you do will affect all the things around you. Everything must be conserved, including solar energy. Here are some suggestions to throw in your little efforts to achieve this goal.

1. Plant trees. Nature works wonders. Every element around us affects everything else. By planting trees, you will be able to maximize the energy coming from the sun. This will be directed to help the plants grow and produce harvests. With healthy plants and trees rooted to the soil, the soil will be firm. This will be able to hold its structure even in times of natural disasters.

2. Limit your use of the energy coming from the sun. With today's innovations, there are lots of things that are being developed to use solar energy as a power source. The source may be free. But to be able to turn it to such power source, there are things that are utilized for this reason. If you will abuse the use of such technology, the crash of the materials used to put this up will be fast. This will take a toll on you especially if you rely a lot on this advancement.

3. Teach kids about the importance of solar energy. You can gain knowledge through research and through your everyday interaction with other people about this thing called the solar energy. You must tell your kids about its importance, they must be educated about it at an early age. They are the future of the nation. What you teach them now will be instilled to them until they grow old. At such a young age, they must know about how they can contribute to conserve energy.

4. Take good care of nature. This is the most important thing that you can do to help advance such cause. The sun can cause damage to people and nature if people won't do the necessary steps to care for nature in the first place. There are lots of things that you get from the environment. It wouldn't hurt to look back every now and then and see what you can do to give back to what it has already given to you. The idea here is that everything in this life must be conserved. You cannot abuse the power that you possess to gain so much without even thinking how your actions affect the world around you. It is all right to go with the flow of the continuing advancement of the technology. Look at the options available to you nowadays with regards to solar energy. This can be used to power homes and vehicles. This can give light, heat water and cook your food. This can give you satellite television and phones for supreme entertainment and communications enjoyment. This can give you luxuries like spas and warm water at pools. You must learn everything on how to conserve solar energy so that you can do your part in making sure that such resource will be available as long as you live.

How Does Solar Energy Work:

Ever wondered how solar energy is converted into electricity? Well, this will give you an idea how it works. First, solar panels are installed over a flat surface like the roof of your home. Once activated, it absorbs the sun's rays since the panels are made of semi-conducting materials such as silicon. Electrons are then knocked off loose from their atoms so it can produce electricity. This process by which light is converted into electricity is better known as the photovoltaic effect. From there, you now have direct current electricity and when this enters an inverter, it is converted into 220 volt AC which is the electricity needed to power the home. Of course this is connected to the utility panel in the house so the lights and the appliances will work when these are switched on. If you are not using that much electricity from the solar energy generated, it is stored in a battery so will be able to supply the house with power during a power outage or at night. Should the battery be full, the excess electricity is then exported to the utility grid if your system happens to be connected to it. When your solar energy runs out, utility supplied electricity kicks in.

If you are not using that much electricity from the solar energy generated, it is stored in a battery so will be able to supply the house with power during a power outage or at night. Should the battery be full, the excess electricity is then exported to the utility grid if your system happens to be connected to it. When your solar energy runs out, utility supplied electricity kicks in. The flow of electricity of solar energy is measured using a utility meter which spins backward and forward. It will go backward when you are producing more energy than you need and forward when you need additional power from the utility company. These two are only offset when you pay for the additional energy from the utility company. Any surplus is sold back to what is known as net metering

A smaller version of this is used to power a water heater inside the home. Using the same principles, homeowners get to convert sunlight into heat to get warm water. As you can see, transforming sunlight into solar energy is very easy. But why do countries like Germany and Japan use it more often than the US? The answer is because it is much cheaper for them to use this form of alternative energy compared to oil. Also, although the US initiated this during the 1973 oil crisis, it is not as popular as it was back then because the government neither increased the budget in research for alternative forms of energy nor gave incentives so people will be encourage into doing that again.

Most state regulations also prohibit individuals from installing their own devices even if this is used to give you warm water. Chances are, you won't even find anyone to do it so you will probably have to do it yourself. Just remember that if there is a problem with the plumbing, your insurance will not cover it. Should the state allow you to install such a system, you will not be entitled to the rebate. Using solar cells is just one way to make the most out of solar energy. Your other option is passive solar energy which helps avoid heat loss so those inside will not feel too cold or too hot throughout the day. This is used by a lot of homeowners living in the southwest since they do not need that much insulation compared to homeowners who live in other parts of the US.

Net Metering and Solar Energy:

You can't help but get into net metering when you decide to invest in solar energy because you sometimes consume more or less than what you actually generate. When you consume less energy, your electric meter spins backward, if you use more then it goes forward. Net metering is simply a special metering and billing agreement between you and the electric service provider. You are eligible for this if you reside in a residential area and generate some form of energy using solar, wind energy or a combination of both. It also has to be located on your premises and connected to the grid. For this to work, you need to have a meter capable of moving in both directions. Most meters these days can do that but if your provider wants to use two meters, they will have to pay for it.

However, if you enter into a time of use billing agreement, you will have to be one to buy the unit. The net metering agreement works by letting you use the electricity you generate first before you use what you normally get from your electric service provider. Your meter should show the net which is measured as the difference between the electricity you purchased and what you actually purchased. The benefit of the net metering system is that it allows you to store electricity when you are not there and then use it the moment you get home. Since there is a law that expands net metering, you can take advantage of it by generating electricity during peak hours and then using it during off peak periods. Another benefit is the fact that you only pay the net electricity that you use. If you consume below the baseline, you pay less and more if you go over it. If what you use offsets what you normally get from a provider, then you will most likely pay a lower rate. Since you entered into an agreement with your provider, you will still be billed monthly.

This will state the amount of power you generated and the amount you actually consumed. On the anniversary of your agreement, you will be billed for the previous 12 months but you can also request for this on a monthly basis. Keep in mind that you will not be paid for the excess generation of electricity in a given year although some do. If you want to use solar energy, you have to contact your electric service provider and ask if they offer net metering. When the papers are drawn up, remember that they cannot require you to pay for any meters beyond the bi-directional meter. They cannot conduct any tests or impose any requirements if it meets existing national standards for grid-interconnected systems. Lastly, you don't have to buy additional insurance or buy power from any of their affiliates.

Net metering is a policy and also an incentive when you decide to use solar energy. This is because you reduce the number of kilowatts used by your electric service provider which in turn decreases the emissions of carbon dioxide into the air.

Solar energy in households:

The sun is a great source of energy. It would be great to use solar energy in your homes especially nowadays when the prices of oil and gas continue to increase. Because of the high fuel and gas prices, more and more people are experimenting on the use of solar energy in their households in their attempts to minimize the costs of basic utilities. The sun's energy can be harnessed in different ways depending on how you would utilize the end product. There are so called solar collectors which are placed on the roof tops or used in buildings. The main purpose of these solar collectors is to provide heating and even ventilation for the houses and buildings.

These collectors harness the sun's energy by magnifying the sunlight several times and transferring that heat to air or water. That heated air or water is stored and will provide the building or home heating and hot water whenever needed. The only problem here is that not all places have equal amounts of sunlight.As you go farther from the equator, the strength of the sun is reduced. But still, this is a much better solution than relying on electric grids which do not reach remote areas. It is just a mater of storing the heat generated from the solar collector properly. For example, some buildings in Sweden utilized an underground storage facility where solar energy is stored resulting to savings from heating the building and their water. In areas where gas and fuel are out of reach of the pockets of poor communities, residents have to rely on solar cooking for their meals. They use this bowl shaped discs equipped with mirrors or reflectors which directs all the sunlight on the middle where a pot is placed.

The same technology is being used in India, Sri Lanka, and Nepal. This serves are a good alternative from conventional fuels like coal, firewood, and gas. They can use these solar stoves during a sunny day and use traditional fuels when the weather is not that good. This reliance by communities on solar cooking should encourage more studies on how to make photovoltaic cells cheaper for an ordinary household. At this time, the use of solar cells is not economically friendly for a single household. However, the approach here is to install a series of solar panels which would be shared by the whole community. This could be a good idea depending on your usage, but for basic lighting purposes these could work in small poor communities. In some areas, community cooperatives have found ways to bring electricity to households out of reach of power grids.

In the Philippines for example, a local cooperative provided households loans to enable them to install a basic solar power module which can produce enough electricity for three light bulbs. This ay be laughable in our standards but to these people who have been living all their lives with the flickering light of the candles, three electric light bulbs make a great deal of a difference.

The story is the same in other countries. In Israel, the high costs of photovoltaic cells have clamped down the growth of solar energy in the country. It if fortunate, therefore, that the Israeli government is now providing incentives for households that would use solar energy. However, according to industry analysts, the costs of solar cells production will go down as the demand increase.

Also, most are hopeful that recent discoveries and advancement in technologies will find a way to bring down costs of using solar energy. Ordinary households using solar energy is an ideal scenario that we should all strive to achieve.

Solar energy simplified:

The sun shines, we collect the sunlight, we convert the sunlight into usable forms, and we enjoy the benefits. You can't get any simpler than that. But okay, I know you need more explanations. You've been looking all over the web for information and you need, no you deserve, more than just a single sentence. The following would be my attempt in simplifying the concept of solar energy and I just hope you get something out of it. The sun produces huge amounts of energy. But what the earth gets is a pretty small share of that energy. However, even if we get only a miniscule amount, the energy we receive from the sun is more than enough for our needs. Believe it or not, a day's worth of sunlight when harnessed properly can power a big country like the US for more than a year.

So if that's how much energy we can get from the sun, why do we rely too much on fossil fuels which will disappear in 40 to 50 years time? The main problem is that the sun shines all throughout the world. That energy is so spread out that harnessing it is really a challenge. But still, there are other factors at work here, political, economical, and even cultural in nature which contributes to the slow progress of solar technologies. But that will need a whole chapter, nay, a whole book to discuss so let's leave that alone for a moment. There are various ways how we harness sunlight and the specific way may depend on how we plan to use that energy. But we can divide the usage into two general concepts, converting solar power into heat and the other one is converting it into electricity.

Using solar power to heat homes is a pretty good example of the first category. There are two ways that can be used, the first one relies on the positioning of the house's windows and the second one involves the use of some mechanical devices to distribute the heat throughout the house. Solar water heaters are also now available. What you do is provide a solar collector where the heat from the sun is trapped and collected. That heat is then transferred to the after that goes out of your faucets and showers. Converting solar power into electricity, however, needs a little bit more explanation. There are basically two ways we can get electricity out of solar power. The first one involves the use of photovoltaic cells and the second one is using various solar thermal systems. Photovoltaic cells are more commonly known as solar cells. These cells are made from silicon wafers and phosphorous.

When sunlight strikes the surface of the silicon wafers, free electrons are produced. The electrons are then harnessed via attaching a wire to the cells. As the electrons leave the cells and pass through the wire, an electronic current is produced. One major flaw of the photovoltaic cells is that they can be quite expensive plus they only convert a small amount of sunlight. Hopefully these cells can be cheaper, more efficient and more suitable to the needs of consumers in the future.

The great thing about solar energy is that it does not produce any kinds of pollution unlike fossil fuels which spit out substantive amounts of pollutants in the air and even in the water. Plus the sun is pretty much in good health aid it is still very far from dying. We can utilize more than enough energy from the sun that will last us for a lifetime.

Solar Energy, How Does It Benefit the Agricultural Sector:

What is solar energy? To put it simply, this is the energy coming from the sun. The heat and light that the sun provides are essential to life. Can you even imagine life without the sun? It will not be normal and there are lots of things and experiences that people can no longer indulge into if ever that will be the case. Everybody relies on the sun for its benefits. Did you know that the earth gets 1740 watts of insolation or the incoming radiation from the sun? This happens at the upper part of the atmosphere. Almost 30% gets reflected back to the space. The rest of the percentage is being absorbed by the clouds, land masses and oceans.

The Agricultural Sector :

If you can think of one industry that won't survive without the energy coming from the sun, what will be the first thing on your mind? There may be many sectors that must rely on the sun's benefits. But the agricultural and horticulture industry will not thrive without it. They have no other options. If the sun will be gone, these sectors will die. The sun is need by the agricultural and horticulture departments to be able to grow their produce. The latter is needed by people as well as animals. These sectors' productivity will depend on the amount of energy that they are getting from the sun. It must be balanced in all ways. It can never too little. And it must also not be so much. If it is too little, the plans may not be able to grow accordingly. The farmers won't achieve the required harvests in order to feed the population. And if it is too much, this will damage the crops. This will also cause bad effects on people's health. But if the latter is the case, people can think of ways in order to achieve the needed produce by manually trying to reduce the amount of heat that can be directed on the plants. But if the situation becomes unbearable, it might lead to drought and deaths. Farmers must know when the sun will be up, when sunny days will be long and factors like that so that they can settle for what kinds of plants they must plant to survive the kind of weather condition.

Here are only some of the things that they resort to in order to optimize the full benefits of the energy coming from the sun.
- Timed planting cycles
- Timed planting cycles
- Tailored row orientation
- Mixing different varieties of crops to improve the yields

Do you ever wonder what farmers did in times like the Little Ice Age? It is said that English and French farmers resorted to fruit walls. These fruit walls help in maximizing the collection of the energy from the sun. These serve as the thermal masses. These walls help in keeping the plants warm to speed up the process of growing and ripening of produce.

The sun's energy is also being utilized in these sectors in vital activities such as drying the crops, pumping of water, drying animals' manure, brooding of chicks and a lot more. It is hard to imagine the agriculture and horticulture sectors to survive without the solar energy. If there are anybody who knows the importance of the sun, these people are the first in line.

Solar Energy is the Future:

We consume fossil fuels at a greater rate than we have ever had over the past 50 years. That demand is fueled by the increase of cars on the street,the number of planes that take to the air and the number of homes that need electricity. Sadly, we will have depleted these resources by the end of this century which is why we have to come up with other ways to get power and solar energy may be the future. Solar energy is simply extracting the sun's energy for power. Just to tell you how powerful the sun is, it can burn scrub lands and give you sunburn if you are out in the sun without any protection. In fact, the Greeks and the Chinese used this to set fire until the 1880's by Charles Fritts made the first solar cell.

Instead of using a heater to warm up the home, sunlight can be used to control the temperature. You will just need large windows and shades to control the amount of sunlight that will go inside and keep the heat absorbed during the day to remain at night. Solar energy can also provide warm water as it warms up cold water that passes down through the closed flat panels called collectors. But solar energy does not only give warmth to the home.

It can also be used to help power it which reduces our dependence on non-renewable resources like oil or coal. This occurs when solar cells are installed on the roof so it will be able to capture as much solar rays as possible and then converts this into electricity. You will need 10 or 12 to capture at least a kilowatt of power and more if you are powering more than just your home. The only limitation which challenges the use of solar energy is that it can only generate power during the day. The answer to this is to put an auxiliary system in place that will store the energy and kick when the sun is not available. This comes in the form of batteries which will provide power in the evening or a brownout. Advances in technology have taken solar energy to the next level.

NASA uses it to power satellites in orbit, solar panels installed onboard aircraft allow it to fly across oceans while cars can travel speeds up to 40 miles per hour. It is used to power a lighthouse so seafarers will be able to find their way at sea while aircraft can land in an airport in the middle of the frozen desert. Solar energy is safe for the environment since it does not emit any harmful gases or chemicals into the air. It is a renewable resource that has not yet been fully tapped by a lot of countries which makes it very viable for the future.

But is it the only answer to reduce our dependence on oil? No because solar energy is just one of the options. We can also harness the power of the wind, the wave in the oceans, geothermal heat, hydroelectricity and a lot more instead of relying on coal or even nuclear energy that may harm the environment. It is something we have to push for the next generation.

Technologies for harnessing solar energy:

Harnessing the sun's energy efficiently is not an easy feat. The sunlight is so widespread that finding the most effective way of capturing it requires advanced knowledge and technology. There are several technologies for utilizing solar energy and all are unique and are dedicated for specific applications. First up are the photovoltaic cells or commonly known as solar cells. These are probably the best known way of harnessing the energy's sun. Whenever one talk about solar power, the first things that come to mind include having panels and panels of photovoltaic cells or PV. These cells contain semi-conductors, commonly are made from silicon, which absorbs the light from the sun. When sunlight hit the surface of the silicon, new free electrons are created. As the electrons are channeled out of the silicon, electric current is created. The second solar power technology is the concentrating solar power systems. This one involves using mirrors to reflect sunlight to one area. Some systems incorporate high tech devices to track the movement of the sun and adjust the mirrors to maximize the amount of sunlight the system receives. The sunlight reflected from the mirrors is used to heat or power a conventional power plant. Other systems channel the light from the mirrors to an area filled with photovoltaic cells. There are several kinds of concentrated solar power systems, the most popular ones are the solar trough, parabolic dish and solar power tower. The solar trough uses large, U-shaped (parabolic) reflectors to point the sunlight to a tower at the center of the mirrors. At the center tower, hot oil is heated by the sun's energy and help boil water to create steam which is then used to power convention plants. The power tower system uses the same concept as solar troughs.

Mirrors are used to reflect sunlight to a center tower where a liquid is heated and utilized for the creation of steam which will power a power. The parabolic dish system uses mirrored dishes to focus and concentrate sunlight onto a receiver. The size of the dish varies but it is commonly 10 times bigger than an ordinary cable satellite dish. Another solar power technology used today is the solar water heating systems. This is a simple one. The process involves collecting the energy directly from the sun to heat water or liquids which in turn heats up the water.

This is more common in households are ideal for family use. In order to capture the sunlight, solar panels have to be installed in your home or in the place where you will be needing hot water like a swimming pool area. You will need a big space for this but in the long run, you will be able to save lots of money from your electric bill. For commercial establishments, an ideal solar power technology is the transpired solar collector or otherwise known as the solar wall. It involves using perforated solar collectors where outside air passes before it enters the building.

These are but a few of the technologies around which can be used for utilizing the power of the sun. The technologies for harnessing solar energy continue to evolve as new technologies and discoveries are being accomplished. Everything might change in a few years time. Plus, the whole solar power technologies will become more price competitive which will benefit the general consumers.

The downsides of solar energy:

Not that I'm against using solar energy or anything but there are some downsides of using solar energy. My intention is to illustrate these disadvantages so that people can realize the other side of the coin to prepare them and not so much as to dissuade them from using solar energy. I am for everything that can save the planet. View this explanation as an introduction where we can still improve the current technologies involving solar energy. One of the first and major drawbacks of using solar power is the costs. The expense is considerably higher than the conventional electric installation. From the purchase to the initial installations of the solar panel unit, the cost is a significant factor to consider.

The high costs of solar power panels lie on the expensive semi-conductor materials that convert sunlight into electricity. However, as technology progresses and as the need slowly increases, the costs of solar panels are expected to go down, something on the level of being competitive with other energy resources. Another to consider is space. We're talking about installing a solar panel which is not small. It requires a significant amount of space which also helps maximize the amount of sunlight it can collect and convert into electricity. Some households will have the panels installed on their roof others will designate a place for it on the year or on top of a pole. The same space problems will need to be readdressed once you decide to add panels when your current setup is no longer enough for your family's needs. Positioning is also vital.

The solar panels will need to be facing a direction where it will receive the most amount of sunlight in a day. However, there is always a solution. If space does not permit such installations, there are some add-ons that can help maximize sun exposure. Positioning is also vital.

The solar panels will need to be facing a direction where it will receive the most amount of sunlight in a day. However, there is always a solution. If space does not permit such installations, there are some add-ons that can help maximize sun exposure. At night, you might encounter a problem with relying solely on solar power. Although the solution here is to purchase batteries which you can charge during the day and use at night. You will need a couple of batteries though to be able to sustain your electricity needs through cloudy, stormy or smoggy or foggy times during the day. As far as solar powered transportation services go, there are still some quirks that need to be fixed before mass production of such vehicles is rolled out.

The most noticeable difference is the speed. Solar powered cars are far slower that their counterparts. But again, due to the fast development of the solar car and the technologies that go with it, this drawback will soon disappear. When you look at the things that I mentioned about the disadvantages of solar energy, you will see that most of them have solutions while others you just need to compromise a bit. I still think that harnessing the power of the sun is the way to go, so these downsides of solar energy are just a small obstacle that we need to overcome.

The future of solar energy on transportation:

INTRODUCTION TO SOLAR ENERGY

Are you familiar with the World Solar Challenge? It is a race specifically for solar cars. Solar cars basically have arrays of photovoltaic cells which converts the sun's rays into usable electrical energy. The purpose of the race is to raise awareness on the use of the sun's energy on transportation and the development of other alternative forms of energy particularly the solar cells. The future of using solar energy on transportation services may still be a little hazy given the practical difficulties involve in converting ordinary cars into solar cars but the idea is here to stay and hopefully develops into something promising and useful. At this point, solar cars have been built to join solar car races. Very few have been constructed for practical and commercial purposes.

There are several reasons why the solar car remains on the background. The design of a solar car relies on the electrical system of the vehicle. The system controls the electricity the flows from the photovoltaic cells to the batteries, to the wheels, and to the controls. The electric motor that moves the vehicle is powered purely by the electricity produced by the solar cells.

The solar cells, depending on the number installed on the vehicle, can produce more or less 1000 watts of power from the sun's rays. To give you an idea, 1000 watts is just enough electricity to power an electric iron or even a toaster. And since the sun will most likely be covered by clouds at one time or the other, or the car goes through a tunnel or something, solar cars are equipped with batteries to serve as backup power supply for the motor. The battery packs are charged by the solar cells. However, the batteries are not charge while driving the solar car unless you intend to go very slow. Just like a gas pedal in conventional motors, a motor controller regulates the amount of electricity that enters the motor to speed up or slow down the vehicle whenever needed. Solar cars are not that slow as perceived by almost everyone.

These cars can go to as fast as 80-85 mph. With this, you can see why solar cars are not yet into commercial production. Nowadays, solar cells can harness more than 21% of the sun's energy that hit the surface. If the time comes that the cells can actually get more energy from the sun then maybe we can see solar cars on the streets. But at this time, it is quite difficult to make a commercial production model of a solar car. Nevertheless, there are companies who have already created some concept solar cars and are testing how road worthy they are. There's even a scooter that is street legal and runs from batteries charged from photovoltaic cells. Other possible application of solar car technologies is on golf carts which runs pretty slow in the first place and can be appreciated by golfers as well.

The future of solar energy on transportation is still not that clear. The application of solar energy on homes and buildings has been moving forward in recent years so hopefully we can find new ways of converting the sun's energy into usable electricity. And this time something that can be economically and efficiently installed in conventional cars.

The Future of Solar Energy, How It Looks and How It Affects Nature:

The future of solar energy lies on the indigenous hands of people who never tire out from thinking of ways in order to make life easier to live. With the advancement in the technology, the boom of the Internet age and a lot of other things, there will come a time when people will turn their backs on whatever is conventional. This can be good and bad in many ways, depending on who is looking at it and from what perspective. But people's quest for the advancement and development of everything that surrounds them provides lots of negative effects as well.

Here are only some.

1.Sometimes, people neglect the environment and how to properly take care of it for the mere fact that they are greedy to get their ideas done no matter what the consequences to the nature will be. Such advancements create harmful effects in the whole state and balance of nature. How many times have you heard about forest denudation or grave floods that kill people? All these occurrences can also be rooted to the activities of men that suffice for their own good without so much consideration for their natural habitat and the nature.

2. With the continuing advancement of everything that surrounds people, the generational gap becomes wider and wider. Old folks will fight for the benefits of the conventional tools and mediums. The newer generations cannot afford to sit on those old ways to do things. They are a slave to the continuing technological developments. It is okay to initiate change. It is good to find better ways to do things. But people must be cautious in achieving this. They must think about everything around them before they even start on their venture to newer and better ways to achieve greatness. The Innovations As of today, solar energy is one of the best options that people have with regards

to alternative power sources. This has already evolved. There was a time when you can only avail such power source when the sun is present and that is during daytime. With the genius of the people behind the development of this resource, they were able to create green gas that can produce electricity. This is done by splitting water properties into hydrogen and oxygen. Both gasses will then be grouped into a cell that will be the electricity source. The same geniuses estimated that the entire planet can rely to an hour of sunlight for its one year electricity consumption. Solar cells have been developed to produce electricity from the energy coming from the sun. The panels for such technology can also be used to heat water and cook food. There are now the solar heating, solar cookers and solar furnaces as add-ons to this innovative venture. There are now hydrogen based cars. These are fueled by the split hydrogen in water. The solar cells also power the satellites that orbit through the surface of the Earth. This is the reason why there are advancements that people benefit from such as satellite phones and TV, accurate weather forecasting, even the development of the GPS technology and a lot more. There are a lot of benefits that people can gain from the future of solar energy. You just have to think that whatever you do or however you use such technology for your own good, you must always think of ways to protect your environment first to be able to get the most out of such improvements.

The Benefits of Solar Energy:

Solar energy will benefit a lot of people and not only the rich. This is why some governments have increased funding for this type of technology because they are aware of its many benefits. For one, solar energy is very cheap compared to other technologies. It is also renewable unlike coal or the rest which are non-renewable and hard to maintain. It also improves the health of people since it does not produce any carbon dioxide emissions unlike kerosene lamps that give out fumes which are just as deadly as smoking 2 packs of cigarettes a day. It also reduces the incidents of fire that are often associated with the use of kerosene, candles,diesel fuel and gasoline for generators. Solar energy is almost maintenance free because the solar cells used will last for 20 years or more before it has to be replaced.

You just have to keep the panels clean so it is able to absorb sunlight and convert that into electricity. These are also very useful in remote locations where power lines are not yet available. Some examples of these include fish houses, highway signs,marine applications, remote lighting and telecommunication. If countries focus on solar energy and other renewable techniques, they will be able to conserve their foreign exchange because they no longer have to use it to pay for foreign oil. This money can then be used for other things such as health care, infrastructure projects and education.

Solar energy will also reduce your electricity bills because you are no longer dependent on electricity coming from the power company. The only downside to solar energy is the initial cost in setting it up. Yes you will have to buy a lot of solar panels which are quite expensive but in the long run, you will be able to save more because you don't have to pay for anything else to keep them running. Should the cost of solar cells be beyond your budget, you can probably invest in used systems first then try to acquire the brand new ones later on. Another benefit of using solar energy is that you get to conserve fossil fuels and other natural resources that are quickly diminishing as a direct result of an increase in the world's population which could compromise the needs of the future generations. So should people get into solar energy? The answer is yes because it is safe, cheap and good for the environment. You only have to worry when the sun isn't shining because when this happens, rays from the sun won't be able to produce electricity so you have to rely on other means to get power. The same also goes when there is a blackout or brownout because you will soon lose power from your solar system.

The demand for solar energy is increasing and you should join in. Aside from reducing your electric bill, homeowners who use solar energy may claim up to $2,000 in federal investment tax credit in the first year while businesses may claim a 30% federal investment tax credit.

Believe it or not, solar energy has one other benefit and that it increases the value of your home. According to home appraisers, a dollar decrease in your energy bill results in a $20 increase in its property value so do the match and you can easily figure out how much your home will be worth after you decide to invest in solar energy.

The History of Solar Energy:

Solar energy is for everyone simply because the sun shines in every corner of the planet. In fact, the history of solar energy can be traced back to the Greeks that were then passed on to the Romans which marked the first people to ever use the passive solar design. Passive solar design is a way to warm the home based on the dwelling's design. They may not have had glass windows back then but their architecture made it possible for the people to use the sun's rays to light and heat indoor spaces. As a result, there was no need to burn food that often which was in short supply. In 1861, Auguste Mouchout invented the first active solar motor. Unfortunately, its expensive price made it impossible to produce commercially. Less than 20 years later, Charles Fritts invented solar cells,which will later on be used to power homes, heaters, satellites and other devices today. Since what he invented was very primitive, other people experimented on solar energy. One such person was

Albert Einstein who won the Nobel Prize for physics in his research on the photoelectric effect which is a phenomenon associated with the generation of electricity through solar cells. In 1953, Bell Laboratories which we know today as AT&T labs developed the first silicon solar cell capable of generating a measurable electric current. Three years later, solar cells ran $300 per watt. With the Cold War and the Space Race on, this was used to power satellites and crafts. But the biggest event in the development of solar energy occurred during the oil crisis of 1973. This prompted the US government to invest heavily in the solar electric cell that was developed by Bell Laboratories 20 years ago.

By the 1990's, research towards solar energy came to a standstill as the price of oil dropped in the world market. Funds were diverted elsewhere and the United States which was probably the leader in this form of alternative energy was soon surpassed by other nations mainly Germany and Japan. In 2002 for example, Japan had installed 25,000 solar panels on rooftops. Because of that, the price of solar panels went down as the demand for it was on the rise.

To date, solar energy is growing at a modest 30% per year. Although there have been improvements in solar energy, its fundamentals are still the same. The sun's rays are collected and then converted into electricity. Aside from powering homes or office buildings, the technology has been used to power aircraft, cars and boats. Unfortunately, none of these have been made available yet for public use. We still rely heavily on oil for electricity, gasoline for our cars, fuel for planes and ships.

In fact, the US is one of the biggest oil users in the world. To prove a point, the department of Defense consumes 395,000 barrels per This has to change because our oil reserves are almost depleted and many experts believe that global supply for these non-renewable resources will be gone before the end of the century. We have to do our share to push for renewable energy and one of them happens to be solar energy.

The Pros and Cons of Solar Energy:

Solar energy is one of the best forms of renewable energy. But why don't we rely on it so much compared to other countries? The answer is simply that there are pros and cons with using this form of alternative energy. The pros of using solar energy is that the system is easy to install, there are no energy costs once it is set up, there are no emissions like air pollutants or greenhouse gas and the sun is widely available. The pros of using solar energy is that the system is easy to install, there are no energy costs once it is set up, there are no emissions like air pollutants or greenhouse gas and the sun is widely available. A solar energy system is composed of the solar panels, the inverter, battery, charge controller, wires and support structure. For you to produce a kilowatt of power, you will need 10 to 12 solar panels that will occupy an area of 100 square feet.

If you are worried that this will cause damage to your roof, don't because it is made of light weight materials. When you call a contractor, it will usually take a day or two to install and cost around $10,000. Not that many people will have cash on hand to pay for it so they can avail of a home equity loan to pay for it. If you use a kilowatt of solar energy, you can save 170 lbs. of coal from being burned, about 300lbs of carbon dioxide from being released into the atmosphere or 105 gallons of water that most homeowners use up every month.

The cons are solar cells are expensive, the rays can only be collected during the day time, the weather and where you are located will play a factor in how much sunlight you can get and you will need a big area to collect the power. But some experts believe that price of these cells and its ability to collect power will improve in the future. Right now, a kilowatt of solar energy can only produce 1,600 kilowatts of hours per year in sunny climate. That means you will receive 5.5 hours of electricity per day. If you produce about 750 kilowatts of power, you will only get 2.5 hours of power per day.

Solar panels come in various colors and usually have a 5 year warranty.Since manufacturers are aware that solar energy can only work when the sun is out, they have installed batteries so you get more than 5 hours of power even during cloudy days and nights. This is because the batteries are designed to absorb, insulate, transmit and reflect rays coming from the sun.

But solar energy can be applied to other things and not just powering our homes. It can be used to power small devices like calculators to bigger things like planes, satellites and cars. Since these are easy to maintain, you don't have to worry about anything. People should take this seriously especially when this is not a renewable source of energy.

Things We Should Know Before Investing in Solar Energy:

There is no doubt that there are a lot of benefits in using solar energy. Aside from protecting the environment, you get to save a great deal of money. But before you switch to solar energy, here are a few things you should consider. First, is your roof right for solar power? Most solar power systems can be installed as long as the roof is flat and made of material such as bitumen, composite shingle, cement tile, metal or tar and gravel. If this is how your roof is positioned, then there shouldn't be any problems. The solar panels will be installed parallel to the roof surface.

If you are concerned that the weight could be too heavy for your roof, don't be since this is very light and quite rare that you have to do some structural work before installing the system. When you are looking for a contractor, find out how much it will cost to install the system. You should compare these first before you decide in picking the best one. But you should know right now that installing solar powered cells are a bit expensive. There are also no financing programs you can avail of. Your best bet if you don't have enough money is to apply for a home equity loan. If you are planning to install this in a commercial establishment, the various loans you can avail of include the capital equipment loan, equipment secured loan, property secured loan or the SAFE-BIDCO energy efficiency loan.

Non-profit organizations may also avail of special loans for solar energy and the best one is through third party financing. In this case, the non-profit organization and the contractor will purchase the system and make use of the tax credits. The third party will then pass on the charges for the produced power to the non-profit and after the system has depreciated, this is sold to the non-profit at a discount. The end result is that you pay for less than what you are currently paying for because it is maintenance free. Will installing a solar system have any effect on your property? The answer is yes. In fact, it will increase the resale value of your property without having to pay much more in terms of property taxes. If you have a lot of space to spare, you may even be able to zero out your electric bill as long as the sun comes out so you can convert sunlight into electricity.

Aside from increasing the properly value, you will also be able to avail of tax credits from the government. Solar energy can power your home in the same way you get electricity from the grid. You won't be able to use it when there is a power outage or when the sun is shining but fortunately, this doesn't happen daily so it is still an alternative form of energy worth considering.

Using solar energy goes way back:

Recollecting the history of solar energy brings us back to the 1970s energy crisis and oil embargo which caused long lines in gasoline stations, high gasoline prices, and even caused panic among consumers and investors alike in the United States. Knowledge about oil being a non-renewable resource has been around since the 1800s.

But it was only during and after the 70s energy crisis that people really began to realize the consequences of depending too much on an already depleting energy resource. However, utilizing the sun's energy is not really a recent development. It has been used by ancient civilizations for warmth, for food and crop preparations and various agricultural purposes. What's new are the technologies involved in harnessing this energy and utilizing it for man's daily use. The technology began in the 1830's when Edmund Becquerel made public his studies on how solar light can be harnessed into usable energy. However, nobody followed up on this idea nor explore any practical use.

The next breakthrough on solar power came after thirty years Becquerel published his works. In 1860s, the French Monarch commissioned Augusted Mouchout to find other sources of energy. And Mouchout looked up in the sky for inspiration. His series of solar powered contractions were quite impressive back then. His inventions included a motor that run on solar energy, a steam engine that uses the sun's light, and an ice maker that fully rely on solar power. After Mouchout, there were several other notable achievements in the line of solar power. Among these is the works of William Adams in the 1870s which utilized mirrors to channel the power of the sun to make a steam engine run. Adams' power tower design concept is still in use today.

Another notable work is by Charles Fritz in the early 1880s. His studies were attuned on turning sunlight into electricity, which he later accomplished. But one of the most significant development in modern solar energy occurred in the 1950s. Early in the decade, R.S. Ohl discovered that sunlight produces large numbers of free electrons when it strikes silicon. Then in the mid-1950s Gerald Pearson, Calvin Fuller, and Daryl Chaplin was able to capture those free electrons and convert them in electricity.

Today, silicon cells are used to make solar cells and solar panels for harnessing the sun's energy. Immediately these solar cells were made into good use and the first among to use them was the field of space aeronautics. These silicon based solar cells were used to power satellites that orbit the earth. The satellite Vanguard I was the first one launched out to space which rely on solar cells for power. More satellites followed. Nowadays, more and more research and studies are being conducted on how best to utilize the sun's energy. Especially today where it is said that about 30-50 years from the now, the world oil reserves will be totally depleted. Thus, the search for alternative sources of energy continuous.

The sun is expected to die out in a couple of thousand of years, it's too long to worry about and man can have all the sun's energy until that day. The challenge today is creating solar energy power in more efficient and cost effective e way. Admittedly, the costs of those photo cells are not that cheap to be accessible by most of the ordinary consumers. The movement today in the science and technology committee is to be able to provide cheap alternative source of energy.

What is Solar Energy?

Solar energy is a form of renewable energy as it utilizes the radiant energy coming from the sun. This is done by converting sunlight into electricity using solar cells. Solar cells or photovoltaics were invented in the 1880's by Charles Fritts. Although it did not convert a lot of sunlight into electricity at the time, this started a revolution that continued on to the 20th century. The greatest example is perhaps the Vanguard 1 which was a satellite fitted with solar cells that enabled it to transmit back to earth after its chemical battery was exhausted. Its success prompted NASA and its Russian counterpart to the same with other satellites including Telstar hich continues to serve as the backbone of the telecommunications structure today.The most significant event that stimulated the demand for solar energy was the 1973 oil crisis.

Early on, power companies would charge the consumer a hundred dollars per watt. In the 1980's, it became only $7 per watt. Unfortunately, the lack of government funding did not sustain its growth so the growth of solar energy was only 15% annually from 1984 to 1996. There have been a decline in the demand for solar energy in the US but this increased in Japan and Germany. From 31.2 megawatts of power in 1994, this increased to 318 megawatts in 1999 and world wide production growth increased by 30% towards the end of the 20th century.

Next to these two countries, Spain is the third largest user of solar energy followed by France, Italy and South Korea.

There are three basic approaches to get the most out of solar energy. It is namely passive, active and solar photovoltaic systems.

1. In passive, it has to do a lot with the building design. This will enable the building to avoid heat loss so people inside will feel a great degree of comfort with the help of controlled ventilation and day lighting. Homes that apply this will greatly reduce their heating requirements by as much as 80% with minimal cost.

2. Active solar heating is used to convert sunlight into heat which provides space or water heating. Used extensively in Europe, getting the right size will cover 50% to 60% of your hot water heating requirements.

3. Lastly is photovoltaic which converts solar radiation into electricity. This is done by installing solar cells in the ground and the greater the intensity of the light, the greater the flow of electricity. These are available in different sizes and some are installed in consumer devices like calculators and watches.

Some vehicles are now powered using solar energy. Cars although not yet produced commercially compete in the World Solar Challenge which invites competitors from around the world to compete in this annual event in Australia.

There are also unmanned aerial vehicles and balloons. To date, solar energy has only been successful in passenger boats.

Many of us take the sun for granted and if we are really serious about preserving the environment and reducing our demand for oil, solar energy is just one of the options we have on the table. We have to lobby and convince our government leaders to do more because it is the cheapest means of providing our home with electricity compared to rechargeable batteries, kerosene or candles.

Wind power vs Solar energy an even match:

Today in center stage is a battle for the ages. On the right corner, packing a hurricane punch yet is known to move softly as a breeze is wind power. On the left corner, with a scorching hot aura, moves in a speed of light, is solar energy. Wind power versus solar energy, which one is going to be declared the champion of the alternative energy movement?! Let's get ready to rumble! Or something like that. I apologize for that intro but I just can't help. I figured that if I was going to match one alternative energy resource against the other, then I'll make some extravagant introduction. Just imagine the drum rolls. Actually, there is an existing debate among environmentalists and even scientists on which energy resource should be developed first given their advantages and drawbacks. Staying away from the personal biases, numerous studies have shown that overall, wind power is more cost effective than harnessing the sun's energy.

Let's see the reasons behind that conclusion. Harnessing the sun's energy can be done by a number of ways. But probably the simplest way which can be applied in a small home is by using photovoltaic cells or PV or solar cells. What happens is that sunlight hit the surface of a photovoltaic (PV) panel which responds by creating free electrons which is channelled to generate an electric current. Wind power on the other hand utilizes a propeller and a shaft system which has a magnet wrapped by a coil of wire inside. As the wind turns the propeller and the magnet inside, the electrons in the wire are forced to move along the wire producing an electrical current. Both ways are quite simple but the complexities now lies on the costs of producing the necessary equipment especially the mechanisms that will maximize the power output. When costs of production of photovoltaic cells and wind turbine are compared, the latter is much cheaper to produce. Although, manufacturers of photovoltaic cells stress that as the demand on PV cells increase, the costs of production decreases. So its just a matter of time before PV cells become price competitive.

Other problems include the logistics of placing the equipment. A solar panel requires quite a large space plus, your location on the globe will affect the amount of sunlight you receive and consequently the amount of power you produce. The further away from the equator you are, the less amount of sunlight you can harness. Also, on the average, the PV cells have a 15-20% efficiency rate. The problem with wind power on the other hand is that not all areas will have winds favorable for a turbine. And if you do locate a place where winds are strong and the turbine can be maximized, you'll find that the area (more often than not) is inhabited by various species of birds. You don't want to kill birds with your turbine, do you? Now going back to our wind power vs. solar energy match-up, indeed we do have to agree that wind power is more cost efficient. However, both alternative energy resource will play a big role in our future.

It is, therefore, in my humble opinion that we both develop the two technologies simultaneously for each one has their advantages and disadvantages and each one can be properly utilized for specific areas.

We Can Have a Home Powered By Solar Energy:

Do you like to live in a home that is energy efficient? The good news is you can given there are technologies these days that can make that happen and one good example happens to be solar energy. Solar energy is the process of using the sun's radiant rays to power your home. For this to work, you will need to get some solar panels and then have this install by a contractor. Ideally, you will need a flat area measuring about a hundred square feet. This is good to install between 10 to 12 solar panels that can produce about a kilowatt of power. If you think 1 kilowatt is small, think again because this is equivalent to 1,600 kilowatts of hours per year. That translates to 5.5 hours of electricity per day if you are using it to the max. Otherwise, excess power will be stored in the battery which will help bring electricity to the house during a blackout or at night.

Aside from the solar panels, you will also need the inverter, battery, charge controller, wires and support structure. Each of these parts are important since the system will not work without the other so whoever you choose as a contractor should have everything ready prior to installation. Once everything is set up, you can already enjoy your solar powered home.

Since it requires minimal maintenance, it can last up to 20 years before you have to replace anything. If you have a larger area to work with, why not invest in a solar thermal roof? The difference between this and the first one mentioned is that you convert the entire roof into a giant collector. It is quite expensive and takes a couple of days to complete but worth every penny. The only reason why not that many people invest in such a system is because most roofs are not oriented towards the south with the steep pitch needed to maximize solar energy especially during the winter.

You will have to do some major construction work to make this happen. Solar energy is just one way for you to stop relying on power coming from the grid. When the sun isn't shining, you have to be ready by preparing other ways to generate electricity. One example that can be used at home is wind energy. Here, you use fans to collect the wind's kinetic energy similar to windmills that you see in the farm. The only difference is that the blades are connected to a drive shaft that turns an electric generator to produce electricity.

You just have to do some research to find out if solar energy is feasible for your home. You should know how much power you consume on a monthly basis and also where exactly is your house located.

Should your study show it is possible to live on solar energy, it is best to apply for a home equity loan to pay for the installation costs because you will surely get a return on your investment later on in the form of tax credit and a utility bill that won't exceed $10. So what are you waiting for? If you don't want to rely on power from the electric company, go ahead and invest in solar energy.

Why Are Solar Panels So Popular?

Over the past 20 years solar panels have become extremely popular with homeowners, business and the agricultural industry.

There are many different reasons why people are interested in solar but we have narrowed them down to **3 main reasons**.

Money:

Firstly, the most common reason why solar is popular is because of money.

Solar panels can provide homeowners with a massive saving toward their energy bill (if not completely reduce it altogether).

When people catch wind of their neighbors slashing their energy bill in half, they simply want a piece of the pie. By having a reduced energy bill it means that you will free up your cash flow each month to spend on stuff that you like or your family.

The finance side of solar is the main reason why it has become so popular in today's age.

Environment:

The second most popular reason is because of the environment.

Solar panels are being installed to help take a stance against climate change. People are willing to invest their money into something that will not pollute the planet we live on. Installing solar panels will help by generating clean energy that can also be sold.

This is much better than burning fossil fuels and oils which has a negative effect on the planet. We are realising the sustainability of solar panels which is making them more popular.

Government Incentives :

Thirdly, solar panels are getting a name for themselves through government incentives.

It is pretty hard to resist when the government is offering to buy back any excess solar energy you produce...

Plus lets not forget the massive reduction in the upfront cost, an interest free loan to help reduce the cost even more and then a STC certificate that can be sold for money!

Even with commercial solar for businesses there are rebates and grants being offered as incentives to help with the move to solar.

We Need a PV System to Generate Solar Energy : Solar energy has been around for quite some time. In fact, now is the best time to get it if you want to cut your electric bill and do your share to protect the environment. For that to happen, you will need to buy a PV system. This is designed to reduce or eliminate the amount of electricity you purchase from the utility especially when there could be a price increase in the next few months. The best part about the PV system is that it generates clean electricity which is clean, reliable and renewable since it does not emit any harmful gases into the atmosphere. The PV system must be placed in an area that is free from any obstruction otherwise, it will not be able to capture the sun's rays. A lot of experts say that the south facing roof is best while the east and west is sufficient. If the roof is not available, it can be mounted on the ground. You should know that PV systems come in various sizes so you should get the one that matches our electrical needs. If you consume about 6,500 kilowatts a year, then a PV system within the 3 to 4 kilowatt range is right for your home. You can measure this by reviewing your past electric bills and making some projections Naturally, the size of the PV system will determine the amount of space needed. If you do not use that much electricity, 50 square feet may be sufficient. However, a larger system may require a little over 600 square feet. Just remember that a kilowatt of electricity requires an area of 100 square feet. Solar energy is converted with the help of an inverter since this is what changes direct current to alternating current. You will also need batteries so excess energy may be stored so you can still use solar energy during the evening or during a power outage. The size of the PV system is also in direct proportion with the cost. Most cost from $1 to $1.5 per watt and when you include installation, the bill may reach be from $1,500 to $2,500. The cost of the PV system should not discourage you from investing in solar energy. People who use it are able to get tax rebates and it will also increase the value of your home. With that, the only thing to do now is to call a reputable solar energy provider. One other thing you should know about the PV system is that this should also be connected to your grid. For this to work, you have to enter into an interconnection agreement with your utility. This agreement will address the issue with regards to the terms and conditions under which your system is tied up with them. This also includes what is known as net metering which allows you to bank any surplus electricity that your system generates on the electric grid in the same manner that you will be charged accordingly should you consume more electricity than what you have banked. You need a PV system to generate solar energy. You just need to know what size of a system you require so this can be installed by your solar provider.

An Overview on the Interesting Facts about Solar Energy:

There are lots of interesting facts about solar energy. Educating yourself about this will prove to be beneficial in the long run. You can share the information to your loved ones. You can teach them of ways on how they can help to conserve the energy. You can also do your share to help this method to advance if you are a genius in the field. But if you are an ordinary citizen who only wants to enjoy, then feast on. But remember that you also have responsibilities to the environment that you must accomplish in order to do your part in the whole scheme of things. The Facts that Matter

1. Solar radiation makes it possible for the energy coming from the sun to be used as power source and energy that can in turn be used for many purposes. The technology on this aspect is characterized in two ways. They can either be passive or active. This will depend on the methods that are used to get, convert and allocate sunlight. What are active solar techniques? These utilize pumps, photovoltaic panels and fans to renovate sunlight into useful resources. These aim to increase the energy supply that is why these can also be referred as supply side technologies. The passive solar techniques, on the other hand, use only selected resources with constructive thermal properties, utilize the kind of spaces that can circulate air naturally and apply the position of buildings and structures towards the sun. These will lessen the need for other sources and can also be referred as the demand side technology.

2. Solar energy has influenced many factors that surround people. This can be referred in planning and designing buildings. This process can be rooted back at the early days of the architectural history. The Greeks and the Chinese first used such factor in building and constructing their architectural pieces and on their planning methods.

3. Solar energy is also being utilized by the agricultural sector because they rely heavily on its benefits in order to gain more harvest. They developed ways in order to plant the kind of crops that will grow according to the amount of sun that they will be getting for the season. This can also be used to dry the crops, pump water, brooding of chicks and to dry animal manures that can later be used as fertilizers.

4. On seasons like the Little Ice Age, fruit walls were used by French and Chinese farmers to be able to collect and store solar energy to help them keep the plants warm and to speedy up the process of ripening of fruits. These walls

serve as the thermal masses. The fruit walls that were first developed were perpendicular to the ground and faced the south direction. Over time, innovations were done and slopping walls were used to gain more advantage from the sun. 5. To convert the solar light into heat, people have developed green houses. These enable the production and cultivation of specialty crops all year round. Such innovation made it possible for crops to be produced in untimely seasons and in places where you think that those plants won't grow. And these are only some of the interesting facts about solar energy. These give you a good peek at how wonderful nature is and how people have developed ways to use it to advance in many aspects of their lives.

5. To convert the solar light into heat, people have developed green houses. These enable the production and cultivation of specialty crops all year round. Such innovation made it possible for crops to be produced in untimely seasons and in places where you think that those plants won't grow. And these are only some of the interesting facts about solar energy. These give you a good peek at how wonderful nature is and how people have developed ways to use it to advance in many aspects of their lives.

Analysing the benefits of solar energy:

We all know that using solar energy is a good thing to do. We have heard, and there are quite a number of them, all about the benefits of solar energy and we can't agree why we can't turn this alternative form of energy source to a primary one. But despite the advantages, solar power has yet to fully make it in the mainstream. Let's go back and discuss a couple of the advantages of solar energy and see why keep going back to fossil fuels for energy resource. In the long run, solar power saves money. Initial costs of installation and operations may be more expensive that other energy forms but after settling the expenses, you have an energy resource that is free. Nobody charges for using sunlight, right? The return of investment can also be shorter depending on how much energy you use. You won't spend too much on maintenance either plus those photovoltaic cells can last for 15 to 20 years. There are no mechanical or moving parts to oil and maintain nor are there parts that need to be replaced yearly. Of course solar power is environmental friendly. First its renewable not like fossil fuels which according to studies will be gone in four to five decades. The process of converting energy to usable electricity does not involve the release of toxic chemicals which can harm the environment. Carbon dioxide, nitrogen oxide, sulphur dioxide, lead, and mercury emissions will be a memory of the past when everyone goes solar. Relying on the sun for power also helps reduce global warming. Aside from the toxic wastes and pollutants, using solar power will limit other aspects of the energy industry like hazards of working with and transporting oil or natural gas. Also, other health risks are present in the use of other fuels like kerosene and candles which are still popular in third world countries. With solar energy, these risks will be minimized if not totally eliminated. The use of solar panels is also good for remote areas where providing basic electricity services is troublesome if not totally impossible at all. Solar energy can be transported to far flung villages and once installed they can be left alone for years with little or without maintenance. Communities in Asian countries have successfully installed solar panels in their community and have been enjoying the benefits of clean and reliable power for years.

For a poor country, producing electricity through solar energy can mean independence from oil producing countries which controls the supply and prices of oil. With such independence, new policies on energy can be created which will maximize the benefit for its citizens. Countries will also not be wary on natural disasters which hampers delivery of oil. With this new found independence, countries can invest its national budget on other programs aside from purchasing oil from foreign sources. There are several disadvantages of using solar power and one of which is the costs. But thinking about it in the long run, you'll see that the benefits of solar energy outweigh the disadvantages. Plus, with the current development in the field of science and technology, solar power is becoming more and more convenient and it would not be surprising to find solar energy as a primary source of power in the next few years

Arguments against solar energy:

We all know that solar energy is a good renewable energy resource and that we should start to utilize it more especially when the Earth's fossil fuel reserves are slowly dwindling and will run out in 30 to 50 years. We better look at the various alternative energies and begin a fast tracking of development to hasten our independence on non-renewable fossil fuels. And solar energy is as good as any other alternative energy resource out there. However, several arguments against solar energy have been raised through the years. But probably the most convincing argument is the high costs of solar energy utilization. The problem with solar energy is that you can only harness it during the daytime. And even when the sun is up, the sunlight will be interrupted by occasional cloud covers, rains, fog, and even smog. So in order to harness the sun's energy we need equipment that can get as much solar power as possible at a given time and we need some way of storing that energy so we can use them without any interruptions. We do have the technology to harness the sun's energy, convert it into usable electricity, and store them for future use. And that technology itself is the primary reason why solar power has not caught on even today.

The process of making solar panels as well as the technology for storing that harnessed power remains to be quite expensive. The good thing about this fact today is that due to the recent increase in the costs of fuel and gas, solar power is no longer a far fetched alternative. The gap between the costs has gone down considerably and hopefully in the near future, the costs of solar energy production will be quite competitive. Furthermore, the costs of photovoltaic cells are indeed quite expensive that contemporary oil and gas equipment. But one of the flaws of the argument of costs is that people tend to limit their perspective of solar energy as to only referring to photovoltaic cells. There are other means of harnessing solar energy and not all of them are as expensive as PV cell manufacturing. One way of getting the sun's energy and converting it into usable electricity is the concept of solar thermal plants. In solar thermal technology, various solar collectors are utilized to generate heat which can be applied from the simplest heating and ventilation of houses to the production of massive amounts of electricity.

The use of mirrors or lenses to reflect sunlight to towers equipped with liquids that heat up and produce steam. The steam then turns turbines which in turn generates the electricity needed. The process adds another step compared to photovoltaics which converts solar energy directly into electricity. Nevertheless, solar thermal systems of power production is cheaper that the production of PV cells. For a larger consumer market, it seems that solar thermal energy is the way to go. Regardless, the point here really is to emphasize that solar energy has more to offer. The cost of production is a valid argument against solar energy but still there are ways around it. Costs can be minimized by using other techniques of harnessing solar energy or future developments in the field of science and technology will produce products that are more cost efficient that what are available today.

Countries on the helm of solar energy technology:

The US is not a leading user of solar energy for a very obvious reason: they can still afford to buy fossil fuels from the international market. In other countries the oil prices are ten times higher in the US and sometimes going for the alternative is a lot better in the long run. Today, more and more countries are looking at solar energy as a primary source of power. There are several countries which can be considered as at the helm of solar energy technology.The number one use of solar energy is Germany. It captures almost 50% of the world market of photovoltaic cells. Nowhere else in the world can you find the most number of households with solar panels installed on their roof tops. Germany has this Renewable Energies Laws (EEG) which passed in 2000. The law certainly helped Germans feel the need to go renewable.

According to statistics, Germans invested nearly US$5 billion in solar photovoltaic systems and have contributed considerable in the growth of the solar energy market. Although most of the things that we see are solar panels, it doesn't mean that Germany's solar industry is not limited to the production of photovoltaic cells for electricity. Other notable usage in Germany includes solar panels for home water heating system. Some news indicate that the German solar hot water market earns U.S.$1.5 billion per year. The "solar park" in Arnstein, Bavaria, Germany is one of the biggest photovoltaic plants in the world. It became operational in 2006 and with more than 1,400 PV solar panels, it can produce 12 megawatts of energy.The next biggest country in terms of usage of solar energy is Spain. The solar energy usage in the country, more specifically the photovoltaic cells usage, has a world market share of 27%. Spain has no sign of slowing down its aggressive and pro-active approach in solar energy. Solar fields are being constructed one of the latest ones is the 60 MW solar field in Olmedilla de Alarcón, near Cuenca. There are other big solar plants in Spain and these include the solar park 12 miles outside of Salamanca, Salamanca, Spain which have 70,000 PV panels divided into three 36-hectare arrays. The arrays produce an output is 13.8 megawatts and has been powering roughly 5,000 homes since it opened in 2007. And the rest of the world follow Germany and Spain. Japan and the US still have a market share in the photovoltaic world market. The two countries both have an 8% market share, a far cry from Germany and Spain. Nevertheless, it is quite important that countries continue to improve their status in the world solar market. Other notable country that uses solar power includes Algeria, Australia, Italy, and Portugal. Aside from the rich European countries, people in Israel. and India are realizing the importance of having alternative sources of energy. These are the countries on the helm of solar energy technology. But, other countries are slowly catching up. The government of Israel, for example, required all residential buildings to install solar water heating systems in the early 90s. Today, business establishments like hotels and office buildings are trying to use solar power as an alternative from using fossil fuels whose prices continue to soar in the world market. India is facing a similar energy crisis and they are also looking at solar energy to get them through it.

Facts about Solar Energy, Some Things to Ponder and why?:

What are the facts about solar energy that we know? It is given that this comes from the sun. This was developed by people in order to take advantage and benefit from everything that the sun can provide. You can also easily guess the goals of these people why they opt to develop such technology. For one, they want to make lives easier to live. Second, they want to find other resources that people can use in their everyday lives. Maybe they also want to profit from the experience because if this will all be successful, people, businesses and industries will gain a lot from what is being developed. During the first years of its introduction, people deem that this technological advancement can only be used by wealthy people. It used to cater mostly for the can afford types of individuals. What if it can heat pool and can run spas? .But the evolution of the solar energy is just starting.

Nowadays, the benefits can be felt even by ordinary citizens. Researchers keep thinking of ways to arrive at this state. And this is proving to be good for everybody's sake. The scientists developed solar panels that can power up homes. They made this available not only for the rich and famous, but they sold the idea to governments. The latter used the innovation to bring electricity to people in their countries who still haven't experienced to live in the comfort of having this kind of power source. As a result, many people experience how it is like to have lights. They have also resorted to businesses that can be aided by such technology. The maintenance is still on-going while the technology is still being pursued. But the fact remains that this has been made available even for the ordinary Person. 2. Aside from electricity, solar energy can be used to heat water and cook food. Life is really becoming easier as people find ways to achieve such state. While the developments are still under way, people are finding ways to make such resource available for everybody.

Different organizations and government agencies help in making this product affordable for everyone no matter what your status in life is. As time passes by, people will be able to develop more and more gadgets and tools to make lives easier. There will come a time when almost everybody can benefit from this. The first notion that the solar energy is only for the wealthy will cease to be remembered. The responsibility now lies on to people's hands to take care of nature. They must give back to nature for everything that they have also gotten in the process. Technological advancements can be better achieved if people will consider how these can affect the natural habitat in general. It is okay to get what people want and what people need. But this must always be done with precaution and by thinking of the effects that these will have on everything. It is fun to learn some facts about solar energy every once in a while. These will excite you about the process. But more so, these must open your eyes to the whole scheme of nature and how important it is to take care of our surroundings to be able to benefit more in the long run.

How to Conserve Solar Energy through Your Little Ways:

As an ordinary person who lives according to what the day brings, have you ever thought about how to conserve solar energy? Do you even care? You may think you are an ordinary worker, or a simple wife or mother. Should you even care about such things? The answer is yes.You must bear in mind that you are part of a whole spectrum of nature.Whatever you do will affect all the things around you. Everything must be conserved, including solar energy. Here are some suggestions to throw in your little efforts to achieve this goal.

1. Plant trees. Nature works wonders. Every element around us affects everything else. By planting trees, you will be able to maximize the energy coming from the sun. This will be directed to help the plants grow and produce harvests. With healthy plants and trees rooted to the soil, the soil will be firm. This will be able to hold its structure even in times of natural disasters.

2. Limit your use of the energy coming from the sun. With today's innovations, there are lots of things that are being developed to use solar energy as a power source. The source may be free. But to be able to turn it to such power

source, there are things that are utilized for this reason. If you will abuse the use of such technology, the crash of the materials used to put this up will be fast. This will take a toll on you especially if you rely a lot on this advancement.

3. Teach kids about the importance of solar energy. You can gain knowledge through research and through your everyday interaction with other people about this thing called the solar energy. You must tell your kids about its importance, they must be educated about it at an early age. They are the future of the nation. What you teach them now will be instilled to them until they grow old. At such a young age, they must know about how they can contribute to conserve energy.

4. Take good care of nature. This is the most important thing that you can do to help advance such cause. The sun can cause damage to people and nature if people won't do the necessary steps to care for nature in the first place. There are lots of things that you get from the environment. It wouldn't hurt to look back every now and then and see what you can do to give back to what it has already given to you. The idea here is that everything in this life must be conserved. You cannot abuse the power that you possess to gain so much without even thinking how your actions affect the world around you. It is all right to go with the flow of the continuing advancement of the technology. Look at the options available to you nowadays with regards to solar energy. This can be used to power homes and vehicles. This can give light, heat water and cook your food. This can give you satellite television and phones for supreme entertainment and communications enjoyment. This can give you luxuries like spas and warm water at pools. You must learn everything on how to conserve solar energy so that you can do your part in making sure that such resource will be available as long as you live.

How Does Solar Energy Work:

Ever wondered how solar energy is converted into electricity? Well, this will give you an idea how it works. First, solar panels are installed over a flat surface like the roof of your home. Once activated, it absorbs the sun's rays since the panels are made of semi-conducting materials such as silicon. Electrons are then knocked off loose from their atoms so it can produce electricity. This process by which light is converted into electricity is better known as the photovoltaic effect. From there, you now have direct current electricity and when this enters an inverter, it is converted into 220 volt AC which is the electricity needed to power the home. Of course this is connected to the utility panel in the house so the lights and the appliances will work when these are switched on. If you are not using that much electricity from the solar energy generated, it is stored in a battery so will be able to supply the house with power during a power outage or at night. Should the battery be full, the excess electricity is then exported to the utility grid if your system happens to be connected to it. When your solar energy runs out, utility supplied electricity kicks in.

If you are not using that much electricity from the solar energy generated, it is stored in a battery so will be able to supply the house with power during a power outage or at night. Should the battery be full, the excess electricity is then exported to the utility grid if your system happens to be connected to it.When your solar energy runs out, utility supplied electricity kicks in. The flow of electricity of solar energy is measured using a utility meter which spins backward and forward. It will go backward when you are producing more energy than you need and forward when you need additional power from the utility company. These two are only offset when you pay for the additional energy from the utility company. Any surplus is sold back to what is known as net metering

A smaller version of this is used to power a water heater inside the home. Using the same principles, homeowners get to convert sunlight into heat to get warm water. As you can see, transforming sunlight into solar energy is very easy. But why do countries like Germany and Japan use it more often than the US? The answer is because it is much cheaper for them to use this form of alternative energy compared to oil. Also, although the US initiated this during the 1973 oil crisis, it is not as popular as it was back then because the government neither increased the budget in research for alternative forms of energy nor gave incentives so people will be encourage into doing that again.

Most state regulations also prohibit individuals from installing their own devices even if this is used to give you warm water. Chances are, you won't even find anyone to do it so you will probably have to do it yourself. Just remember that if there is a problem with the plumbing, your insurance will not cover it. Should the state allow you to install such a system, you will not be entitled to the rebate. Using solar cells is just one way to make the most out of solar energy. Your other option is passive solar energy which helps avoid heat loss so those inside will not feel too cold or too hot throughout the day. This is used by a lot of homeowners living in the southwest since they do not need that much insulation compared to homeowners who live in other parts of the US.

Net Metering and Solar Energy:

You can't help but get into net metering when you decide to invest in solar energy because you sometimes consume more or less than what you actually generate. When you consume less energy, your electric meter spins backward, if you use more then it goes forward. Net metering is simply a special metering and billing agreement between you and the electric service provider. You are eligible for this if you reside in a residential area and generate some form of energy using solar, wind energy or a combination of both. It also has to be located on your premises and connected to the grid. For this to work, you need to have a meter capable of moving in both directions. Most meters these days can do that but if your provider wants to use two meters, they will have to pay for it.

However, if you enter into a time of use billing agreement, you will have to be one to buy the unit. The net metering agreement works by letting you use the electricity you generate first before you use what you normally get from your electric service provider. Your meter should show the net which is measured as the difference between the electricity you purchased and what you actually purchased. The benefit of the net metering system is that it allows you to store electricity when you are not there and then use it the moment you get home. Since there is a law that expands net metering, you can take advantage of it by generating electricity during peak hours and then using it during off peak periods. Another benefit is the fact that you only pay the net electricity that you use. If you consume below the baseline, you pay less and more if you go over it. If what you use offsets what you normally get from a provider, then you will most likely pay a lower rate. Since you entered into an agreement with your provider, you will still be billed monthly.

This will state the amount of power you generated and the amount you actually consumed. On the anniversary of your agreement, you will be billed for the previous 12 months but you can also request for this on a monthly basis. Keep in mind that you will not be paid for the excess generation of electricity in a given year although some do. If you want to use solar energy, you have to contact your electric service provider and ask if they offer net metering. When the papers are drawn up, remember that they cannot require you to pay for any meters beyond the bi-directional meter. They cannot conduct any tests or impose any requirements if it meets existing national standards for grid-interconnected systems. Lastly, you don't have to buy additional insurance or buy power from any of their affiliates.

Net metering is a policy and also an incentive when you decide to use solar energy. This is because you reduce the number of kilowatts used by your electric service provider which in turn decreases the emissions of carbon dioxide into the air.

Solar energy in households:

The sun is a great source of energy. It would be great to use solar energy in your homes especially nowadays when the prices of oil and gas continue to increase. Because of the high fuel and gas prices, more and more people are experimenting on the use of solar energy in their households in their attempts to minimize the costs of basic utilities. The sun's energy can be harnessed in different ways depending on how you would utilize the end product. There are so called solar collectors which are placed on the roof tops or used in buildings. The main purpose of these solar collectors is to provide heating and even ventilation for the houses and buildings.

These collectors harness the sun's energy by magnifying the sunlight several times and transferring that heat to air or water. That heated air or water is stored and will provide the building or home heating and hot water whenever needed. The only problem here is that not all places have equal amounts of sunlight.As you go farther from the equator, the strength of the sun is reduced. But still, this is a much better solution than relying on electric grids which do not reach remote areas. It is just a mater of storing the heat generated from the solar collector properly. For example, some buildings in Sweden utilized an underground storage facility where solar energy is stored resulting to savings from heating the building and their water. In areas where gas and fuel are out of reach of the pockets of poor communities, residents have to rely on solar cooking for their meals. They use this bowl shaped discs equipped with mirrors or reflectors which directs all the sunlight on the middle where a pot is placed.

The same technology is being used in India, Sri Lanka, and Nepal. This serves are a good alternative from conventional fuels like coal, firewood, and gas. They can use these solar stoves during a sunny day and use traditional fuels when the weather is not that good. This reliance by communities on solar cooking should encourage more studies on how to make photovoltaic cells cheaper for an ordinary household. At this time, the use of solar cells is not economically friendly for a single household. However, the approach here is to install a series of solar panels which would be shared by the whole community. This could be a good idea depending on your usage, but for basic lighting purposes these could work in small poor communities. In some areas, community cooperatives have found ways to bring electricity to households out of reach of power grids.

In the Philippines for example, a local cooperative provided households loans to enable them to install a basic solar power module which can produce enough electricity for three light bulbs. This ay be laughable in our standards but to these people who have been living all their lives with the flickering light of the candles, three electric light bulbs make a great deal of a difference.

The story is the same in other countries. In Israel, the high costs of photovoltaic cells have clamped down the growth of solar energy in the country. It if fortunate, therefore, that the Israeli government is now providing incentives for households that would use solar energy. However, according to industry analysts, the costs of solar cells production will go down as the demand increase.

Also, most are hopeful that recent discoveries and advancement in technologies will find a way to bring down costs of using solar energy. Ordinary households using solar energy is an ideal scenario that we should all strive to achieve.

Solar energy simplified:

The sun shines, we collect the sunlight, we convert the sunlight into usable forms, and we enjoy the benefits. You can't get any simpler than that. But okay, I know you need more explanations. You've been looking all over the web for information and you need, no you deserve, more than just a single sentence. The following would be my attempt in simplifying the concept of solar energy and I just hope you get something out of it. The sun produces huge amounts of energy. But what the earth gets is a pretty small share of that energy. However, even if we get only a miniscule amount, the energy we receive from the sun is more than enough for our needs. Believe it or not, a day's worth of sunlight when harnessed properly can power a big country like the US for more than a year.

So if that's how much energy we can get from the sun, why do we rely too much on fossil fuels which will disappear in 40 to 50 years time? The main problem is that the sun shines all throughout the world. That energy is so spread out that harnessing it is really a challenge. But still, there are other factors at work here, political, economical, and even cultural in nature which contributes to the slow progress of solar technologies. But that will need a whole chapter, nay, a whole book to discuss so let's leave that alone for a moment. There are various ways how we harness sunlight and the specific way may depend on how we plan to use that energy. But we can divide the usage into two general concepts, converting solar power into heat and the other one is converting it into electricity.

Using solar power to heat homes is a pretty good example of the first category. There are two ways that can be used, the first one relies on the positioning of the house's windows and the second one involves the use of some mechanical devices to distribute the heat throughout the house. Solar water heaters are also now available. What you do is provide a solar collector where the heat from the sun is trapped and collected. That heat is then transferred to the after that goes out of your faucets and showers. Converting solar power into electricity, however, needs a little bit more explanation. There are basically two ways we can get electricity out of solar power. The first one involves the use of photovoltaic cells and the second one is using various solar thermal systems. Photovoltaic cells are more commonly known as solar cells. These cells are made from silicon wafers and phosphorous.

When sunlight strikes the surface of the silicon wafers, free electrons are produced. The electrons are then harnessed via attaching a wire to the cells. As the electrons leave the cells and pass through the wire, an electronic current is produced. One major flaw of the photovoltaic cells is that they can be quite expensive plus they only convert a small amount of sunlight. Hopefully these cells can be cheaper, more efficient and more suitable to the needs of consumers in the future.

The great thing about solar energy is that it does not produce any kinds of pollution unlike fossil fuels which spit out substantive amounts of pollutants in the air and even in the water. Plus the sun is pretty much in good health aid it is still very far from dying. We can utilize more than enough energy from the sun that will last us for a lifetime.

Solar Energy, How Does It Benefit the Agricultural Sector:

What is solar energy? To put it simply, this is the energy coming from the sun. The heat and light that the sun provides are essential to life. Can you even imagine life without the sun? It will not be normal and there are lots of things and experiences that people can no longer indulge into if ever that will be the case. Everybody relies on the sun for its benefits. Did you know that the earth gets 1740 watts of insolation or the incoming radiation from the sun? This happens at the upper part of the atmosphere. Almost 30% gets reflected back to the space. The rest of the percentage is being absorbed by the clouds, land masses and oceans.

The Agricultural Sector :

If you can think of one industry that won't survive without the energy coming from the sun, what will be the first thing on your mind? There may be many sectors that must rely on the sun's benefits. But the agricultural and horticulture industry will not thrive without it. They have no other options. If the sun will be gone, these sectors will die. The sun is need by the agricultural and horticulture departments to be able to grow their produce. The latter is needed by people as well as animals. These sectors' productivity will depend on the amount of energy that they are getting from the sun. It must be balanced in all ways. It can never too little. And it must also not be so much. If it is too little, the plans may not be able to grow accordingly. The farmers won't achieve the required harvests in order to feed the population. And if it is too much, this will damage the crops. This will also cause bad effects on people's health. But if the latter is the case, people can think of ways in order to achieve the needed produce by manually trying to reduce the amount of heat that can be directed on the plants. But if the situation becomes unbearable, it might lead to drought and deaths. Farmers must know when the sun will be up, when sunny days will be long and factors like that so that they can settle for what kinds of plants they must plant to survive the kind of weather condition.

Here are only some of the things that they resort to in order to optimize the full benefits of the energy coming from the sun.

- Timed planting cycles
- Timed planting cycles
- Tailored row orientation
- Mixing different varieties of crops to improve the yields

Do you ever wonder what farmers did in times like the Little Ice Age? It is said that English and French farmers resorted to fruit walls. These fruit walls help in maximizing the collection of the energy from the sun. These serve as the thermal masses. These walls help in keeping the plants warm to speed up the process of growing and ripening of produce.

The sun's energy is also being utilized in these sectors in vital activities such as drying the crops, pumping of water, drying animals' manure, brooding of chicks and a lot more. It is hard to imagine the agriculture and horticulture sectors to survive without the solar energy. If there are anybody who knows the importance of the sun, these people are the first in line.

Solar Energy is the Future:

We consume fossil fuels at a greater rate than we have ever had over the past 50 years. That demand is fueled by the increase of cars on the street,the number of planes that take to the air and the number of homes that need electricity. Sadly, we will have depleted these resources by the end of this century which is why we have to come up with other ways to get power and solar energy may be the future. Solar energy is simply extracting the sun's energy for power. Just to tell you how powerful the sun is, it can burn scrub lands and give you sunburn if you are out in the sun without any protection. In fact, the Greeks and the Chinese used this to set fire until the 1880's by Charles Fritts made the first solar cell.

Instead of using a heater to warm up the home, sunlight can be used to control the temperature. You will just need large windows and shades to control the amount of sunlight that will go inside and keep the heat absorbed during the day to remain at night. Solar energy can also provide warm water as it warms up cold water that passes down through the closed flat panels called collectors. But solar energy does not only give warmth to the home.

It can also be used to help power it which reduces our dependence on non-renewable resources like oil or coal. This occurs when solar cells are installed on the roof so it will be able to capture as much solar rays as possible and then converts this into electricity. You will need 10 or 12 to capture at least a kilowatt of power and more if you are powering more than just your home. The only limitation which challenges the use of solar energy is that it can only generate power during the day. The answer to this is to put an auxiliary system in place that will store the energy and kick when the sun is not available. This comes in the form of batteries which will provide power in the evening or a brownout. Advances in technology have taken solar energy to the next level.

NASA uses it to power satellites in orbit, solar panels installed onboard aircraft allow it to fly across oceans while cars can travel speeds up to 40 miles per hour. It is used to power a lighthouse so seafarers will be able to find their way at sea while aircraft can land in an airport in the middle of the frozen desert. Solar energy is safe for the environment since it does not emit any harmful gases or chemicals into the air. It is a renewable resource that has not yet been fully tapped by a lot of countries which makes it very viable for the future.

But is it the only answer to reduce our dependence on oil? No because solar energy is just one of the options. We can also harness the power of the wind, the wave in the oceans, geothermal heat, hydroelectricity and a lot more instead of relying on coal or even nuclear energy that may harm the environment. It is something we have to push for the next generation.

Technologies for harnessing solar energy:

Harnessing the sun's energy efficiently is not an easy feat. The sunlight is so widespread that finding the most effective way of capturing it requires advanced knowledge and technology. There are several technologies for utilizing solar energy and all are unique and are dedicated for specific applications. First up are the photovoltaic cells or commonly known as solar cells. These are probably the best known way of harnessing the energy's sun. Whenever one talk about solar power, the first things that come to mind include having panels and panels of photovoltaic cells or PV. These cells contain semi-conductors, commonly are made from silicon, which absorbs the light from the sun. When sunlight hit the surface of the silicon, new free electrons are created. As the electrons are channeled out of the silicon, electric current is created. The second solar power technology is the concentrating solar power systems. This one involves using mirrors to reflect sunlight to one area. Some systems incorporate high tech devices to track the movement of the sun and adjust the mirrors to maximize the amount of sunlight the system receives. The sunlight reflected from the mirrors is used to heat or power a conventional power plant. Other systems channel the light from the mirrors to an area filled with photovoltaic cells. There are several kinds of concentrated solar power systems, the most popular ones are the solar trough, parabolic dish and solar power tower. The solar trough uses large, U-shaped (parabolic) reflectors to point the sunlight to a tower at the center of the mirrors. At the center tower, hot oil is heated by the sun's energy and help boil water to create steam which is then used to power convention plants. The power tower system uses the same concept as solar troughs.

Mirrors are used to reflect sunlight to a center tower where a liquid is heated and utilized for the creation of steam which will power a power. The parabolic dish system uses mirrored dishes to focus and concentrate sunlight onto a receiver. The size of the dish varies but it is commonly 10 times bigger than an ordinary cable satellite dish. Another solar power technology used today is the solar water heating systems. This is a simple one. The process involves collecting the energy directly from the sun to heat water or liquids which in turn heats up the water.

This is more common in households are ideal for family use. In order to capture the sunlight, solar panels have to be installed in your home or in the place where you will be needing hot water like a swimming pool area. You will need a big space for this but in the long run, you will be able to save lots of money from your electric bill. For commercial establishments, an ideal solar power technology is the transpired solar collector or otherwise known as the solar wall. It involves using perforated solar collectors where outside air passes before it enters the building.

These are but a few of the technologies around which can be used for utilizing the power of the sun. The technologies for harnessing solar energy continue to evolve as new technologies and discoveries are being accomplished. Everything might change in a few years time. Plus, the whole solar power technologies will become more price competitive which will benefit the general consumers.

The downsides of solar energy:

Not that I'm against using solar energy or anything but there are some downsides of using solar energy. My intention is to illustrate these disadvantages so that people can realize the other side of the coin to prepare them and not so much as to dissuade them from using solar energy. I am for everything that can save the planet. View this explanation as an introduction where we can still improve the current technologies involving solar energy. One of the first and major drawbacks of using solar power is the costs. The expense is considerably higher than the conventional electric installation. From the purchase to the initial installations of the solar panel unit, the cost is a significant factor to consider.

The high costs of solar power panels lie on the expensive semi-conductor materials that convert sunlight into electricity. However, as technology progresses and as the need slowly increases, the costs of solar panels are expected to go down, something on the level of being competitive with other energy resources. Another to consider is space. We're talking about installing a solar panel which is not small. It requires a significant amount of space which also helps maximize the amount of sunlight it can collect and convert into electricity. Some households will have the panels installed on their roof others will designate a place for it on the year or on top of a pole. The same space problems will need to be readdressed once you decide to add panels when your current setup is no longer enough for your family's needs. Positioning is also vital.

The solar panels will need to be facing a direction where it will receive the most amount of sunlight in a day. However, there is always a solution. If space does not permit such installations, there are some add-ons that can help maximize sun exposure. Positioning is also vital.

The solar panels will need to be facing a direction where it will receive the most amount of sunlight in a day. However, there is always a solution. If space does not permit such installations, there are some add-ons that can help maximize sun exposure. At night, you might encounter a problem with relying solely on solar power. Although the solution here is to purchase batteries which you can charge during the day and use at night. You will need a couple of batteries though to be able to sustain your electricity needs through cloudy, stormy or smoggy or foggy times during the day. As far as solar powered transportation services go, there are still some quirks that need to be fixed before mass production of such vehicles is rolled out.

The most noticeable difference is the speed. Solar powered cars are far slower that their counterparts. But again, due to the fast development of the solar car and the technologies that go with it, this drawback will soon disappear. When you look at the things that I mentioned about the disadvantages of solar energy, you will see that most of them have solutions while others you just need to compromise a bit. I still think that harnessing the power of the sun is the way to go, so these downsides of solar energy are just a small obstacle that we need to overcome.

The future of solar energy on transportation:

Are you familiar with the World Solar Challenge? It is a race specifically for solar cars. Solar cars basically have arrays of photovoltaic cells which converts the sun's rays into usable electrical energy. The purpose of the race is to raise awareness on the use of the sun's energy on transportation and the development of other alternative forms of energy particularly the solar cells. The future of using solar energy on transportation services may still be a little hazy given the practical difficulties involve in converting ordinary cars into solar cars but the idea is here to stay and hopefully develops into something promising and useful. At this point, solar cars have been built to join solar car races. Very few have been constructed for practical and commercial purposes.

There are several reasons why the solar car remains on the background. The design of a solar car relies on the electrical system of the vehicle. The system controls the electricity the flows from the photovoltaic cells to the batteries, to the wheels, and to the controls. The electric motor that moves the vehicle is powered purely by the electricity produced by the solar cells.

The solar cells, depending on the number installed on the vehicle, can produce more or less 1000 watts of power from the sun's rays. To give you an idea, 1000 watts is just enough electricity to power an electric iron or even a toaster. And since the sun will most likely be covered by clouds at one time or the other, or the car goes through a tunnel or something, solar cars are equipped with batteries to serve as backup power supply for the motor. The battery packs are charged by the solar cells. However, the batteries are not charge while driving the solar car unless you intend to go very slow. Just like a gas pedal in conventional motors, a motor controller regulates the amount of electricity that enters the motor to speed up or slow down the vehicle whenever needed. Solar cars are not that slow as perceived by almost everyone.

These cars can go to as fast as 80-85 mph. With this, you can see why solar cars are not yet into commercial production. Nowadays, solar cells can harness more than 21% of the sun's energy that hit the surface. If the time comes that the cells can actually get more energy from the sun then maybe we can see solar cars on the streets. But at this time, it is quite difficult to make a commercial production model of a solar car. Nevertheless, there are companies who have already created some concept solar cars and are testing how road worthy they are. There's even a scooter that is street legal and runs from batteries charged from photovoltaic cells. Other possible application of solar car technologies is on golf carts which runs pretty slow in the first place and can be appreciated by golfers as well.

The future of solar energy on transportation is still not that clear. The application of solar energy on homes and buildings has been moving forward in recent years so hopefully we can find new ways of converting the sun's energy into usable electricity. And this time something that can be economically and efficiently installed in conventional cars.

The Future of Solar Energy, How It Looks and How It Affects Nature:

The future of solar energy lies on the indigenous hands of people who never tire out from thinking of ways in order to make life easier to live. With the advancement in the technology, the boom of the Internet age and a lot of other things, there will come a time when people will turn their backs on whatever is conventional. This can be good and bad in many ways, depending on who is looking at it and from what perspective. But people's quest for the advancement and development of everything that surrounds them provides lots of negative effects as well.

Here are only some.

1.Sometimes, people neglect the environment and how to properly take care of it for the mere fact that they are greedy to get their ideas done no matter what the consequences to the nature will be. Such advancements create harmful effects in the whole state and balance of nature. How many times have you heard about forest denudation or grave floods that kill people? All these occurrences can also be rooted to the activities of men that suffice for their own good without so much consideration for their natural habitat and the nature.

2. With the continuing advancement of everything that surrounds people, the generational gap becomes wider and wider. Old folks will fight for the benefits of the conventional tools and mediums. The newer generations cannot afford to sit on those old ways to do things. They are a slave to the continuing technological developments. It is okay to initiate change. It is good to find better ways to do things. But people must be cautious in achieving this. They must think about everything around them before they even start on their venture to newer and better ways to achieve greatness. The Innovations As of today, solar energy is one of the best options that people have with regards to alternative power sources. This has already evolved. There was a time when you can only avail such power source when the sun is present and that is during daytime. With the genius of the people behind the development of this resource, they were able to create green gas that can produce electricity. This is done by splitting water properties into hydrogen and oxygen. Both gasses will then be grouped into a cell that will be the electricity source. The same geniuses estimated that the entire planet can rely to an hour of sunlight for its one year electricity consumption. Solar cells have been developed to produce electricity from the energy coming from the sun. The panels for such technology can also be used to heat water and cook food. There are now the solar heating, solar cookers and solar furnaces as add-ons to this innovative venture. There are now hydrogen based cars. These are fueled by the split hydrogen in water. The solar cells also power the satellites that orbit through the surface of the Earth. This is the reason why there are advancements that people benefit from such as satellite phones and TV, accurate weather forecasting, even the development of the GPS technology and a lot more. There are a lot of benefits that people can gain from the future of solar energy. You just have to think that whatever you do or however you use such technology for your own good, you must always think of ways to protect your environment first to be able to get the most out of such improvements.

The Benefits of Solar Energy:

Solar energy will benefit a lot of people and not only the rich. This is why some governments have increased funding for this type of technology because they are aware of its many benefits. For one, solar energy is very cheap compared to other technologies. It is also renewable unlike coal or the rest which are non-renewable and hard to maintain. It also improves the health of people since it does not produce any carbon dioxide emissions unlike kerosene lamps that give out fumes which are just as deadly as smoking 2 packs of cigarettes a day. It also reduces the incidents of fire that are often associated with the use of kerosene, candles,diesel fuel and gasoline for generators. Solar energy is almost maintenance free because the solar cells used will last for 20 years or more before it has to be replaced.

You just have to keep the panels clean so it is able to absorb sunlight and convert that into electricity. These are also very useful in remote locations where power lines are not yet available. Some examples of these include fish houses, highway signs,marine applications, remote lighting and telecommunication. If countries focus on solar energy and other renewable techniques, they will be able to conserve their foreign exchange because they no longer have to use it to pay for foreign oil. This money can then be used for other things such as health care, infrastructure projects and education.

Solar energy will also reduce your electricity bills because you are no longer dependent on electricity coming from the power company. The only downside to solar energy is the initial cost in setting it up. Yes you will have to buy a lot of solar panels which are quite expensive but in the long run, you will be able to save more because you don't have to pay for anything else to keep them running. Should the cost of solar cells be beyond your budget, you can probably invest in used systems first then try to acquire the brand new ones later on. Another benefit of using solar energy is that you get to conserve fossil fuels and other natural resources that are quickly diminishing as a direct result of an increase in the world's population which could compromise the needs of the future generations. So should people get into solar energy? The answer is yes because it is safe, cheap and good for the environment. You only have to worry when the sun isn't shining because when this happens, rays from the sun won't be able to produce electricity so you have to rely on other means to get power. The same also goes when there is a blackout or brownout because you will soon lose power from your solar system.

The demand for solar energy is increasing and you should join in. Aside from reducing your electric bill, homeowners who use solar energy may claim up to $2,000 in federal investment tax credit in the first year while businesses may claim a 30% federal investment tax credit.

Believe it or not, solar energy has one other benefit and that it increases the value of your home. According to home appraisers, a dollar decrease in your energy bill results in a $20 increase in its property value so do the match and you can easily figure out how much your home will be worth after you decide to invest in solar energy.

The History of Solar Energy:

Solar energy is for everyone simply because the sun shines in every corner of the planet. In fact, the history of solar energy can be traced back to the Greeks that were then passed on to the Romans which marked the first people to ever use the passive solar design. Passive solar design is a way to warm the home based on the dwelling's design. They may not have had glass windows back then but their architecture made it possible for the people to use the sun's rays to light and heat indoor spaces. As a result, there was no need to burn food that often which was in short supply. In 1861, Auguste Mouchout invented the first active solar motor. Unfortunately, its expensive price made it impossible to produce commercially. Less than 20 years later, Charles Fritts invented solar cells,which will later on be used to power homes, heaters, satellites and other devices today. Since what he invented was very primitive, other people experimented on solar energy. One such person was

Albert Einstein who won the Nobel Prize for physics in his research on the photoelectric effect which is a phenomenon associated with the generation of electricity through solar cells. In 1953, Bell Laboratories which we know today as AT&T labs developed the first silicon solar cell capable of generating a measurable electric current. Three years later, solar cells ran $300 per watt. With the Cold War and the Space Race on, this was used to power satellites and crafts. But the biggest event in the development of solar energy occurred during the oil crisis of 1973. This prompted the US government to invest heavily in the solar electric cell that was developed by Bell Laboratories 20 years ago.

By the 1990's, research towards solar energy came to a standstill as the price of oil dropped in the world market. Funds were diverted elsewhere and the United States which was probably the leader in this form of alternative energy was soon surpassed by other nations mainly Germany and Japan. In 2002 for example, Japan had installed 25,000 solar panels on rooftops. Because of that, the price of solar panels went down as the demand for it was on the rise.

To date, solar energy is growing at a modest 30% per year. Although there have been improvements in solar energy, its fundamentals are still the same. The sun's rays are collected and then converted into electricity. Aside from powering homes or office buildings, the technology has been used to power aircraft, cars and boats. Unfortunately, none of these have been made available yet for public use. We still rely heavily on oil for electricity, gasoline for our cars, fuel for planes and ships.

In fact, the US is one of the biggest oil users in the world. To prove a point, the department of Defense consumes 395,000 barrels per This has to change because our oil reserves are almost depleted and many experts believe that global supply for these non-renewable resources will be gone before the end of the century. We have to do our share to push for renewable energy and one of them happens to be solar energy.

The Pros and Cons of Solar Energy:

Solar energy is one of the best forms of renewable energy. But why don't we rely on it so much compared to other countries? The answer is simply that there are pros and cons with using this form of alternative energy. The pros of using solar energy is that the system is easy to install, there are no energy costs once it is set up, there are no emissions like air pollutants or greenhouse gas and the sun is widely available. The pros of using solar energy is that the system is easy to install, there are no energy costs once it is set up, there are no emissions like air pollutants or greenhouse gas and the sun is widely available. A solar energy system is composed of the solar panels, the inverter, battery, charge controller, wires and support structure. For you to produce a kilowatt of power, you will need 10 to 12 solar panels that will occupy an area of 100 square feet.

If you are worried that this will cause damage to your roof, don't because it is made of light weight materials. When you call a contractor, it will usually take a day or two to install and cost around $10,000. Not that many people will have cash on hand to pay for it so they can avail of a home equity loan to pay for it. If you use a kilowatt of solar energy, you can save 170 lbs. of coal from being burned, about 300lbs of carbon dioxide from being released into the atmosphere or 105 gallons of water that most homeowners use up every month.

The cons are solar cells are expensive, the rays can only be collected during the day time, the weather and where you are located will play a factor in how much sunlight you can get and you will need a big area to collect the power. But some experts believe that price of these cells and its ability to collect power will improve in the future. Right now, a kilowatt of solar energy can only produce 1,600 kilowatts of hours per year in sunny climate. That means you will receive 5.5 hours of electricity per day. If you produce about 750 kilowatts of power, you will only get 2.5 hours of power per day.

Solar panels come in various colors and usually have a 5 year warranty.Since manufacturers are aware that solar energy can only work when the sun is out, they have installed batteries so you get more than 5 hours of power even during cloudy days and nights. This is because the batteries are designed to absorb, insulate, transmit and reflect rays coming from the sun.

But solar energy can be applied to other things and not just powering our homes. It can be used to power small devices like calculators to bigger things like planes, satellites and cars. Since these are easy to maintain, you don't have to worry about anything. People should take this seriously especially when this is not a renewable source of energy.

Things We Should Know Before Investing in Solar Energy:

There is no doubt that there are a lot of benefits in using solar energy. Aside from protecting the environment, you get to save a great deal of money. But before you switch to solar energy, here are a few things you should consider. First, is your roof right for solar power? Most solar power systems can be installed as long as the roof is flat and made of material such as bitumen, composite shingle, cement tile, metal or tar and gravel. If this is how your roof is positioned, then there shouldn't be any problems. The solar panels will be installed parallel to the roof surface.

If you are concerned that the weight could be too heavy for your roof, don't be since this is very light and quite rare that you have to do some structural work before installing the system. When you are looking for a contractor, find out how much it will cost to install the system. You should compare these first before you decide in picking the best one. But you should know right now that installing solar powered cells are a bit expensive. There are also no financing programs you can avail of. Your best bet if you don't have enough money is to apply for a home equity loan.

If you are planning to install this in a commercial establishment, the various loans you can avail of include the capital equipment loan, equipment secured loan, property secured loan or the SAFE-BIDCO energy efficiency loan.

Non-profit organizations may also avail of special loans for solar energy and the best one is through third party financing. In this case, the non-profit organization and the contractor will purchase the system and make use of the tax credits. The third party will then pass on the charges for the produced power to the non-profit and after the system has depreciated, this is sold to the non-profit at a discount. The end result is that you pay for less than what you are currently paying for because it is maintenance free. Will installing a solar system have any effect on your property? The answer is yes. In fact, it will increase the resale value of your property without having to pay much more in terms of property taxes. If you have a lot of space to spare, you may even be able to zero out your electric bill as long as the sun comes out so you can convert sunlight into electricity.

Aside from increasing the properly value, you will also be able to avail of tax credits from the government. Solar energy can power your home in the same way you get electricity from the grid. You won't be able to use it when there is a power outage or when the sun is shining but fortunately, this doesn't happen daily so it is still an alternative form of energy worth considering.

Using solar energy goes way back:

Recollecting the history of solar energy brings us back to the 1970s energy crisis and oil embargo which caused long lines in gasoline stations, high gasoline prices, and even caused panic among consumers and investors alike in the United States. Knowledge about oil being a non-renewable resource has been around since the 1800s.

But it was only during and after the 70s energy crisis that people really began to realize the consequences of depending too much on an already depleting energy resource. However, utilizing the sun's energy is not really a recent development. It has been used by ancient civilizations for warmth, for food and crop preparations and various agricultural purposes. What's new are the technologies involved in harnessing this energy and utilizing it for man's daily use. The technology began in the 1830's when Edmund Becquerel made public his studies on how solar light can be harnessed into usable energy. However, nobody followed up on this idea nor explore any practical use.

The next breakthrough on solar power came after thirty years Becquerel published his works. In 1860s, the French Monarch commissioned Augusted Mouchout to find other sources of energy. And Mouchout looked up in the sky for inspiration. His series of solar powered contractions were quite impressive back then. His inventions included a motor that run on solar energy, a steam engine that uses the sun's light, and an ice maker that fully rely on solar power. After Mouchout, there were several other notable achievements in the line of solar power. Among these is the works of William Adams in the 1870s which utilized mirrors to channel the power of the sun to make a steam engine run. Adams' power tower design concept is still in use today.

Another notable work is by Charles Fritz in the early 1880s. His studies were attuned on turning sunlight into electricity, which he later accomplished. But one of the most significant development in modern solar energy occurred in the 1950s. Early in the decade, R.S. Ohl discovered that sunlight produces large numbers of free electrons when it strikes silicon. Then in the mid-1950s Gerald Pearson, Calvin Fuller, and Daryl Chaplin was able to capture those free electrons and convert them in electricity.

Today, silicon cells are used to make solar cells and solar panels for harnessing the sun's energy. Immediately these solar cells were made into good use and the first among to use them was the field of space aeronautics. These silicon based solar cells were used to power satellites that orbit the earth. The satellite Vanguard I was the first one launched out to space which rely on solar cells for power. More satellites followed. Nowadays, more and more research and studies are being conducted on how best to utilize the sun's energy. Especially today where it is said that about 30-50 years from the now, the world oil reserves will be totally depleted. Thus, the search for alternative sources of energy continuous.

The sun is expected to die out in a couple of thousand of years, it's too long to worry about and man can have all the sun's energy until that day. The challenge today is creating solar energy power in more efficient and cost effective e way. Admittedly, the costs of those photo cells are not that cheap to be accessible by most of the ordinary consumers. The movement today in the science and technology committee is to be able to provide cheap alternative source of energy.

What is Solar Energy?

Solar energy is a form of renewable energy as it utilizes the radiant energy coming from the sun. This is done by converting sunlight into electricity using solar cells. Solar cells or photovoltaics were invented in the 1880's by Charles Fritts. Although it did not convert a lot of sunlight into electricity at the time, this started a revolution that continued on to the 20th century. The greatest example is perhaps the Vanguard 1 which was a satellite fitted with solar cells that enabled it to transmit back to earth after its chemical battery was exhausted. Its success prompted NASA and its Russian counterpart to the same with other satellites including Telstar hich continues to serve as the backbone of the telecommunications structure today.The most significant event that stimulated the demand for solar energy was the 1973 oil crisis.

Early on, power companies would charge the consumer a hundred dollars per watt. In the 1980's, it became only $7 per watt. Unfortunately, the lack of government funding did not sustain its growth so the growth of solar energy was only 15% annually from 1984 to 1996. There have been a decline in the demand for solar energy in the US but this increased in Japan and Germany. From 31.2 megawatts of power in 1994, this increased to 318 megawatts in 1999 and world wide production growth increased by 30% towards the end of the 20th century.

Next to these two countries, Spain is the third largest user of solar energy followed by France, Italy and South Korea.

There are three basic approaches to get the most out of solar energy. It is namely passive, active and solar photovoltaic systems.

1.In passive, it has to do a lot with the building design. This will enable the building to avoid heat loss so people inside will feel a great degree of comfort with the help of controlled ventilation and day lighting. Homes that apply this will greatly reduce their heating requirements by as much as 80% with minimal cost.

2. Active solar heating is used to convert sunlight into heat which provides space or water heating. Used extensively in Europe, getting the right size will cover 50% to 60% of your hot water heating requirements.

3. Lastly is photovoltaic which converts solar radiation into electricity. This is done by installing solar cells in the ground and the greater the intensity of the light, the greater the flow of electricity. These are available in different sizes and some are installed in consumer devices like calculators and watches.

Some vehicles are now powered using solar energy. Cars although not yet produced commercially compete in the World Solar Challenge which invites competitors from around the world to compete in this annual event in Australia. There are also unmanned aerial vehicles and balloons. To date,solar energy has only been successful in passenger boats.

Many of us take the sun for granted and if we are really serious about preserving the environment and reducing our demand for oil, solar energy is just one of the options we have on the table. We have to lobby and convince our government leaders to do more because it is the cheapest means of providing our home with electricity compared to rechargeable batteries, kerosene or candles.

Wind power vs Solar energy an even match:

Today in center stage is a battle for the ages. On the right corner, packing a hurricane punch yet is known to move softly as a breeze is wind power. On the left corner, with a scorching hot aura, moves in a speed of light, is solar energy. Wind power versus solar energy, which one is going to be declared the champion of the alternative energy movement?! Let's get ready to rumble! Or something like that. I apologize for that intro but I just can't help. I figured that if I was going to match one alternative energy resource against the other, then I'll make some extravagant introduction. Just imagine the drum rolls. Actually, there is an existing debate among environmentalists and even scientists on which energy resource should be developed first given their advantages and drawbacks. Staying away from the personal biases, numerous studies have shown that overall, wind power is more cost effective than harnessing the sun's energy.

Let's see the reasons behind that conclusion. Harnessing the sun's energy can be done by a number of ways. But probably the simplest way which can be applied in a small home is by using photovoltaic cells or PV or solar cells. What happens is that sunlight hit the surface of a photovoltaic (PV) panel which responds by creating free electrons which is channelled to generate an electric current. Wind power on the other hand utilizes a propeller and a shaft system which has a magnet wrapped by a coil of wire inside. As the wind turns the propeller and the magnet inside, the electrons in the wire are forced to move along the wire producing an electrical current. Both ways are quite simple but the complexities now lies on the costs of producing the necessary equipment especially the mechanisms that will maximize the power output. When costs of production of photovoltaic cells and wind turbine are compared, the latter is much cheaper to produce. Although, manufacturers of photovoltaic cells stress that as the demand on PV cells increase, the costs of production decreases. So its just a matter of time before PV cells become price competitive.

Other problems include the logistics of placing the equipment. A solar panel requires quite a large space plus, your location on the globe will affect the amount of sunlight you receive and consequently the amount of power you produce. The further away from the equator you are, the less amount of sunlight you can harness. Also, on the average, the PV cells have a 15-20% efficiency rate. The problem with wind power on the other hand is that not all areas will have winds favorable for a turbine. And if you do locate a place where winds are strong and the turbine can be maximized, you'll find that the area (more often than not) is inhabited by various species of birds. You don't want to kill birds with your turbine, do you? Now going back to our wind power vs. solar energy match-up, indeed we do have to agree that wind power is more cost efficient. However, both alternative energy resource will play a big role in our future.

It is, therefore, in my humble opinion that we both develop the two technologies simultaneously for each one has their advantages and disadvantages and each one can be properly utilized for specific areas.

We Can Have a Home Powered By Solar Energy:

Do you like to live in a home that is energy efficient? The good news is you can given there are technologies these days that can make that happen and one good example happens to be solar energy. Solar energy is the process of using the sun's radiant rays to power your home. For this to work, you will need to get some solar panels and then have this install by a contractor. Ideally, you will need a flat area measuring about a hundred square feet. This is good to install between 10 to 12 solar panels that can produce about a kilowatt of power. If you think 1 kilowatt is small, think again because this is equivalent to 1,600 kilowatts of hours per year. That translates to 5.5 hours of electricity per day if you are using it to the max. Otherwise, excess power will be stored in the battery which will help bring electricity to the house during a blackout or at night.

Aside from the solar panels, you will also need the inverter, battery, charge controller, wires and support structure. Each of these parts are important since the system will not work without the other so whoever you choose as a contractor should have everything ready prior to installation. Once everything is set up, you can already enjoy your solar powered home.

Since it requires minimal maintenance, it can last up to 20 years before you have to replace anything. If you have a larger area to work with, why not invest in a solar thermal roof? The difference between this and the first one mentioned is that you convert the entire roof into a giant collector. It is quite expensive and takes a couple of days to complete but worth every penny. The only reason why not that many people invest in such a system is because most roofs are not oriented towards the south with the steep pitch needed to maximize solar energy especially during the winter.

You will have to do some major construction work to make this happen. Solar energy is just one way for you to stop relying on power coming from the grid. When the sun isn't shining, you have to be ready by preparing other ways to generate electricity. One example that can be used at home is wind energy. Here, you use fans to collect the wind's kinetic energy similar to windmills that you see in the farm. The only difference is that the blades are connected to a drive shaft that turns an electric generator to produce electricity.

You just have to do some research to find out if solar energy is feasible for your home. You should know how much power you consume on a monthly basis and also where exactly is your house located.

Should your study show it is possible to live on solar energy, it is best to apply for a home equity loan to pay for the installation costs because you will surely get a return on your investment later on in the form of tax credit and a utility bill that won't exceed $10. So what are you waiting for? If you don't want to rely on power from the electric company, go ahead and invest in solar energy.

Why Are Solar Panels So Popular?

Over the past 20 years solar panels have become extremely popular with homeowners, business and the agricultural industry.

There are many different reasons why people are interested in solar but we have narrowed them down to **3 main reasons.**

Money:

Firstly, the most common reason why solar is popular is because of money.

Solar panels can provide homeowners with a massive saving toward their energy bill (if not completely reduce it altogether).

When people catch wind of their neighbors slashing their energy bill in half, they simply want a piece of the pie. By having a reduced energy bill it means that you will free up your cash flow each month to spend on stuff that you like or your family.

The finance side of solar is the main reason why it has become so popular in today's age.

Environment:

The second most popular reason is because of the environment.

Solar panels are being installed to help take a stance against climate change. People are willing to invest their money into something that will not pollute the planet we live on. Installing solar panels will help by generating clean energy that can also be sold.

This is much better than burning fossil fuels and oils which has a negative effect on the planet. We are realising the sustainability of solar panels which is making them more popular.

Government Incentives :

Thirdly, solar panels are getting a name for themselves through government incentives.

It is pretty hard to resist when the government is offering to buy back any excess solar energy you produce...

Plus lets not forget the massive reduction in the upfront cost, an interest free loan to help reduce the cost even more and then a STC certificate that can be sold for money!

Even with commercial solar for businesses there are rebates and grants being offered as incentives to help with the move to solar.

We Need a PV System to Generate Solar Energy : Solar energy has been around for quite some time. In fact, now is the best time to get it if you want to cut your electric bill and do your share to protect the environment. For that to happen, you will need to buy a PV system. This is designed to reduce or eliminate the amount of electricity you purchase from the utility especially when there could be a price increase in the next few months. The best part about the PV system is that it generates clean electricity which is clean, reliable and renewable since it does not emit any harmful gases into the atmosphere. The PV system must be placed in an area that is free from any obstruction otherwise, it will not be able to capture the sun's rays. A lot of experts say that the south facing roof is best while the east and west is sufficient. If the roof is not available, it can be mounted on the ground. You should know that PV systems come in various sizes so you should get the one that matches our electrical needs. If you consume about 6,500 kilowatts a year, then a PV system within the 3 to 4 kilowatt range is right for your home. You can measure this by reviewing your past electric bills and making some projections Naturally, the size of the PV system will determine the amount of space needed. If you do not use that much electricity, 50 square feet may be sufficient. However, a larger system may require a little over 600 square feet. Just remember that a kilowatt of electricity requires an area of 100 square feet. Solar energy is converted with the help of an inverter since this is what changes direct current to alternating current. You will also need batteries so excess energy may be stored so you can still use solar energy during the evening or during a power outage. The size of the PV system is also in direct proportion with the cost. Most cost from $1 to $1.5 per watt and when you include installation, the bill may reach be from $1,500 to $2,500. The cost of the PV system should not discourage you from investing in solar energy. People who use it are able to get tax rebates and it will also increase the value of your home. With that, the only thing to do now is to call a reputable solar energy provider. One other thing you should know about the PV system is that this should also be connected to your grid. For this to work, you have to enter into an interconnection agreement with your utility. This agreement will address the issue with regards to the terms and conditions under which your system is tied up with them. This also includes what is known as net metering which allows you to bank any surplus electricity that your system generates on the electric grid in the same manner that you will be charged accordingly should you consume more electricity than what you have banked. You need a PV system to generate solar energy. You just need to know what size of a system you require so this can be installed by your solar provider.

An Overview on the Interesting Facts about Solar Energy:

There are lots of interesting facts about solar energy. Educating yourself about this will prove to be beneficial in the long run. You can share the information to your loved ones. You can teach them of ways on how they can help to conserve the energy. You can also do your share to help this method to advance if you are a genius in the field. But if you are an ordinary citizen who only wants to enjoy, then feast on. But remember that you also have responsibilities to the environment that you must accomplish in order to do your part in the whole scheme of things. The Facts that Matter

1. Solar radiation makes it possible for the energy coming from the sun to be used as power source and energy that can in turn be used for many purposes. The technology on this aspect is characterized in two ways. They can either be passive or active. This will depend on the methods that are used to get, convert and allocate sunlight. What are active solar techniques? These utilize pumps, photovoltaic panels and fans to renovate sunlight into useful resources. These aim to increase the energy supply that is why these can also be referred as supply side technologies. The passive solar techniques, on the other hand, use only selected resources with constructive thermal properties, utilize the kind of spaces that can circulate air naturally and apply the position of buildings and structures towards the sun. These will lessen the need for other sources and can also be referred as the demand side technology.

2. Solar energy has influenced many factors that surround people. This can be referred in planning and designing buildings. This process can be rooted back at the early days of the architectural history. The Greeks and the Chinese first used such factor in building and constructing their architectural pieces and on their planning methods.

3. Solar energy is also being utilized by the agricultural sector because they rely heavily on its benefits in order to gain more harvest. They developed ways in order to plant the kind of crops that will grow according to the amount of sun that they will be getting for the season. This can also be used to dry the crops, pump water, brooding of chicks and to dry animal manures that can later be used as fertilizers.

4. On seasons like the Little Ice Age, fruit walls were used by French and Chinese farmers to be able to collect and store solar energy to help them keep the plants warm and to speedy up the process of ripening of fruits. These walls serve as the thermal masses. The fruit walls that were first developed were perpendicular to the ground and faced the south direction. Over time, innovations were done and slopping walls were used to gain more advantage from the sun. 5. To convert the solar light into heat, people have developed green houses. These enable the production and cultivation of specialty crops all year round. Such innovation made it possible for crops to be produced in untimely seasons and in places where you think that those plants won't grow. And these are only some of the interesting facts about solar energy. These give you a good peek at how wonderful nature is and how people have developed ways to use it to advance in many aspects of their lives.

5. To convert the solar light into heat, people have developed green houses. These enable the production and cultivation of specialty crops all year round. Such innovation made it possible for crops to be produced in untimely seasons and in places where you think that those plants won't grow. And these are only some of the interesting facts about solar energy. These give you a good peek at how wonderful nature is and how people have developed ways to use it to advance in many aspects of their lives.

Analysing the benefits of solar energy:

We all know that using solar energy is a good thing to do. We have heard, and there are quite a number of them, all about the benefits of solar energy and we can't agree why we can't turn this alternative form of energy source to a primary one. But despite the advantages, solar power has yet to fully make it in the mainstream. Let's go back and discuss a couple of the advantages of solar energy and see why keep going back to fossil fuels for energy resource. In the long run, solar power saves money. Initial costs of installation and operations may be more expensive that other energy forms but after settling the expenses, you have an energy resource that is free. Nobody charges for using sunlight, right? The return of investment can also be shorter depending on how much energy you use. You won't spend too much on maintenance either plus those photovoltaic cells can last for 15 to 20 years. There are no mechanical or moving parts to oil and maintain nor are there parts that need to be replaced yearly. Of course solar power is environmental friendly. First its renewable not like fossil fuels which according to studies will be gone in four to five decades. The process of converting energy to usable electricity does not involve the release of toxic chemicals which can harm the environment. Carbon dioxide, nitrogen oxide, sulphur dioxide, lead, and mercury emissions will be a memory of the past when everyone goes solar. Relying on the sun for power also helps reduce global warming. Aside from the toxic wastes and pollutants, using solar power will limit other aspects of the energy industry like hazards of working with and transporting oil or natural gas. Also, other health risks are present in the use of other fuels like kerosene and candles which are still popular in third world countries. With solar energy, these risks will be minimized if not totally eliminated. The use of solar panels is also good for remote areas where providing basic electricity services is troublesome if not totally impossible at all. Solar energy can be transported to far flung villages and once installed they can be left alone for years with little or without maintenance. Communities in Asian countries have successfully installed solar panels in their community and have been enjoying the benefits of clean and reliable power for years.

For a poor country, producing electricity through solar energy can mean independence from oil producing countries which controls the supply and prices of oil. With such independence, new policies on energy can be created which will maximize the benefit for its citizens. Countries will also not be wary on natural disasters which hampers delivery of oil. With this new found independence, countries can invest its national budget on other programs aside from purchasing oil from foreign sources. There are several disadvantages of using solar power and one of which is the costs. But thinking about it in the long run, you'll see that the benefits of solar energy outweigh the disadvantages. Plus, with the current development in the field of science and technology, solar power is becoming more and more convenient and it would not be surprising to find solar energy as a primary source of power in the next few years

Arguments against solar energy:

We all know that solar energy is a good renewable energy resource and that we should start to utilize it more especially when the Earth's fossil fuel reserves are slowly dwindling and will run out in 30 to 50 years. We better look at the various alternative energies and begin a fast tracking of development to hasten our independence on non-renewable fossil fuels. And solar energy is as good as any other alternative energy resource out there. However, several arguments against solar energy have been raised through the years. But probably the most convincing argument is the high costs of solar energy utilization. The problem with solar energy is that you can only harness it during the daytime. And even when the sun is up, the sunlight will be interrupted by occasional cloud covers, rains, fog, and even smog. So in order to harness the sun's energy we need equipment that can get as much solar power as possible at a given time and we need some way of storing that energy so we can use them without any interruptions. We do have the technology to harness the sun's energy, convert it into usable electricity, and store them for future use. And that technology itself is the primary reason why solar power has not caught on even today.

The process of making solar panels as well as the technology for storing that harnessed power remains to be quite expensive. The good thing about this fact today is that due to the recent increase in the costs of fuel and gas, solar power is no longer a far fetched alternative. The gap between the costs has gone down considerably and hopefully in the near future, the costs of solar energy production will be quite competitive. Furthermore, the costs of photovoltaic cells are indeed quite expensive that contemporary oil and gas equipment. But one of the flaws of the argument of costs is that people tend to limit their perspective of solar energy as to only referring to photovoltaic cells. There are other means of harnessing solar energy and not all of them are as expensive as PV cell manufacturing. One way of getting the sun's energy and converting it into usable electricity is the concept of solar thermal plants. In solar thermal technology, various solar collectors are utilized to generate heat which can be applied from the simplest heating and ventilation of houses to the production of massive amounts of electricity.

The use of mirrors or lenses to reflect sunlight to towers equipped with liquids that heat up and produce steam. The steam then turns turbines which in turn generates the electricity needed. The process adds another step compared to photovoltaics which converts solar energy directly into electricity. Nevertheless, solar thermal systems of power production is cheaper that the production of PV cells. For a larger consumer market, it seems that solar thermal energy is the way to go. Regardless, the point here really is to emphasize that solar energy has more to offer. The cost of production is a valid argument against solar energy but still there are ways around it. Costs can be minimized by using other techniques of harnessing solar energy or future developments in the field of science and technology will produce products that are more cost efficient that what are available today.

Countries on the helm of solar energy technology:

The US is not a leading user of solar energy for a very obvious reason: they can still afford to buy fossil fuels from the international market. In other countries the oil prices are ten times higher in the US and sometimes going for the alternative is a lot better in the long run. Today, more and more countries are looking at solar energy as a primary source of power. There are several countries which can be considered as at the helm of solar energy technology.The number one use of solar energy is Germany. It captures almost 50% of the world market of photovoltaic cells. Nowhere else in the world can you find the most number of households with solar panels installed on their roof tops. Germany has this Renewable Energies Laws (EEG) which passed in 2000. The law certainly helped Germans feel the need to go renewable.

According to statistics, Germans invested nearly US$5 billion in solar photovoltaic systems and have contributed considerable in the growth of the solar energy market. Although most of the things that we see are solar panels, it doesn't mean that Germany's solar industry is not limited to the production of photovoltaic cells for electricity. Other notable usage in Germany includes solar panels for home water heating system. Some news indicate that the German solar hot water market earns U.S.$1.5 billion per year. The "solar park" in Arnstein, Bavaria, Germany is one of the biggest photovoltaic plants in the world. It became operational in 2006 and with more than 1,400 PV solar panels, it can produce 12 megawatts of energy.The next biggest country in terms of usage of solar energy is Spain. The solar energy usage in the country, more specifically the photovoltaic cells usage, has a world market share of 27%. Spain has no sign of slowing down its aggressive and pro-active approach in solar energy. Solar fields are being constructed one of the latest ones is the 60 MW solar field in Olmedilla de Alarcón, near Cuenca. There are other big solar plants in Spain and these include the solar park 12 miles outside of Salamanca, Salamanca, Spain which have 70,000 PV panels divided into three 36-hectare arrays. The arrays produce an output is 13.8 megawatts and has been powering roughly 5,000 homes since it opened in 2007. And the rest of the world follow Germany and Spain. Japan and the US still have a market share in the photovoltaic world market. The two countries both have an 8% market share, a far cry from Germany and Spain. Nevertheless, it is quite important that countries continue to improve their status in the world solar market. Other notable country that uses solar power includes Algeria, Australia, Italy, and Portugal. Aside from the rich European countries, people in Israel. and India are realizing the importance of having alternative sources of energy. These are the countries on the helm of solar energy technology. But, other countries are slowly catching up. The government of Israel, for example, required all residential buildings to install solar water heating systems in the early 90s. Today, business establishments like hotels and office buildings are trying to use solar power as an alternative from using fossil fuels whose prices continue to soar in the world market. India is facing a similar energy crisis and they are also looking at solar energy to get them through it.

Facts about Solar Energy, Some Things to Ponder and why?:

What are the facts about solar energy that we know? It is given that this comes from the sun. This was developed by people in order to take advantage and benefit from everything that the sun can provide. You can also easily guess the goals of these people why they opt to develop such technology. For one, they want to make lives easier to live. Second, they want to find other resources that people can use in their everyday lives. Maybe they also want to profit from the experience because if this will all be successful, people, businesses and industries will gain a lot from what is being developed. During the first years of its introduction, people deem that this technological advancement can only be used by wealthy people. It used to cater mostly for the can afford types of individuals. What if it can heat pool and can run spas? .But the evolution of the solar energy is just starting.

Nowadays, the benefits can be felt even by ordinary citizens. Researchers keep thinking of ways to arrive at this state. And this is proving to be good for everybody's sake. The scientists developed solar panels that can power up homes. They made this available not only for the rich and famous, but they sold the idea to governments. The latter used the innovation to bring electricity to people in their countries who still haven't experienced to live in the

comfort of having this kind of power source. As a result, many people experience how it is like to have lights. They have also resorted to businesses that can be aided by such technology. The maintenance is still on-going while the technology is still being pursued. But the fact remains that this has been made available even for the ordinary Person.
2. Aside from electricity, solar energy can be used to heat water and cook food. Life is really becoming easier as people find ways to achieve such state. While the developments are still under way, people are finding ways to make such resource available for everybody.

Different organizations and government agencies help in making this product affordable for everyone no matter what your status in life is. As time passes by, people will be able to develop more and more gadgets and tools to make lives easier. There will come a time when almost everybody can benefit from this. The first notion that the solar energy is only for the wealthy will cease to be remembered. The responsibility now lies on to people's hands to take care of nature. They must give back to nature for everything that they have also gotten in the process. Technological advancements can be better achieved if people will consider how these can affect the natural habitat in general. It is okay to get what people want and what people need. But this must always be done with precaution and by thinking of the effects that these will have on everything. It is fun to learn some facts about solar energy every once in a while. These will excite you about the process. But more so, these must open your eyes to the whole scheme of nature and how important it is to take care of our surroundings to be able to benefit more in the long run.

How to Conserve Solar Energy through Your Little Ways:

As an ordinary person who lives according to what the day brings, have you ever thought about how to conserve solar energy? Do you even care? You may think you are an ordinary worker, or a simple wife or mother. Should you even care about such things? The answer is yes.You must bear in mind that you are part of a whole spectrum of nature.Whatever you do will affect all the things around you. Everything must be conserved, including solar energy. Here are some suggestions to throw in your little efforts to achieve this goal.

1. Plant trees. Nature works wonders. Every element around us affects everything else. By planting trees, you will be able to maximize the energy coming from the sun. This will be directed to help the plants grow and produce harvests. With healthy plants and trees rooted to the soil, the soil will be firm. This will be able to hold its structure even in times of natural disasters.

2. Limit your use of the energy coming from the sun. With today's innovations, there are lots of things that are being developed to use solar energy as a power source. The source may be free. But to be able to turn it to such power source, there are things that are utilized for this reason. If you will abuse the use of such technology, the crash of the materials used to put this up will be fast. This will take a toll on you especially if you rely a lot on this advancement.

3. Teach kids about the importance of solar energy. You can gain knowledge through research and through your everyday interaction with other people about this thing called the solar energy. You must tell your kids about its importance, they must be educated about it at an early age. They are the future of the nation. What you teach them now will be instilled to them until they grow old. At such a young age, they must know about how they can contribute to conserve energy.

4. Take good care of nature. This is the most important thing that you can do to help advance such cause. The sun can cause damage to people and nature if people won't do the necessary steps to care for nature in the first place. There are lots of things that you get from the environment. It wouldn't hurt to look back every now and then and see what you can do to give back to what it has already given to you. The idea here is that everything in this life must be conserved. You cannot abuse the power that you possess to gain so much without even thinking how your actions affect the world around you. It is all right to go with the flow of the continuing advancement of the technology. Look at the options available to you nowadays with regards to solar energy. This can be used to power homes and vehicles. This can give light, heat water and cook your food. This can give you satellite television and phones for supreme entertainment and communications enjoyment. This can give you luxuries like spas and warm water at pools. You must learn everything on how to conserve solar energy so that you can do your part in making sure that such resource will be available as long as you live.

How Does Solar Energy Work:

INTRODUCTION TO SOLAR ENERGY

Ever wondered how solar energy is converted into electricity? Well, this will give you an idea how it works. First, solar panels are installed over a flat surface like the roof of your home. Once activated, it absorbs the sun's rays since the panels are made of semi-conducting materials such as silicon. Electrons are then knocked off loose from their atoms so it can produce electricity. This process by which light is converted into electricity is better known as the photovoltaic effect. From there, you now have direct current electricity and when this enters an inverter, it is converted into 220 volt AC which is the electricity needed to power the home. Of course this is connected to the utility panel in the house so the lights and the appliances will work when these are switched on. If you are not using that much electricity from the solar energy generated, it is stored in a battery so will be able to supply the house with power during a power outage or at night. Should the battery be full, the excess electricity is then exported to the utility grid if your system happens to be connected to it. When your solar energy runs out, utility supplied electricity kicks in.

If you are not using that much electricity from the solar energy generated, it is stored in a battery so will be able to supply the house with power during a power outage or at night. Should the battery be full, the excess electricity is then exported to the utility grid if your system happens to be connected to it.When your solar energy runs out, utility supplied electricity kicks in. The flow of electricity of solar energy is measured using a utility meter which spins backward and forward. It will go backward when you are producing more energy than you need and forward when you need additional power from the utility company. These two are only offset when you pay for the additional energy from the utility company. Any surplus is sold back to what is known as net metering

A smaller version of this is used to power a water heater inside the home. Using the same principles, homeowners get to convert sunlight into heat to get warm water. As you can see, transforming sunlight into solar energy is very easy. But why do countries like Germany and Japan use it more often than the US? The answer is because it is much cheaper for them to use this form of alternative energy compared to oil. Also, although the US initiated this during the 1973 oil crisis, it is not as popular as it was back then because the government neither increased the budget in research for alternative forms of energy nor gave incentives so people will be encourage into doing that again.

Most state regulations also prohibit individuals from installing their own devices even if this is used to give you warm water. Chances are, you won't even find anyone to do it so you will probably have to do it yourself. Just remember that if there is a problem with the plumbing, your insurance will not cover it. Should the state allow you to install such a system, you will not be entitled to the rebate. Using solar cells is just one way to make the most out of solar energy. Your other option is passive solar energy which helps avoid heat loss so those inside will not feel too cold or too hot throughout the day. This is used by a lot of homeowners living in the southwest since they do not need that much insulation compared to homeowners who live in other parts of the US.

Net Metering and Solar Energy:

You can't help but get into net metering when you decide to invest in solar energy because you sometimes consume more or less than what you actually generate. When you consume less energy, your electric meter spins backward, if you use more then it goes forward. Net metering is simply a special metering and billing agreement between you and the electric service provider. You are eligible for this if you reside in a residential area and generate some form of energy using solar, wind energy or a combination of both. It also has to be located on your premises and connected to the grid. For this to work, you need to have a meter capable of moving in both directions. Most meters these days can do that but if your provider wants to use two meters, they will have to pay for it.

However, if you enter into a time of use billing agreement, you will have to be one to buy the unit. The net metering agreement works by letting you use the electricity you generate first before you use what you normally get from your electric service provider. Your meter should show the net which is measured as the difference between the electricity you purchased and what you actually purchased. The benefit of the net metering system is that it allows you to store electricity when you are not there and then use it the moment you get home. Since there is a law that expands net metering, you can take advantage of it by generating electricity during peak hours and then using it during off peak periods. Another benefit is the fact that you only pay the net electricity that you use. If you consume below the baseline, you pay less and more if you go over it. If what you use offsets what you normally get from a provider, then you will most likely pay a lower rate. Since you entered into an agreement with your provider, you will still be billed monthly.

This will state the amount of power you generated and the amount you actually consumed. On the anniversary of your agreement, you will be billed for the previous 12 months but you can also request for this on a monthly basis. Keep in mind that you will not be paid for the excess generation of electricity in a given year although some do. If you want to use solar energy, you have to contact your electric service provider and ask if they offer net metering. When the papers are drawn up, remember that they cannot require you to pay for any meters beyond the bi-directional meter. They cannot conduct any tests or impose any requirements if it meets existing national standards for grid-interconnected systems. Lastly, you don't have to buy additional insurance or buy power from any of their affiliates.

Net metering is a policy and also an incentive when you decide to use solar energy. This is because you reduce the number of kilowatts used by your electric service provider which in turn decreases the emissions of carbon dioxide into the air.

Solar energy in households:

The sun is a great source of energy. It would be great to use solar energy in your homes especially nowadays when the prices of oil and gas continue to increase. Because of the high fuel and gas prices, more and more people are experimenting on the use of solar energy in their households in their attempts to minimize the costs of basic utilities. The sun's energy can be harnessed in different ways depending on how you would utilize the end product. There are so called solar collectors which are placed on the roof tops or used in buildings. The main purpose of these solar collectors is to provide heating and even ventilation for the houses and buildings.

These collectors harness the sun's energy by magnifying the sunlight several times and transferring that heat to air or water. That heated air or water is stored and will provide the building or home heating and hot water whenever needed. The only problem here is that not all places have equal amounts of sunlight. As you go farther from the equator, the strength of the sun is reduced. But still, this is a much better solution than relying on electric grids which do not reach remote areas. It is just a mater of storing the heat generated from the solar collector properly. For example, some buildings in Sweden utilized an underground storage facility where solar energy is stored resulting to savings from heating the building and their water. In areas where gas and fuel are out of reach of the pockets of poor communities, residents have to rely on solar cooking for their meals. They use this bowl shaped discs equipped with mirrors or reflectors which directs all the sunlight on the middle where a pot is placed.

The same technology is being used in India, Sri Lanka, and Nepal. This serves are a good alternative from conventional fuels like coal, firewood, and gas. They can use these solar stoves during a sunny day and use traditional fuels when the weather is not that good. This reliance by communities on solar cooking should encourage more studies on how to make photovoltaic cells cheaper for an ordinary household. At this time, the use of solar cells is not economically friendly for a single household. However, the approach here is to install a series of solar panels which would be shared by the whole community. This could be a good idea depending on your usage, but for basic lighting purposes these could work in small poor communities. In some areas, community cooperatives have found ways to bring electricity to households out of reach of power grids.

In the Philippines for example, a local cooperative provided households loans to enable them to install a basic solar power module which can produce enough electricity for three light bulbs. This ay be laughable in our standards but to these people who have been living all their lives with the flickering light of the candles, three electric light bulbs make a great deal of a difference.

The story is the same in other countries. In Israel, the high costs of photovoltaic cells have clamped down the growth of solar energy in the country. It if fortunate, therefore, that the Israeli government is now providing incentives for households that would use solar energy. However, according to industry analysts, the costs of solar cells production will go down as the demand increase.

Also, most are hopeful that recent discoveries and advancement in technologies will find a way to bring down costs of using solar energy. Ordinary households using solar energy is an ideal scenario that we should all strive to achieve.

Solar energy simplified:

The sun shines, we collect the sunlight, we convert the sunlight into usable forms, and we enjoy the benefits. You can't get any simpler than that. But okay, I know you need more explanations. You've been looking all over the web for information and you need, no you deserve, more than just a single sentence. The following would be my attempt in simplifying the concept of solar energy and I just hope you get something out of it. The sun produces huge amounts of energy. But what the earth gets is a pretty small share of that energy. However, even if we get only a miniscule amount, the energy we receive from the sun is more than enough for our needs. Believe it or not, a day's worth of sunlight when harnessed properly can power a big country like the US for more than a year.

So if that's how much energy we can get from the sun, why do we rely too much on fossil fuels which will disappear in 40 to 50 years time? The main problem is that the sun shines all throughout the world. That energy is so spread out that harnessing it is really a challenge. But still, there are other factors at work here, political, economical, and even cultural in nature which contributes to the slow progress of solar technologies. But that will need a whole chapter, nay, a whole book to discuss so let's leave that alone for a moment. There are various ways how we harness sunlight and the specific way may depend on how we plan to use that energy. But we can divide the usage into two general concepts, converting solar power into heat and the other one is converting it into electricity.

Using solar power to heat homes is a pretty good example of the first category. There are two ways that can be used, the first one relies on the positioning of the house's windows and the second one involves the use of some mechanical devices to distribute the heat throughout the house. Solar water heaters are also now available. What you do is provide a solar collector where the heat from the sun is trapped and collected. That heat is then transferred to the after that goes out of your faucets and showers. Converting solar power into electricity, however, needs a little bit more explanation. There are basically two ways we can get electricity out of solar power. The first one involves the use of photovoltaic cells and the second one is using various solar thermal systems. Photovoltaic cells are more commonly known as solar cells. These cells are made from silicon wafers and phosphorous.

When sunlight strikes the surface of the silicon wafers, free electrons are produced. The electrons are then harnessed via attaching a wire to the cells. As the electrons leave the cells and pass through the wire, an electronic current is produced. One major flaw of the photovoltaic cells is that they can be quite expensive plus they only convert a small amount of sunlight. Hopefully these cells can be cheaper, more efficient and more suitable to the needs of consumers in the future.

The great thing about solar energy is that it does not produce any kinds of pollution unlike fossil fuels which spit out substantive amounts of pollutants in the air and even in the water. Plus the sun is pretty much in good health aid it is still very far from dying. We can utilize more than enough energy from the sun that will last us for a lifetime.

Solar Energy, How Does It Benefit the Agricultural Sector:

What is solar energy? To put it simply, this is the energy coming from the sun. The heat and light that the sun provides are essential to life. Can you even imagine life without the sun? It will not be normal and there are lots of things and experiences that people can no longer indulge into if ever that will be the case. Everybody relies on the sun for its benefits. Did you know that the earth gets 1740 watts of insolation or the incoming radiation from the sun? This happens at the upper part of the atmosphere. Almost 30% gets reflected back to the space. The rest of the percentage is being absorbed by the clouds, land masses and oceans.

The Agricultural Sector :

If you can think of one industry that won't survive without the energy coming from the sun, what will be the first thing on your mind? There may be many sectors that must rely on the sun's benefits. But the agricultural and horticulture industry will not thrive without it. They have no other options. If the sun will be gone, these sectors will die. The sun is need by the agricultural and horticulture departments to be able to grow their produce. The latter is needed by people as well as animals. These sectors' productivity will depend on the amount of energy that they are getting from the sun. It must be balanced in all ways. It can never too little. And it must also not be so much. If it is too little, the plans may not be able to grow accordingly. The farmers won't achieve the required harvests in order to feed the population. And if it is too much, this will damage the crops. This will also cause bad effects on people's health. But if the latter is the case, people can think of ways in order to achieve the needed produce by manually trying to reduce the amount of heat that can be directed on the plants. But if the situation becomes unbearable, it might lead to drought and deaths. Farmers must know when the sun will be up, when sunny days will be long and factors like that so that they can settle for what kinds of plants they must plant to survive the kind of weather condition.

Here are only some of the things that they resort to in order to optimize the full benefits of the energy coming from the sun.
- Timed planting cycles
- Timed planting cycles
- Tailored row orientation
- Mixing different varieties of crops to improve the yields

Do you ever wonder what farmers did in times like the Little Ice Age? It is said that English and French farmers resorted to fruit walls. These fruit walls help in maximizing the collection of the energy from the sun. These serve as the thermal masses. These walls help in keeping the plants warm to speed up the process of growing and ripening of produce.

The sun's energy is also being utilized in these sectors in vital activities such as drying the crops, pumping of water, drying animals' manure, brooding of chicks and a lot more. It is hard to imagine the agriculture and horticulture sectors to survive without the solar energy. If there are anybody who knows the importance of the sun, these people are the first in line.

Solar Energy is the Future:

We consume fossil fuels at a greater rate than we have ever had over the past 50 years. That demand is fueled by the increase of cars on the street,the number of planes that take to the air and the number of homes that need electricity. Sadly, we will have depleted these resources by the end of this century which is why we have to come up with other ways to get power and solar energy may be the future. Solar energy is simply extracting the sun's energy for power. Just to tell you how powerful the sun is, it can burn scrub lands and give you sunburn if you are out in the sun without any protection. In fact, the Greeks and the Chinese used this to set fire until the 1880's by Charles Fritts made the first solar cell.

Instead of using a heater to warm up the home, sunlight can be used to control the temperature. You will just need large windows and shades to control the amount of sunlight that will go inside and keep the heat absorbed during the day to remain at night. Solar energy can also provide warm water as it warms up cold water that passes down through the closed flat panels called collectors. But solar energy does not only give warmth to the home.

It can also be used to help power it which reduces our dependence on non-renewable resources like oil or coal. This occurs when solar cells are installed on the roof so it will be able to capture as much solar rays as possible and then converts this into electricity. You will need 10 or 12 to capture at least a kilowatt of power and more if you are powering more than just your home. The only limitation which challenges the use of solar energy is that it can only generate power during the day. The answer to this is to put an auxiliary system in place that will store the energy and kick when the sun is not available. This comes in the form of batteries which will provide power in the evening or a brownout. Advances in technology have taken solar energy to the next level.

NASA uses it to power satellites in orbit, solar panels installed onboard aircraft allow it to fly across oceans while cars can travel speeds up to 40 miles per hour. It is used to power a lighthouse so seafarers will be able to find their way at sea while aircraft can land in an airport in the middle of the frozen desert. Solar energy is safe for the environment since it does not emit any harmful gases or chemicals into the air. It is a renewable resource that has not yet been fully tapped by a lot of countries which makes it very viable for the future.

But is it the only answer to reduce our dependence on oil? No because solar energy is just one of the options. We can also harness the power of the wind, the wave in the oceans, geothermal heat, hydroelectricity and a lot more instead of relying on coal or even nuclear energy that may harm the environment. It is something we have to push for the next generation.

Technologies for harnessing solar energy:

Harnessing the sun's energy efficiently is not an easy feat. The sunlight is so widespread that finding the most effective way of capturing it requires advanced knowledge and technology. There are several technologies for utilizing solar energy and all are unique and are dedicated for specific applications. First up are the photovoltaic cells or commonly known as solar cells. These are probably the best known way of harnessing the energy's sun. Whenever one talk about solar power, the first things that come to mind include having panels and panels of photovoltaic cells or PV. These cells contain semi-conductors, commonly are made from silicon, which absorbs the light from the sun. When sunlight hit the surface of the silicon, new free electrons are created. As the electrons are channeled out of the silicon, electric current is created. The second solar power technology is the concentrating solar power systems. This one involves using mirrors to reflect sunlight to one area. Some systems incorporate high tech devices to track the movement of the sun and adjust the mirrors to maximize the amount of sunlight the system receives. The sunlight reflected from the mirrors is used to heat or power a conventional power plant. Other systems channel the light from the mirrors to an area filled with photovoltaic cells. There are several kinds of concentrated solar power systems, the most popular ones are the solar trough, parabolic dish and solar power tower. The solar trough uses large, U-shaped (parabolic) reflectors to point the sunlight to a tower at the center of the mirrors. At the center tower, hot oil is heated by the sun's energy and help boil water to create steam which is then used to power convention plants. The power tower system uses the same concept as solar troughs.

Mirrors are used to reflect sunlight to a center tower where a liquid is heated and utilized for the creation of steam which will power a power. The parabolic dish system uses mirrored dishes to focus and concentrate sunlight onto a receiver. The size of the dish varies but it is commonly 10 times bigger than an ordinary cable satellite dish. Another solar power technology used today is the solar water heating systems. This is a simple one. The process involves collecting the energy directly from the sun to heat water or liquids which in turn heats up the water.

This is more common in households are ideal for family use. In order to capture the sunlight, solar panels have to be installed in your home or in the place where you will be needing hot water like a swimming pool area. You will need a big space for this but in the long run, you will be able to save lots of money from your electric bill. For commercial establishments, an ideal solar power technology is the transpired solar collector or otherwise known as the solar wall. It involves using perforated solar collectors where outside air passes before it enters the building.

These are but a few of the technologies around which can be used for utilizing the power of the sun. The technologies for harnessing solar energy continue to evolve as new technologies and discoveries are being accomplished. Everything might change in a few years time. Plus, the whole solar power technologies will become more price competitive which will benefit the general consumers.

The downsides of solar energy:

Not that I'm against using solar energy or anything but there are some downsides of using solar energy. My intention is to illustrate these disadvantages so that people can realize the other side of the coin to prepare them and not so much as to dissuade them from using solar energy. I am for everything that can save the planet. View this explanation as an introduction where we can still improve the current technologies involving solar energy. One of the first and major drawbacks of using solar power is the costs. The expense is considerably higher than the conventional electric installation. From the purchase to the initial installations of the solar panel unit, the cost is a significant factor to consider.

The high costs of solar power panels lie on the expensive semi-conductor materials that convert sunlight into electricity. However, as technology progresses and as the need slowly increases, the costs of solar panels are expected to go down, something on the level of being competitive with other energy resources. Another to consider is space. We're talking about installing a solar panel which is not small. It requires a significant amount of space which also helps maximize the amount of sunlight it can collect and convert into electricity. Some households will have the panels installed on their roof others will designate a place for it on the year or on top of a pole. The same space problems will need to be readdressed once you decide to add panels when your current setup is no longer enough for your family's needs. Positioning is also vital.

The solar panels will need to be facing a direction where it will receive the most amount of sunlight in a day. However, there is always a solution. If space does not permit such installations, there are some add-ons that can help maximize sun exposure. Positioning is also vital.

The solar panels will need to be facing a direction where it will receive the most amount of sunlight in a day. However, there is always a solution. If space does not permit such installations, there are some add-ons that can help maximize sun exposure. At night, you might encounter a problem with relying solely on solar power. Although the solution here is to purchase batteries which you can charge during the day and use at night. You will need a couple of batteries though to be able to sustain your electricity needs through cloudy, stormy or smoggy or foggy times during the day. As far as solar powered transportation services go, there are still some quirks that need to be fixed before mass production of such vehicles is rolled out.

The most noticeable difference is the speed. Solar powered cars are far slower that their counterparts. But again, due to the fast development of the solar car and the technologies that go with it, this drawback will soon disappear. When you look at the things that I mentioned about the disadvantages of solar energy, you will see that most of them have solutions while others you just need to compromise a bit. I still think that harnessing the power of the sun is the way to go, so these downsides of solar energy are just a small obstacle that we need to overcome.

The future of solar energy on transportation:

Are you familiar with the World Solar Challenge? It is a race specifically for solar cars. Solar cars basically have arrays of photovoltaic cells which converts the sun's rays into usable electrical energy. The purpose of the race is to raise awareness on the use of the sun's energy on transportation and the development of other alternative forms of energy particularly the solar cells. The future of using solar energy on transportation services may still be a little hazy given the practical difficulties involve in converting ordinary cars into solar cars but the idea is here to stay and hopefully develops into something promising and useful. At this point, solar cars have been built to join solar car races. Very few have been constructed for practical and commercial purposes.

There are several reasons why the solar car remains on the background. The design of a solar car relies on the electrical system of the vehicle. The system controls the electricity the flows from the photovoltaic cells to the batteries, to the wheels, and to the controls. The electric motor that moves the vehicle is powered purely by the electricity produced by the solar cells.

The solar cells, depending on the number installed on the vehicle, can produce more or less 1000 watts of power from the sun's rays. To give you an idea, 1000 watts is just enough electricity to power an electric iron or even a toaster. And since the sun will most likely be covered by clouds at one time or the other, or the car goes through a tunnel or something, solar cars are equipped with batteries to serve as backup power supply for the motor. The battery packs are charged by the solar cells. However, the batteries are not charge while driving the solar car unless you intend to go very slow. Just like a gas pedal in conventional motors, a motor controller regulates the amount of electricity that enters the motor to speed up or slow down the vehicle whenever needed. Solar cars are not that slow as perceived by almost everyone.

These cars can go to as fast as 80-85 mph. With this, you can see why solar cars are not yet into commercial production. Nowadays, solar cells can harness more than 21% of the sun's energy that hit the surface. If the time comes that the cells can actually get more energy from the sun then maybe we can see solar cars on the streets. But at this time, it is quite difficult to make a commercial production model of a solar car. Nevertheless, there are companies who have already created some concept solar cars and are testing how road worthy they are. There's even a scooter that is street legal and runs from batteries charged from photovoltaic cells. Other possible application of solar car technologies is on golf carts which runs pretty slow in the first place and can be appreciated by golfers as well.

The future of solar energy on transportation is still not that clear. The application of solar energy on homes and buildings has been moving forward in recent years so hopefully we can find new ways of converting the sun's energy into usable electricity. And this time something that can be economically and efficiently installed in conventional cars.

The Future of Solar Energy, How It Looks and How It Affects Nature:

The future of solar energy lies on the indigenous hands of people who never tire out from thinking of ways in order to make life easier to live. With the advancement in the technology, the boom of the Internet age and a lot of other things, there will come a time when people will turn their backs on whatever is conventional. This can be good and bad in many ways, depending on who is looking at it and from what perspective. But people's quest for the advancement and development of everything that surrounds them provides lots of negative effects as well.

Here are only some.

1. Sometimes, people neglect the environment and how to properly take care of it for the mere fact that they are greedy to get their ideas done no matter what the consequences to the nature will be. Such advancements create harmful effects in the whole state and balance of nature. How many times have you heard about forest denudation or grave floods that kill people? All these occurrences can also be rooted to the activities of men that suffice for their own good without so much consideration for their natural habitat and the nature.

2. With the continuing advancement of everything that surrounds people, the generational gap becomes wider and wider. Old folks will fight for the benefits of the conventional tools and mediums. The newer generations cannot afford to sit on those old ways to do things. They are a slave to the continuing technological developments. It is okay to initiate change. It is good to find better ways to do things. But people must be cautious in achieving this. They must think about everything around them before they even start on their venture to newer and better ways to achieve greatness. The Innovations As of today, solar energy is one of the best options that people have with regards to alternative power sources. This has already evolved. There was a time when you can only avail such power source when the sun is present and that is during daytime. With the genius of the people behind the development of this resource, they were able to create green gas that can produce electricity. This is done by splitting water properties into hydrogen and oxygen. Both gasses will then be grouped into a cell that will be the electricity source. The same geniuses estimated that the entire planet can rely to an hour of sunlight for its one year electricity consumption. Solar cells have been developed to produce electricity from the energy coming from the sun. The panels for such technology can also be used to heat water and cook food. There are now the solar heating, solar cookers and solar furnaces as add-ons to this innovative venture. There are now hydrogen based cars. These are fueled by the split hydrogen in water. The solar cells also power the satellites that orbit through the surface of the Earth. This is the reason why there are advancements that people benefit from such as satellite phones and TV, accurate weather forecasting, even the development of the GPS technology and a lot more. There are a lot of benefits that people can gain from the future of solar energy. You just have to think that whatever you do or however you use such technology for your own good, you must always think of ways to protect your environment first to be able to get the most out of such improvements.

The Benefits of Solar Energy:

Solar energy will benefit a lot of people and not only the rich. This is why some governments have increased funding for this type of technology because they are aware of its many benefits. For one, solar energy is very cheap compared to other technologies. It is also renewable unlike coal or the rest which are non-renewable and hard to maintain. It also improves the health of people since it does not produce any carbon dioxide emissions unlike kerosene lamps that give out fumes which are just as deadly as smoking 2 packs of cigarettes a day. It also reduces the incidents of fire that are often associated with the use of kerosene, candles,diesel fuel and gasoline for generators. Solar energy is almost maintenance free because the solar cells used will last for 20 years or more before it has to be replaced.

You just have to keep the panels clean so it is able to absorb sunlight and convert that into electricity. These are also very useful in remote locations where power lines are not yet available. Some examples of these include fish houses, highway signs,marine applications, remote lighting and telecommunication. If countries focus on solar energy and other renewable techniques, they will be able to conserve their foreign exchange because they no longer have to use it to pay for foreign oil. This money can then be used for other things such as health care, infrastructure projects and education.

Solar energy will also reduce your electricity bills because you are no longer dependent on electricity coming from the power company. The only downside to solar energy is the initial cost in setting it up. Yes you will have to buy a lot of solar panels which are quite expensive but in the long run, you will be able to save more because you don't have to pay for anything else to keep them running. Should the cost of solar cells be beyond your budget, you can probably invest in used systems first then try to acquire the brand new ones later on. Another benefit of using solar energy is that you get to conserve fossil fuels and other natural resources that are quickly diminishing as a direct result of an increase in the world's population which could compromise the needs of the future generations. So should people get into solar energy? The answer is yes because it is safe, cheap and good for the environment. You only have to worry when the sun isn't shining because when this happens, rays from the sun won't be able to produce electricity so you have to rely on other means to get power. The same also goes when there is a blackout or brownout because you will soon lose power from your solar system.

The demand for solar energy is increasing and you should join in. Aside from reducing your electric bill, homeowners who use solar energy may claim up to $2,000 in federal investment tax credit in the first year while businesses may claim a 30% federal investment tax credit.

Believe it or not, solar energy has one other benefit and that it increases the value of your home. According to home appraisers, a dollar decrease in your energy bill results in a $20 increase in its property value so do the match and you can easily figure out how much your home will be worth after you decide to invest in solar energy.

The History of Solar Energy:

Solar energy is for everyone simply because the sun shines in every corner of the planet. In fact, the history of solar energy can be traced back to the Greeks that were then passed on to the Romans which marked the first people to ever use the passive solar design. Passive solar design is a way to warm the home based on the dwelling's design. They may not have had glass windows back then but their architecture made it possible for the people to use the sun's rays to light and heat indoor spaces. As a result, there was no need to burn food that often which was in short supply. In 1861, Auguste Mouchout invented the first active solar motor. Unfortunately, its expensive price made it impossible to produce commercially. Less than 20 years later, Charles Fritts invented solar cells,which will later on be used to power homes, heaters, satellites and other devices today. Since what he invented was very primitive, other people experimented on solar energy. One such person was

Albert Einstein who won the Nobel Prize for physics in his research on the photoelectric effect which is a phenomenon associated with the generation of electricity through solar cells. In 1953, Bell Laboratories which we know today as AT&T labs developed the first silicon solar cell capable of generating a measurable electric current. Three years later, solar cells ran $300 per watt. With the Cold War and the Space Race on, this was used to power satellites and crafts. But the biggest event in the development of solar energy occurred during the oil crisis of 1973. This prompted the US government to invest heavily in the solar electric cell that was developed by Bell Laboratories 20 years ago.

By the 1990's, research towards solar energy came to a standstill as the price of oil dropped in the world market. Funds were diverted elsewhere and the United States which was probably the leader in this form of alternative energy was soon surpassed by other nations mainly Germany and Japan. In 2002 for example, Japan had installed 25,000 solar panels on rooftops. Because of that, the price of solar panels went down as the demand for it was on the rise.

To date, solar energy is growing at a modest 30% per year. Although there have been improvements in solar energy, its fundamentals are still the same. The sun's rays are collected and then converted into electricity. Aside from powering homes or office buildings, the technology has been used to power aircraft, cars and boats. Unfortunately, none of these have been made available yet for public use. We still rely heavily on oil for electricity, gasoline for our cars, fuel for planes and ships.

In fact, the US is one of the biggest oil users in the world. To prove a point, the department of Defense consumes 395,000 barrels per This has to change because our oil reserves are almost depleted and many experts believe that global supply for these non-renewable resources will be gone before the end of the century. We have to do our share to push for renewable energy and one of them happens to be solar energy.

The Pros and Cons of Solar Energy:

Solar energy is one of the best forms of renewable energy. But why don't we rely on it so much compared to other countries? The answer is simply that there are pros and cons with using this form of alternative energy. The pros of using solar energy is that the system is easy to install, there are no energy costs once it is set up, there are no emissions like air pollutants or greenhouse gas and the sun is widely available. The pros of using solar energy is that the system is easy to install, there are no energy costs once it is set up, there are no emissions like air pollutants or greenhouse gas and the sun is widely available. A solar energy system is composed of the solar panels, the inverter, battery, charge controller, wires and support structure. For you to produce a kilowatt of power, you will need 10 to 12 solar panels that will occupy an area of 100 square feet.

If you are worried that this will cause damage to your roof, don't because it is made of light weight materials. When you call a contractor, it will usually take a day or two to install and cost around $10,000. Not that many people will have cash on hand to pay for it so they can avail of a home equity loan to pay for it. If you use a kilowatt of solar energy, you can save 170 lbs. of coal from being burned, about 300lbs of carbon dioxide from being released into the atmosphere or 105 gallons of water that most homeowners use up every month.

The cons are solar cells are expensive, the rays can only be collected during the day time, the weather and where you are located will play a factor in how much sunlight you can get and you will need a big area to collect the power. But some experts believe that price of these cells and its ability to collect power will improve in the future. Right now, a kilowatt of solar energy can only produce 1,600 kilowatts of hours per year in sunny climate. That means you will receive 5.5 hours of electricity per day. If you produce about 750 kilowatts of power, you will only get 2.5 hours of power per day.

Solar panels come in various colors and usually have a 5 year warranty.Since manufacturers are aware that solar energy can only work when the sun is out, they have installed batteries so you get more than 5 hours of power even during cloudy days and nights. This is because the batteries are designed to absorb, insulate, transmit and reflect rays coming from the sun.

But solar energy can be applied to other things and not just powering our homes. It can be used to power small devices like calculators to bigger things like planes, satellites and cars. Since these are easy to maintain, you don't have to worry about anything. People should take this seriously especially when this is not a renewable source of energy.

Things We Should Know Before Investing in Solar Energy:

There is no doubt that there are a lot of benefits in using solar energy. Aside from protecting the environment, you get to save a great deal of money. But before you switch to solar energy, here are a few things you should consider. First, is your roof right for solar power? Most solar power systems can be installed as long as the roof is flat and made of material such as bitumen, composite shingle, cement tile, metal or tar and gravel. If this is how your roof is positioned, then there shouldn't be any problems. The solar panels will be installed parallel to the roof surface.

If you are concerned that the weight could be too heavy for your roof, don't be since this is very light and quite rare that you have to do some structural work before installing the system. When you are looking for a contractor, find out how much it will cost to install the system. You should compare these first before you decide in picking the best one. But you should know right now that installing solar powered cells are a bit expensive. There are also no financing programs you can avail of. Your best bet if you don't have enough money is to apply for a home equity loan. If you are planning to install this in a commercial establishment, the various loans you can avail of include the capital equipment loan, equipment secured loan, property secured loan or the SAFE-BIDCO energy efficiency loan.

Non-profit organizations may also avail of special loans for solar energy and the best one is through third party financing. In this case, the non-profit organization and the contractor will purchase the system and make use of the tax credits. The third party will then pass on the charges for the produced power to the non-profit and after the system has depreciated, this is sold to the non-profit at a discount. The end result is that you pay for less than what you are currently paying for because it is maintenance free. Will installing a solar system have any effect on your property? The answer is yes. In fact, it will increase the resale value of your property without having to pay much more in terms of property taxes. If you have a lot of space to spare, you may even be able to zero out your electric bill as long as the sun comes out so you can convert sunlight into electricity.

Aside from increasing the properly value, you will also be able to avail of tax credits from the government. Solar energy can power your home in the same way you get electricity from the grid. You won't be able to use it when there is a power outage or when the sun is shining but fortunately, this doesn't happen daily so it is still an alternative form of energy worth considering.

Using solar energy goes way back:

Recollecting the history of solar energy brings us back to the 1970s energy crisis and oil embargo which caused long lines in gasoline stations, high gasoline prices, and even caused panic among consumers and investors alike in the United States. Knowledge about oil being a non-renewable resource has been around since the 1800s.

But it was only during and after the 70s energy crisis that people really began to realize the consequences of depending too much on an already depleting energy resource. However, utilizing the sun's energy is not really a recent development. It has been used by ancient civilizations for warmth, for food and crop preparations and various agricultural purposes. What's new are the technologies involved in harnessing this energy and utilizing it for man's daily use. The technology began in the 1830's when Edmund Becquerel made public his studies on how solar light can be harnessed into usable energy. However, nobody followed up on this idea nor explore any practical use.

The next breakthrough on solar power came after thirty years Becquerel published his works. In 1860s, the French Monarch commissioned Augusted Mouchout to find other sources of energy. And Mouchout looked up in the sky for inspiration. His series of solar powered contractions were quite impressive back then. His inventions included a motor that run on solar energy, a steam engine that uses the sun's light, and an ice maker that fully rely on solar power. After Mouchout, there were several other notable achievements in the line of solar power. Among these is the works of William Adams in the 1870s which utilized mirrors to channel the power of the sun to make a steam engine run. Adams' power tower design concept is still in use today.

Another notable work is by Charles Fritz in the early 1880s. His studies were attuned on turning sunlight into electricity, which he later accomplished. But one of the most significant development in modern solar energy occurred in the 1950s. Early in the decade, R.S. Ohl discovered that sunlight produces large numbers of free electrons when it strikes silicon. Then in the mid-1950s Gerald Pearson, Calvin Fuller, and Daryl Chaplin was able to capture those free electrons and convert them in electricity.

Today, silicon cells are used to make solar cells and solar panels for harnessing the sun's energy. Immediately these solar cells were made into good use and the first among to use them was the field of space aeronautics. These silicon based solar cells were used to power satellites that orbit the earth. The satellite Vanguard I was the first one launched out to space which rely on solar cells for power. More satellites followed. Nowadays, more and more research and studies are being conducted on how best to utilize the sun's energy. Especially today where it is said that about 30-50 years from the now, the world oil reserves will be totally depleted. Thus, the search for alternative sources of energy continuous.

The sun is expected to die out in a couple of thousand of years, it's too long to worry about and man can have all the sun's energy until that day. The challenge today is creating solar energy power in more efficient and cost effective e way. Admittedly, the costs of those photo cells are not that cheap to be accessible by most of the ordinary consumers. The movement today in the science and technology committee is to be able to provide cheap alternative source of energy.

What is Solar Energy?

Solar energy is a form of renewable energy as it utilizes the radiant energy coming from the sun. This is done by converting sunlight into electricity using solar cells. Solar cells or photovoltaics were invented in the 1880's by Charles Fritts. Although it did not convert a lot of sunlight into electricity at the time, this started a revolution that continued on to the 20th century. The greatest example is perhaps the Vanguard 1 which was a satellite fitted with solar cells that enabled it to transmit back to earth after its chemical battery was exhausted. Its success prompted NASA and its Russian counterpart to the same with other satellites including Telstar hich continues to serve as the backbone of the telecommunications structure today. The most significant event that stimulated the demand for solar energy was the 1973 oil crisis.

Early on, power companies would charge the consumer a hundred dollars per watt. In the 1980's, it became only $7 per watt. Unfortunately, the lack of government funding did not sustain its growth so the growth of solar energy was only 15% annually from 1984 to 1996. There have been a decline in the demand for solar energy in the US but this increased in Japan and Germany. From 31.2 megawatts of power in 1994, this increased to 318 megawatts in 1999 and world wide production growth increased by 30% towards the end of the 20th century.

Next to these two countries, Spain is the third largest user of solar energy followed by France, Italy and South Korea.

There are three basic approaches to get the most out of solar energy. It is namely passive, active and solar photovoltaic systems.

1. In passive, it has to do a lot with the building design. This will enable the building to avoid heat loss so people inside will feel a great degree of comfort with the help of controlled ventilation and day lighting. Homes that apply this will greatly reduce their heating requirements by as much as 80% with minimal cost.

2. Active solar heating is used to convert sunlight into heat which provides space or water heating. Used extensively in Europe, getting the right size will cover 50% to 60% of your hot water heating requirements.

3. Lastly is photovoltaic which converts solar radiation into electricity. This is done by installing solar cells in the ground and the greater the intensity of the light, the greater the flow of electricity. These are available in different sizes and some are installed in consumer devices like calculators and watches.

Some vehicles are now powered using solar energy. Cars although not yet produced commercially compete in the World Solar Challenge which invites competitors from around the world to compete in this annual event in Australia. There are also unmanned aerial vehicles and balloons. To date, solar energy has only been successful in passenger boats.

Many of us take the sun for granted and if we are really serious about preserving the environment and reducing our demand for oil, solar energy is just one of the options we have on the table. We have to lobby and convince our government leaders to do more because it is the cheapest means of providing our home with electricity compared to rechargeable batteries, kerosene or candles.

Wind power vs Solar energy an even match:

Today in center stage is a battle for the ages. On the right corner, packing a hurricane punch yet is known to move softly as a breeze is wind power. On the left corner, with a scorching hot aura, moves in a speed of light, is solar energy. Wind power versus solar energy, which one is going to be declared the champion of the alternative energy movement?! Let's get ready to rumble! Or something like that. I apologize for that intro but I just can't help. I figured that if I was going to match one alternative energy resource against the other, then I'll make some extravagant introduction. Just imagine the drum rolls. Actually, there is an existing debate among environmentalists and even scientists on which energy resource should be developed first given their advantages and drawbacks. Staying away from the personal biases, numerous studies have shown that overall, wind power is more cost effective than harnessing the sun's energy.

Let's see the reasons behind that conclusion. Harnessing the sun's energy can be done by a number of ways. But probably the simplest way which can be applied in a small home is by using photovoltaic cells or PV or solar cells. What happens is that sunlight hit the surface of a photovoltaic (PV) panel which responds by creating free electrons which is channelled to generate an electric current. Wind power on the other hand utilizes a propeller and a shaft system which has a magnet wrapped by a coil of wire inside. As the wind turns the propeller and the magnet inside, the electrons in the wire are forced to move along the wire producing an electrical current. Both ways are quite simple but the complexities now lies on the costs of producing the necessary equipment especially the mechanisms that will maximize the power output. When costs of production of photovoltaic cells and wind turbine are compared, the latter is much cheaper to produce. Although, manufacturers of photovoltaic cells stress that as the demand on PV cells increase, the costs of production decreases. So its just a matter of time before PV cells become price competitive.

Other problems include the logistics of placing the equipment. A solar panel requires quite a large space plus, your location on the globe will affect the amount of sunlight you receive and consequently the amount of power you produce. The further away from the equator you are, the less amount of sunlight you can harness. Also, on the average, the PV cells have a 15-20% efficiency rate. The problem with wind power on the other hand is that not all areas will have winds favorable for a turbine. And if you do locate a place where winds are strong and the turbine can be maximized, you'll find that the area (more often than not) is inhabited by various species of birds. You don't want to kill birds with your turbine, do you? Now going back to our wind power vs. solar energy match-up, indeed we do have to agree that wind power is more cost efficient. However, both alternative energy resource will play a big role in our future.

It is, therefore, in my humble opinion that we both develop the two technologies simultaneously for each one has their advantages and disadvantages and each one can be properly utilized for specific areas.

We Can Have a Home Powered By Solar Energy:

Do you like to live in a home that is energy efficient? The good news is you can given there are technologies these days that can make that happen and one good example happens to be solar energy. Solar energy is the process of using the sun's radiant rays to power your home. For this to work, you will need to get some solar panels and then have this install by a contractor. Ideally, you will need a flat area measuring about a hundred square feet. This is good to install between 10 to 12 solar panels that can produce about a kilowatt of power. If you think 1 kilowatt is small, think again because this is equivalent to 1,600 kilowatts of hours per year. That translates to 5.5 hours of electricity per day if you are using it to the max. Otherwise, excess power will be stored in the battery which will help bring electricity to the house during a blackout or at night.

Aside from the solar panels, you will also need the inverter, battery, charge controller, wires and support structure. Each of these parts are important since the system will not work without the other so whoever you choose as a contractor should have everything ready prior to installation. Once everything is set up, you can already enjoy your solar powered home.

Since it requires minimal maintenance, it can last up to 20 years before you have to replace anything. If you have a larger area to work with, why not invest in a solar thermal roof? The difference between this and the first one mentioned is that you convert the entire roof into a giant collector. It is quite expensive and takes a couple of days to complete but worth every penny. The only reason why not that many people invest in such a system is because most roofs are not oriented towards the south with the steep pitch needed to maximize solar energy especially during the winter.

You will have to do some major construction work to make this happen. Solar energy is just one way for you to stop relying on power coming from the grid. When the sun isn't shining, you have to be ready by preparing other ways to generate electricity. One example that can be used at home is wind energy. Here, you use fans to collect the wind's kinetic energy similar to windmills that you see in the farm. The only difference is that the blades are connected to a drive shaft that turns an electric generator to produce electricity.

You just have to do some research to find out if solar energy is feasible for your home. You should know how much power you consume on a monthly basis and also where exactly is your house located.

Should your study show it is possible to live on solar energy, it is best to apply for a home equity loan to pay for the installation costs because you will surely get a return on your investment later on in the form of tax credit and a utility bill that won't exceed $10. So what are you waiting for? If you don't want to rely on power from the electric company, go ahead and invest in solar energy.

CHAPTER TWO

Advantages & Disadvantages of Solar Panels

Advantages of Solar Panels:

1. Reduce the cost of your energy bill

The most widely known advantage of solar panels is that they will reduce the cost of your electricity bills.

By producing your own power through the sun you will ultimately be buying less power from the grid. This allows you to spend less money buying energy which leads to saving more money on your power bills.

Due to the sun's energy being renewable and free it means that you will not be paying for the energy you generate through your solar panels.

There are endless benefits that come from having spare cash each month to spend on your family or other things. Saving money is one of the biggest advantages of solar.

2. Renewable energy source

Solar power is a renewable source of energy. Renewable energy is a source of power that cannot be used up.

Essentially the sun is generating a mass amount of power all the time that can be harvested by your solar panels without running out.

The plus side of solar being renewable means that everyone can take advantage of free energy given by the sun.

We wouldn't have to worry about the sun's power running out, but instead we can enjoy the rays that hit our solar panels and generate free, clean energy.

Being a renewable source solar power is also clean energy meaning the energy doesn't produce any greenhouse gasses emissions.

3. Increase your property value

Because solar panels have so many benefits for homeowners, installing them on your property will increase its value.

Houses that have solar panels will be more valuable than those that do not.

This is because one home will be highly dependent on the grid whereas the other will be generating its own energy. Enjoying being free from the shackles of increasing energy prices.

Again this is because solar panels do have a high upfront cost and can be seen as a great investment asset.

The money that you spend on solar panels will be invested into your home as well, you may even see a high return on investment from installing solar at your property.

4. Environmentally friendly

Energy that is produced by solar panels is clean, renewable and has zero-emissions. Solar energy does not contribute towards greenhouse gasses or fossil fuels unlike other oils and coals.

Essentially this means that solar panels are environmentally friendly products and will not harm the planet.

Being environmentally friendly means a lot nowadays, and you can gain popularity within communities for taking a stance against climate change.

It is one of the most popular reasons why people take a move towards solar, and is definitely one of the biggest advantages of solar panels.

Homeowners can rest easy knowing their energy is not harming the planet.

5. Wide range of solar products

Another massive advantage of solar panels is the huge range of different solar panel products available.

There are solar panels that are built for performance for those people who are looking for a high-end system to perform for a long time.

For homeowners who are looking for a good budget system then there is a massive range to be browsed from as well.

Thermal solar panels are also available for people who spend most of their energy on heating and want to use solar to help lower the cost.

Solar panels can be purchased with an all-in-one battery system for homeowners who need to store their power to use at night instead.

Having this wide variety of options comes as a massive advantage for homeowners as they can get solar panels specific to their requirements and needs.

6. Low maintenance costs

With new technology being readily available, the maintenance of solar panels are becoming easier and easier.

Warranties are also being included for massive periods of time making the maintenance of solar panels less and less.

This is great because it means homeowners can buy solar without having to fix or check the system every week. Also, low maintenance means low cost.

You won't need to spend anything extra on your solar panels system to keep it working at optimum.

Once in a while it's recommended to get your solar panels cleaned if they have collected any soil or dust.

7. Homeowners can become energy independent

The installation of solar panels to your home could allow you to become completely energy independent.

With a good enough system, you could generate enough energy to power your home without having to buy power from the grid.

Not only is this a great accomplishment, but it also means homeowners won't have to face rising electricity prices again.

Generating your own power will be save you a large amount of money. You also would not be affected if there was a power cut or any maintenance by the grid on their power lines.

Many people who have become energy independent can say that it's a massive advantage of solar panels.

8. Excess solar can be sold to the grid

Any excess energy that is not used in your home can be sold to the grid for extra cash.

Not only this, you are providing your local community with clean, renewable energy. This helps you and your community have cleaner energy supplied to your grid by pulling energy from the sun.

Some homeowners will purposely upgrade their systems just to sell excess energy back to the grid.

The government offers some really good Feed-In Tariffs available for homeowners to get rewarded for any excess power they don't use.

These tariffs usually vary from state to state. The two main tariffs are fixed rate and time varying. The price per KW is decided by these two tariffs, and is a great way to help pay off your system quicker.

Once the system is paid off you will see the return on investment from your solar panels. Solar panels could actually generate you free money, which is a massive advantage.

9. Return on investment

Solar panels are a really good investment to make, and homeowners will be able to get the money they invested back within time.

Although solar panels have a high upfront investment cost, the money that gets saved each month on power bills will help toward paying off that cost of the system.

An easy way to look at it would be: If you saved a large sum of money on your energy bill, then you can put that money towards covering the cost of your system.

Once the solar system is paid off you will still be saving money on your energy bills. Therefore, you are now making a return from the initial investment made on your solar panels.

10. Get rewarded by the government

Government rebates are a great advantage of solar panels.

Being able to sell your energy back to the government for cash is enticing for homeowners to make the move to solar. With pressures on governments to move towards greener solutions, all future rewards are looking bright.

Rates may start to become more profitable and rebates becoming easier to get. However, this may not last forever.

Although these rebates differ from state to state they all offer a big reduction in the cost and most will also offer a no interest loan scheme.

These government incentives actually make solar energy more affordable. This is a step in the right direction and helps first time buyers secure solar.

11. Power can be stored and used at night

This would benefit homeowners that use a majority of power at night. Similar to commercial businesses like supermarkets or schools.

When you store power you become independent from the grid. Rather than buy energy, you can use the energy that has been stored.

This could provide even further savings for homeowners. It's best invested with high end solar panels to see the full benefits of solar battery storage.

High end solar panels tend to have a higher performance and generate more energy, meaning you can store more power quicker.

12. Solar panels have Long lasting warranties

Companies that design, test and manufacturer and solar panels include long lasting warranties with their products.

This shows that they have a lot of confidence in the performance of solar panels and that they are guaranteed to reach a minimum performance for a period of time.

Long lasting warranties are a big benefit of solar panels because they show that they won't break or stop performance within the first 10+ years installing them. Companies like Jinko, LG and SunPower offer great warranties.

Homeowners can feel like moving to solar is less risky, because they are covered by the solar panels warranties.

It also means they can work out their estimated saving given that there are no issues with the solar panels.

13. Solar panel technology is becoming more advanced

I've seen this a lot over the past 5 years. Solar panel technology is taking huge leaps in advancements to allow for some really awesome features. I'd say most important in particular is the availability for flexible solar system designs.

The reason why I like this so much is because you can design a system around your energy bill. Depending on when you use the most energy, you can place panels to capture the most sunlight during that time, maximising on your self consumption and giving you the highest possible savings.

Other features include full visibility and tracking of your system so you know it's performance and SMART features which can learn when you use the most energy and start to export this to the grid or other places like a battery or electric car.

14. Cost of solar panels are becoming more affordable year after year

Solar panels are becoming more and more affordable every year. There is a race towards making solar panels affordable whilst also maintaining the quality of the solar panels.

15. Options to charge your electric vehicle from your solar panel system

This is going to become a massive benefit of solar panels within the next 6 months. At the end of 2021 we've seen a huge spike in the demand for home EV charging systems which can connect and charge from your solar panels.

16. Solar energy was announced the cheapest form of electricity in history

Wooo! Go solar. That's right, solar energy was declared the cheapest form of electricity in history. There has never been a cheaper way to produce high quality, green energy. This was found by the International Energy Agency back in October 2020.

It was highlighted that solar energy is significantly cheaper than coal and gas. It's safe to say, solar panels have a very bright future ahead being the cheapest form of energy in the world right now.

Disadvantages of Solar Panels:

1. High upfront cost

The first initial investment for solar panel installation is quite high, and not everybody will be able to afford them. Although we could argue that solar panels are the most affordable they've ever been… Still they do come with a price tag.

Unfortunately this is a downside to solar panels however the future is bright as prices are coming down.

Solar panels right now are fairly expensive, however with new government schemes and the latest technology the price is becoming more and more affordable.

2. The size of system is dependent on your available space

Available space is a big factor in solar panel installation. If your roof is not big enough, then it means that you may have to downsize your system or rethink about getting solar altogether.

Solar panels are still fairly large products meaning they require a big space to be installed. The size disadvantage means that they cannot be placed into small areas, and actually require a large roof.

This is important for those who are looking to future proof their home with a big enough system to last years.

Some systems however do provide flexible designs for smaller roofs.

3. Requires sunny weather to work best

Energy can only be generated when sunlight is hitting the face of the panel and being converted. Therefore if there is no sun, there will be no energy being produced.

Although solar panels can still generate power on cloudy days (as it's the UV light that generates the energy) they perform best on sunny days. If you are in a location that doesn't get much sun, it's probably best to look at other options for get a system that overcomes shading issues.

Your solar panel performance will be negatively affected if there is not enough sunlight hitting the panels on rainy days.

Just remember, luckily in Australia we get a lot of sun so it makes it worthwhile for us, even for those in Melbourne.

4. Manufacturing of solar panels can harm the environment

Although solar panels produce clean, renewable energy, the process it takes to manufacture them can harm the environment. Mass production of solar panels may result in fossil fuels being burned and plastic waste.

Unfortunately, this is one of the overlooked disadvantages of solar panels. They are not eco-friendly to mass manufacture. Then again, you can ask what is these days? This is quite a shame because solar panels stand for a big movement to fight the climate crisis.

This does become a disadvantage for solar panels although they themselves produce green, renewable energy. Overall, I'd say that they still do more good than they do bad.

5. Low energy conversion rate

Even the most advanced solar panels still only convert around 20-25% of the sun's energy into power. It goes to show how much opportunity there is to develop better technology to optimise the full force of the sun.

However, there are many things that need to be considered like the direction of the panels and location.

Jinko solar panels have claimed the world record a few times. So have Canadian solar panels.

Although, I also want to stress that solar panel efficiency shouldn't be the most important thing. Especially when you're talking about 1-2% difference. Really, I'd be more concerned about the installation or warranties.

6. Cannot be used at night

No energy can be produced by your solar panels at night which essentially means your solar panels can only generate energy 12 hours of a full day. Without any sunlight hitting the solar panels then there will be no energy produced.

This is a disadvantage of solar panels but may be something that is overcome in the future with new technology. There are already talks about an 'anti solar panel' that is able to produce power at night.

7. Solar panels are fixed at their installed location

Panels that are installed on your roof are pretty much installed there for good.

Unless you are looking to pay extra to have your system dismantled, de-wired and transported to another location then solar panels are stuck in one position.

Solar systems are not mobile at all, which means if you purchase solar but decide to sell you will have to leave your system behind.

9. Disposal of old solar panels can be harmful to the environment

Unfortunately, when we dispose of old solar panels it requires them to be melted down which can produce some harmful chemicals in the process. Not only this, but it can be harmful to the local area that this occurs in. Mostly you will see solar panels back at landfill sites which is better than burning. One good thing is that usually solar panels will last around 15-25 years so there isn't an abundance of old panels causing issues.

Advantages of Solar Panels:

1. Reduce the cost of your energy bill

The most widely known advantage of solar panels is that they will reduce the cost of your electricity bills.

By producing your own power through the sun you will ultimately be buying less power from the grid. This allows you to spend less money buying energy which leads to saving more money on your power bills.

Due to the sun's energy being renewable and free it means that you will not be paying for the energy you generate through your solar panels.

There are endless benefits that come from having spare cash each month to spend on your family or other things. Saving money is one of the biggest advantages of solar.

2. Renewable energy source

Solar power is a renewable source of energy. Renewable energy is a source of power that cannot be used up.

Essentially the sun is generating a mass amount of power all the time that can be harvested by your solar panels without running out.

The plus side of solar being renewable means that everyone can take advantage of free energy given by the sun.

We wouldn't have to worry about the sun's power running out, but instead we can enjoy the rays that hit our solar panels and generate free, clean energy.

Being a renewable source solar power is also clean energy meaning the energy doesn't produce any greenhouse gasses emissions.

3. Increase your property value

Because solar panels have so many benefits for homeowners, installing them on your property will increase its value.

Houses that have solar panels will be more valuable than those that do not.

This is because one home will be highly dependent on the grid whereas the other will be generating its own energy. Enjoying being free from the shackles of increasing energy prices.

Again this is because solar panels do have a high upfront cost and can be seen as a great investment asset.

The money that you spend on solar panels will be invested into your home as well, you may even see a high return on investment from installing solar at your property.

4. Environmentally friendly

Energy that is produced by solar panels is clean, renewable and has zero-emissions. Solar energy does not contribute towards greenhouse gasses or fossil fuels unlike other oils and coals.

Essentially this means that solar panels are environmentally friendly products and will not harm the planet.

Being environmentally friendly means a lot nowadays, and you can gain popularity within communities for taking a stance against climate change.

It is one of the most popular reasons why people take a move towards solar, and is definitely one of the biggest advantages of solar panels.

Homeowners can rest easy knowing their energy is not harming the planet.

5. Wide range of solar products

Another massive advantage of solar panels is the huge range of different solar panel products available.

There are solar panels that are built for performance for those people who are looking for a high-end system to perform for a long time.

For homeowners who are looking for a good budget system then there is a massive range to be browsed from as well.

Thermal solar panels are also available for people who spend most of their energy on heating and want to use solar to help lower the cost.

Solar panels can be purchased with an all-in-one battery system for homeowners who need to store their power to use at night instead.

Having this wide variety of options comes as a massive advantage for homeowners as they can get solar panels specific to their requirements and needs.

6. Low maintenance costs

With new technology being readily available, the maintenance of solar panels are becoming easier and easier.

Warranties are also being included for massive periods of time making the maintenance of solar panels less and less.

This is great because it means homeowners can buy solar without having to fix or check the system every week. Also, low maintenance means low cost.

You won't need to spend anything extra on your solar panels system to keep it working at optimum.

Once in a while it's recommended to get your solar panels cleaned if they have collected any soil or dust.

7. Homeowners can become energy independent

The installation of solar panels to your home could allow you to become completely energy independent.

With a good enough system, you could generate enough energy to power your home without having to buy power from the grid.

Not only is this a great accomplishment, but it also means homeowners won't have to face rising electricity prices again.

Generating your own power will be save you a large amount of money. You also would not be affected if there was a power cut or any maintenance by the grid on their power lines.

Many people who have become energy independent can say that it's a massive advantage of solar panels.

8. Excess solar can be sold to the grid

Any excess energy that is not used in your home can be sold to the grid for extra cash.

Not only this, you are providing your local community with clean, renewable energy. This helps you and your community have cleaner energy supplied to your grid by pulling energy from the sun.

Some homeowners will purposely upgrade their systems just to sell excess energy back to the grid.

The government offers some really good Feed-In Tariffs available for homeowners to get rewarded for any excess power they don't use.

These tariffs usually vary from state to state. The two main tariffs are fixed rate and time varying. The price per KW is decided by these two tariffs, and is a great way to help pay off your system quicker.

Once the system is paid off you will see the return on investment from your solar panels. Solar panels could actually generate you free money, which is a massive advantage.

9. Return on investment

Solar panels are a really good investment to make, and homeowners will be able to get the money they invested back within time.

Although solar panels have a high upfront investment cost, the money that gets saved each month on power bills will help toward paying off that cost of the system.

An easy way to look at it would be: If you saved a large sum of money on your energy bill, then you can put that money towards covering the cost of your system.

Once the solar system is paid off you will still be saving money on your energy bills. Therefore, you are now making a return from the initial investment made on your solar panels.

10. Get rewarded by the government

Government rebates are a great advantage of solar panels.

Being able to sell your energy back to the government for cash is enticing for homeowners to make the move to solar. With pressures on governments to move towards greener solutions, all future rewards are looking bright.

Rates may start to become more profitable and rebates becoming easier to get. However, this may not last forever.

Although these rebates differ from state to state they all offer a big reduction in the cost and most will also offer a no interest loan scheme.

These government incentives actually make solar energy more affordable. This is a step in the right direction and helps first time buyers secure solar.

11. Power can be stored and used at night

This would benefit homeowners that use a majority of power at night. Similar to commercial businesses like supermarkets or schools.

When you store power you become independent from the grid. Rather than buy energy, you can use the energy that has been stored.

This could provide even further savings for homeowners. It's best invested with high end solar panels to see the full benefits of solar battery storage.

High end solar panels tend to have a higher performance and generate more energy, meaning you can store more power quicker.

12. Solar panels have Long lasting warranties

Companies that design, test and manufacturer and solar panels include long lasting warranties with their products.

This shows that they have a lot of confidence in the performance of solar panels and that they are guaranteed to reach a minimum performance for a period of time.

Long lasting warranties are a big benefit of solar panels because they show that they won't break or stop performance within the first 10+ years installing them. Companies like Jinko, LG and SunPower offer great warranties.

Homeowners can feel like moving to solar is less risky, because they are covered by the solar panels warranties.

It also means they can work out their estimated saving given that there are no issues with the solar panels.

13. Solar panel technology is becoming more advanced

I've seen this a lot over the past 5 years. Solar panel technology is taking huge leaps in advancements to allow for some really awesome features. I'd say most important in particular is the availability for flexible solar system designs.

The reason why I like this so much is because you can design a system around your energy bill. Depending on when you use the most energy, you can place panels to capture the most sunlight during that time, maximising on your self consumption and giving you the highest possible savings.

Other features include full visibility and tracking of your system so you know it's performance and SMART features which can learn when you use the most energy and start to export this to the grid or other places like a battery or electric car.

14. Cost of solar panels are becoming more affordable year after year

Solar panels are becoming more and more affordable every year. There is a race towards making solar panels affordable whilst also maintaining the quality of the solar panels.

15. Options to charge your electric vehicle from your solar panel system

This is going to become a massive benefit of solar panels within the next 6 months. At the end of 2021 we've seen a huge spike in the demand for home EV charging systems which can connect and charge from your solar panels.

16. Solar energy was announced the cheapest form of electricity in history

Wooo! Go solar. That's right, solar energy was declared the cheapest form of electricity in history. There has never been a cheaper way to produce high quality, green energy. This was found by the International Energy Agency back in October 2020.

It was highlighted that solar energy is significantly cheaper than coal and gas. It's safe to say, solar panels have a very bright future ahead being the cheapest form of energy in the world right now.

Disadvantages of Solar Panels:
1. High upfront cost
The first initial investment for solar panel installation is quite high, and not everybody will be able to afford them. Although we could argue that solar panels are the most affordable they've ever been... Still they do come with a price tag.

Unfortunately this is a downside to solar panels however the future is bright as prices are coming down.

Solar panels right now are fairly expensive, however with new government schemes and the latest technology the price is becoming more and more affordable.

2. The size of system is dependent on your available space
Available space is a big factor in solar panel installation. If your roof is not big enough, then it means that you may have to downsize your system or rethink about getting solar altogether.

Solar panels are still fairly large products meaning they require a big space to be installed. The size disadvantage means that they cannot be placed into small areas, and actually require a large roof.

This is important for those who are looking to future proof their home with a big enough system to last years.

Some systems however do provide flexible designs for smaller roofs.

3. Requires sunny weather to work best
Energy can only be generated when sunlight is hitting the face of the panel and being converted. Therefore if there is no sun, there will be no energy being produced.

Although solar panels can still generate power on cloudy days (as it's the UV light that generates the energy) they perform best on sunny days. If you are in a location that doesn't get much sun, it's probably best to look at other options for get a system that overcomes shading issues.

Your solar panel performance will be negatively affected if there is not enough sunlight hitting the panels on rainy days.

Just remember, luckily in Australia we get a lot of sun so it makes it worthwhile for us, even for those in Melbourne.

4. Manufacturing of solar panels can harm the environment
Although solar panels produce clean, renewable energy, the process it takes to manufacture them can harm the environment. Mass production of solar panels may result in fossil fuels being burned and plastic waste.

Unfortunately, this is one of the overlooked disadvantages of solar panels. They are not eco-friendly to mass manufacture. Then again, you can ask what is these days? This is quite a shame because solar panels stand for a big movement to fight the climate crisis.

This does become a disadvantage for solar panels although they themselves produce green, renewable energy. Overall, I'd say that they still do more good than they do bad.

5. Low energy conversion rate
Even the most advanced solar panels still only convert around 20-25% of the sun's energy into power. It goes to show how much opportunity there is to develop better technology to optimise the full force of the sun.

However, there are many things that need to be considered like the direction of the panels and location.

Jinko solar panels have claimed the world record a few times. So have Canadian solar panels.

Although, I also want to stress that solar panel efficiency shouldn't be the most important thing. Especially when you're talking about 1-2% difference. Really, I'd be more concerned about the installation or warranties.

6. Cannot be used at night
No energy can be produced by your solar panels at night which essentially means your solar panels can only generate energy 12 hours of a full day. Without any sunlight hitting the solar panels then there will be no energy produced.

This is a disadvantage of solar panels but may be something that is overcome in the future with new technology. There are already talks about an 'anti solar panel' that is able to produce power at night.

7. Solar panels are fixed at their installed location
Panels that are installed on your roof are pretty much installed there for good.

Unless you are looking to pay extra to have your system dismantled, de-wired and transported to another location then solar panels are stuck in one position.

Solar systems are not mobile at all, which means if you purchase solar but decide to sell you will have to leave your system behind.

9. Disposal of old solar panels can be harmful to the environment

Unfortunately, when we dispose of old solar panels it requires them to be melted down which can produce some harmful chemicals in the process. Not only this, but it can be harmful to the local area that this occurs in. Mostly you will see solar panels back at landfill sites which is better than burning. One good thing is that usually solar panels will last around 15-25 years so there isn't an abundance of old panels causing issues.

Advantages of Solar Panels:

1. Reduce the cost of your energy bill

The most widely known advantage of solar panels is that they will reduce the cost of your electricity bills.

By producing your own power through the sun you will ultimately be buying less power from the grid. This allows you to spend less money buying energy which leads to saving more money on your power bills.

Due to the sun's energy being renewable and free it means that you will not be paying for the energy you generate through your solar panels.

There are endless benefits that come from having spare cash each month to spend on your family or other things. Saving money is one of the biggest advantages of solar.

2. Renewable energy source

Solar power is a renewable source of energy. Renewable energy is a source of power that cannot be used up.

Essentially the sun is generating a mass amount of power all the time that can be harvested by your solar panels without running out.

The plus side of solar being renewable means that everyone can take advantage of free energy given by the sun.

We wouldn't have to worry about the sun's power running out, but instead we can enjoy the rays that hit our solar panels and generate free, clean energy.

Being a renewable source solar power is also clean energy meaning the energy doesn't produce any greenhouse gasses emissions.

3. Increase your property value

Because solar panels have so many benefits for homeowners, installing them on your property will increase its value.

Houses that have solar panels will be more valuable than those that do not.

This is because one home will be highly dependent on the grid whereas the other will be generating its own energy. Enjoying being free from the shackles of increasing energy prices.

Again this is because solar panels do have a high upfront cost and can be seen as a great investment asset.

The money that you spend on solar panels will be invested into your home as well, you may even see a high return on investment from installing solar at your property.

4. Environmentally friendly

Energy that is produced by solar panels is clean, renewable and has zero-emissions. Solar energy does not contribute towards greenhouse gasses or fossil fuels unlike other oils and coals.

Essentially this means that solar panels are environmentally friendly products and will not harm the planet.

Being environmentally friendly means a lot nowadays, and you can gain popularity within communities for taking a stance against climate change.

It is one of the most popular reasons why people take a move towards solar, and is definitely one of the biggest advantages of solar panels.

Homeowners can rest easy knowing their energy is not harming the planet.

5. Wide range of solar products

Another massive advantage of solar panels is the huge range of different solar panel products available.

There are solar panels that are built for performance for those people who are looking for a high-end system to perform for a long time.

For homeowners who are looking for a good budget system then there is a massive range to be browsed from as well.

Thermal solar panels are also available for people who spend most of their energy on heating and want to use solar to help lower the cost.

Solar panels can be purchased with an all-in-one battery system for homeowners who need to store their power to use at night instead.

Having this wide variety of options comes as a massive advantage for homeowners as they can get solar panels specific to their requirements and needs.

6. Low maintenance costs

With new technology being readily available, the maintenance of solar panels are becoming easier and easier.

Warranties are also being included for massive periods of time making the maintenance of solar panels less and less.

This is great because it means homeowners can buy solar without having to fix or check the system every week. Also, low maintenance means low cost.

You won't need to spend anything extra on your solar panels system to keep it working at optimum.

Once in a while it's recommended to get your solar panels cleaned if they have collected any soil or dust.

7. Homeowners can become energy independent

The installation of solar panels to your home could allow you to become completely energy independent.

With a good enough system, you could generate enough energy to power your home without having to buy power from the grid.

Not only is this a great accomplishment, but it also means homeowners won't have to face rising electricity prices again.

Generating your own power will be save you a large amount of money. You also would not be affected if there was a power cut or any maintenance by the grid on their power lines.

Many people who have become energy independent can say that it's a massive advantage of solar panels.

8. Excess solar can be sold to the grid

Any excess energy that is not used in your home can be sold to the grid for extra cash.

Not only this, you are providing your local community with clean, renewable energy. This helps you and your community have cleaner energy supplied to your grid by pulling energy from the sun.

Some homeowners will purposely upgrade their systems just to sell excess energy back to the grid.

The government offers some really good Feed-In Tariffs available for homeowners to get rewarded for any excess power they don't use.

These tariffs usually vary from state to state. The two main tariffs are fixed rate and time varying. The price per KW is decided by these two tariffs, and is a great way to help pay off your system quicker.

Once the system is paid off you will see the return on investment from your solar panels. Solar panels could actually generate you free money, which is a massive advantage.

9. Return on investment

Solar panels are a really good investment to make, and homeowners will be able to get the money they invested back within time.

Although solar panels have a high upfront investment cost, the money that gets saved each month on power bills will help toward paying off that cost of the system.

An easy way to look at it would be: If you saved a large sum of money on your energy bill, then you can put that money towards covering the cost of your system.

Once the solar system is paid off you will still be saving money on your energy bills. Therefore, you are now making a return from the initial investment made on your solar panels.

10. Get rewarded by the government

Government rebates are a great advantage of solar panels.

Being able to sell your energy back to the government for cash is enticing for homeowners to make the move to solar. With pressures on governments to move towards greener solutions, all future rewards are looking bright.

Rates may start to become more profitable and rebates becoming easier to get. However, this may not last forever.

Although these rebates differ from state to state they all offer a big reduction in the cost and most will also offer a no interest loan scheme.

These government incentives actually make solar energy more affordable. This is a step in the right direction and helps first time buyers secure solar.

11. Power can be stored and used at night

This would benefit homeowners that use a majority of power at night. Similar to commercial businesses like supermarkets or schools.

When you store power you become independent from the grid. Rather than buy energy, you can use the energy that has been stored.

This could provide even further savings for homeowners. It's best invested with high end solar panels to see the full benefits of solar battery storage.

High end solar panels tend to have a higher performance and generate more energy, meaning you can store more power quicker.

12. Solar panels have Long lasting warranties

Companies that design, test and manufacturer and solar panels include long lasting warranties with their products.

This shows that they have a lot of confidence in the performance of solar panels and that they are guaranteed to reach a minimum performance for a period of time.

Long lasting warranties are a big benefit of solar panels because they show that they won't break or stop performance within the first 10+ years installing them. Companies like Jinko, LG and SunPower offer great warranties.

Homeowners can feel like moving to solar is less risky, because they are covered by the solar panels warranties.

It also means they can work out their estimated saving given that there are no issues with the solar panels.

13. Solar panel technology is becoming more advanced

I've seen this a lot over the past 5 years. Solar panel technology is taking huge leaps in advancements to allow for some really awesome features. I'd say most important in particular is the availability for flexible solar system designs.

The reason why I like this so much is because you can design a system around your energy bill. Depending on when you use the most energy, you can place panels to capture the most sunlight during that time, maximising on your self consumption and giving you the highest possible savings.

Other features include full visibility and tracking of your system so you know it's performance and SMART features which can learn when you use the most energy and start to export this to the grid or other places like a battery or electric car.

14. Cost of solar panels are becoming more affordable year after year

Solar panels are becoming more and more affordable every year. There is a race towards making solar panels affordable whilst also maintaining the quality of the solar panels.

15. Options to charge your electric vehicle from your solar panel system

This is going to become a massive benefit of solar panels within the next 6 months. At the end of 2021 we've seen a huge spike in the demand for home EV charging systems which can connect and charge from your solar panels.

16. Solar energy was announced the cheapest form of electricity in history

Wooo! Go solar. That's right, solar energy was declared the cheapest form of electricity in history. There has never been a cheaper way to produce high quality, green energy. This was found by the International Energy Agency back in October 2020.

It was highlighted that solar energy is significantly cheaper than coal and gas. It's safe to say, solar panels have a very bright future ahead being the cheapest form of energy in the world right now.

Disadvantages of Solar Panels:

1. High upfront cost

The first initial investment for solar panel installation is quite high, and not everybody will be able to afford them. Although we could argue that solar panels are the most affordable they've ever been... Still they do come with a price tag.

Unfortunately this is a downside to solar panels however the future is bright as prices are coming down.

Solar panels right now are fairly expensive, however with new government schemes and the latest technology the price is becoming more and more affordable.

2. The size of system is dependent on your available space

Available space is a big factor in solar panel installation. If your roof is not big enough, then it means that you may have to downsize your system or rethink about getting solar altogether.

Solar panels are still fairly large products meaning they require a big space to be installed. The size disadvantage means that they cannot be placed into small areas, and actually require a large roof.

This is important for those who are looking to future proof their home with a big enough system to last years.

Some systems however do provide flexible designs for smaller roofs.

3. Requires sunny weather to work best

Energy can only be generated when sunlight is hitting the face of the panel and being converted. Therefore if there is no sun, there will be no energy being produced.

Although solar panels can still generate power on cloudy days (as it's the UV light that generates the energy) they perform best on sunny days. If you are in a location that doesn't get much sun, it's probably best to look at other options for get a system that overcomes shading issues.

Your solar panel performance will be negatively affected if there is not enough sunlight hitting the panels on rainy days.

Just remember, luckily in Australia we get a lot of sun so it makes it worthwhile for us, even for those in Melbourne.

4. Manufacturing of solar panels can harm the environment

Although solar panels produce clean, renewable energy, the process it takes to manufacture them can harm the environment. Mass production of solar panels may result in fossil fuels being burned and plastic waste.

Unfortunately, this is one of the overlooked disadvantages of solar panels. They are not eco-friendly to mass manufacture. Then again, you can ask what is these days? This is quite a shame because solar panels stand for a big movement to fight the climate crisis.

This does become a disadvantage for solar panels although they themselves produce green, renewable energy. Overall, I'd say that they still do more good than they do bad.

5. Low energy conversion rate

Even the most advanced solar panels still only convert around 20-25% of the sun's energy into power. It goes to show how much opportunity there is to develop better technology to optimise the full force of the sun.

However, there are many things that need to be considered like the direction of the panels and location.

Jinko solar panels have claimed the world record a few times. So have Canadian solar panels.

Although, I also want to stress that solar panel efficiency shouldn't be the most important thing. Especially when you're talking about 1-2% difference. Really, I'd be more concerned about the installation or warranties.

6. Cannot be used at night

No energy can be produced by your solar panels at night which essentially means your solar panels can only generate energy 12 hours of a full day. Without any sunlight hitting the solar panels then there will be no energy produced.

This is a disadvantage of solar panels but may be something that is overcome in the future with new technology. There are already talks about an 'anti solar panel' that is able to produce power at night.

7. Solar panels are fixed at their installed location

Panels that are installed on your roof are pretty much installed there for good.

Unless you are looking to pay extra to have your system dismantled, de-wired and transported to another location then solar panels are stuck in one position.

Solar systems are not mobile at all, which means if you purchase solar but decide to sell you will have to leave your system behind.

9. Disposal of old solar panels can be harmful to the environment

Unfortunately, when we dispose of old solar panels it requires them to be melted down which can produce some harmful chemicals in the process. Not only this, but it can be harmful to the local area that this occurs in. Mostly you will see solar panels back at landfill sites which is better than burning. One good thing is that usually solar panels will last around 15-25 years so there isn't an abundance of old panels causing issues.

www.ingramcontent.com/pod-product-compliance
Lightning Source LLC
LaVergne TN
LVHW081552060526
838201LV00054B/1863